AA308
Thought and Experience:
Themes in the Philosophy of Mind

BOOK 4

Imagination and Creativity

MICHAEL BEANEY

This publication forms part of an Open University course AA308 *Thought and Experience: Themes in the Philosophy of Mind*. Details of this and other Open University courses can be obtained from the Course Information and Advice Centre, PO Box 724, The Open University, Milton Keynes MK7 6ZS, United Kingdom: tel. +44 (0)1908 653231, email general-enquiries@open.ac.uk

Alternatively, you may visit the Open University website at http://www.open.ac.uk where you can learn more about the wide range of courses and packs offered at all levels by The Open University.

To purchase a selection of Open University course materials visit the webshop at www.ouw.co.uk, or contact Open University Worldwide, Michael Young Building, Walton Hall, Milton Keynes MK7 6AA, United Kingdom for a brochure. tel. +44 (0) 1908 858785; fax +44 (0)1908 858787; email ouwenq@open.ac.uk

The Open University
Walton Hall, Milton Keynes
MK7 6AA

First published 2005

Copyright © 2005 The Open University

All rights reserved. No part of this publication may be reproduced, stored in a retrieval system, transmitted or utilized in any form or by any means, electronic, mechanical, photocopying, recording or otherwise, without written permission from the publisher or a licence from the Copyright Licensing Agency Ltd. Details of such licences (for reprographic reproduction) may be obtained from the Copyright Licensing Agency Ltd of 90 Tottenham Court Road, London W1T 4LP.

Edited, designed and typeset by The Open University.

Printed and bound in the United Kingdom by Bath Press, Bath.

ISBN 0 7492 9644 5

1.1

... nothing invigorates the imagination more than a spell of sharp thinking ...
(Eva T.H. Brann, *The World of the Imagination*, 1991, 32)

Contents

Preface	ix
1 Imagination: the missing mystery of philosophy?	1
The varieties of imaginative experience	2
Imagery and supposition	26
Review and preview	35
Further reading	36

PART ONE: IMAGINATION, PERCEPTION AND THOUGHT

2 Imagination and conception	40
Descartes's critique of sensory imagination	41
Descartes's use of intellectual imagination	52
Review and preview	57
Further reading	58
3 Imagination and perception	60
The way of ideas	60
Hume's empire of the imagination	70
Review and preview	81
Further reading	82
4 Imagination and synthesis	83
Kant and the reproductive imagination	84
Kant and the productive imagination	99
Images and schemata	109
Review and preview	121
Further reading	122
5 Imagination and aspect perception	124
Wittgenstein on imagination and images	126
Wittgenstein's discussion of seeing-as	135
Seeing-as and imagination	155
Review and preview	167
Further reading	168

Part Two: Creativity

6 Creativity and originality — 170
    The definition of creativity — 170
    Boden's theory of creativity and Novitz's critique — 177
    Novitz's recombination theory — 187
    Review and preview — 191
    Further reading — 192

7 Creativity and imagination — 193
    The role of imagination in creativity — 193
    The creative imagination — 203
    Review — 212
    Further reading — 213

Appendix 1   Imagination and creativity in Euclidean geometry — 214

Appendix 2   The structure of Kant's *Critique of Pure Reason* — 220

Glossary — 221

Bibliography — 226

Readings

1 Imagination and imagery — 234
    ALAN R. WHITE

2 Imagining and supposing — 240
    ALAN R. WHITE

3 What is creativity? — 242
    MARGARET BODEN

4 Creativity and constraint — 255
    DAVID NOVITZ

5 Is imagery a kind of imagination? — 265
    GREGORY CURRIE and IAN RAVENSCROFT

6	Creativity and imagination BERYS GAUT	268
Index		294

Preface

In much of western thought from the seventeenth to the nineteenth century, the imagination was accorded a central role in human cognitive activity alongside that of perception and thought. Its nature and status were admittedly unclear, but in Romanticism, for example, it was attributed enormous powers, and was seen as underlying all forms of creativity. But perhaps in reaction to the mystification of the imagination found in Romanticism, imagination and creativity were relatively neglected in twentieth-century philosophy. There are notable exceptions. Mental imagery has been a fairly constant topic in philosophy of mind, as has artistic creativity in aesthetics, and both issues have been hotly debated in psychology and cognitive science. But there has been much less concern to offer philosophical clarification of our various concepts of imagination and creativity – of what it means to 'imagine', be 'creative', and so on – and the relationships between these concepts. In recent years, however, this has begun to change, and the central aims of this book are to explore some of the different conceptions of imagination that can be found in western philosophical thought and to introduce and elucidate some of the philosophical issues that arise concerning imagination and creativity.

After an introductory chapter looking at the range of different conceptions of imagination, this book divides into two parts. Part One (chapters 2 to 5) explores some of these conceptions in more detail, through the work of four giants of modern philosophy – Descartes, Hume, Kant and Wittgenstein. The central theme of Part One is the relationship between imagination, perception and thought. Part Two (chapters 6 and 7) is devoted to creativity, discussing what is meant by 'creativity' and considering the relationship between creativity and imagination.

There are six readings associated with chapter 1 and the two chapters of Part Two, which are collected together at the end of the book. In the case of Part One, since the passages I have selected are fairly short and often drawn from different sections of the relevant philosopher's work, I have incorporated them into the text of the chapters themselves. There are activities throughout the book. These are intended to encourage thinking about the philosophical issues and as a guide through the selected passages and readings.

The first chapter offers initial clarification of the concept of imagination and an introduction to the philosophical issues with which this book is concerned.

Chapters 2 and 3 look at Descartes and Hume, respectively, and some of this, at least, should be familiar to anyone who has done first or second level courses in philosophy. Chapter 4, on Kant, and chapter 5, on Wittgenstein, are the most difficult chapters of the book. No account of imagination can even pretend to be adequate without some discussion of Kant, and no understanding of central themes and approaches in contemporary philosophy of mind would be adequate without some appreciation of Wittgenstein's philosophy. The topic of imagination provides a good route into the heart of Kant's and Wittgenstein's ideas. It may be advisable to allow additional time to work through chapters 4 and 5, but I hope that the benefits will outweigh the extra effort that these two chapters may require. Part Two, however, provides a chance to wind down. The debate about the nature of creativity is relatively easier to follow, even if the issues remain controversial; and the final chapter brings together the threads of discussion in earlier chapters in considering the role of the imagination in creativity.

In writing this book, I have benefited from the advice and support of colleagues in the Philosophy Department at the Open University: Alex Barber, Sean Crawford, Keith Frankish, Derek Matravers, Carolyn Price and Peter Wright. I am particularly grateful to Sean Crawford and Carolyn Price for detailed written comments on various drafts of this material, and to the Open University editors Nancy Marten and Peter Wright for suggested improvements to the penultimate draft. Gerry Bolton, Jan Cant and Michelle Wright have assisted in the production process, and Richard Hoyle and Audrey Linkman with the graphic design and illustrations. I have also received helpful comments on drafts of chapters from Tara Beaney, Ian Chowcat, Tim Crane, Berys Gaut, Jens Kulenkampff, Sharon Macdonald and Nick McAdoo. I am especially indebted to Thomas and Harriet Beaney, as well as to Sharon Macdonald and Tara Beaney, who have put up with my obsessions with imagination and creativity over the last few years, and with whom I have discussed many of the ideas and tried out many of the examples and illustrations. I have given talks on some of this material on various occasions, to the Open University Creativity Centre, to the British Society of Aesthetics, and at seminars at the Open University, the University of Erlangen-Nürnberg and the University of Lille. I would like to thank the audiences on these occasions for fruitful discussion. Above all, I would like to thank the imagined readership of this book for shaping what I have created. I hope my imagined readership does not prove to have been imaginary.

CHAPTER 1

Imagination: the missing mystery of philosophy?

> Imagination, a licentious and vagrant faculty, unsusceptible of limitations and impatient of restraint, has always endeavoured to baffle the logician, to perplex the confines of distinction, and burst the enclosures of regularity.
>
> (Samuel Johnson, *Rambler*, no.125, 28 May 1751)

In much of western thought, the imagination has an ambiguous status, seemingly poised between spirit and nature, mediating between mind and body – the mental and the physical – and interceding between one soul and another. For Aristotle, the imagination – or *phantasia* – was a kind of bridge between sensation and thought, supplying the images or 'phantasms' without which thought could not occur. Descartes argued that the imagination was not an essential part of the mind, since it dealt with images in the brain whose existence – unlike that of the mind – could be doubted. Kant, on the other hand, held that the imagination was fundamental to the human mind, not only bringing together our sensory and intellectual faculties but also acting in creative ways, a conception that was to blossom in Romanticism and find poetic expression in the works of Coleridge and Wordsworth. More recently, the role of the imagination in empathy has been stressed: the ability to identify with our fellow human beings and with fictional characters being regarded as crucial in accessing other minds, enriching our own experience and developing our moral sense. In fact, in the history of western thought, the imagination has been seen as performing such a wide range of different functions that it is problematic whether it can be understood as a single faculty at all. In imagination we are able to think of what is absent, unreal or even absurd, and so it appears to grant us almost unlimited conceptual powers. Yet it also seems to inform our perception of what is present and real and everyday, and so permeates the most basic levels of our daily lives. In this first chapter, we will be concerned with some of the different ways in which the imagination is talked of and conceived, exploring just what the imagination might be and what philosophical issues it raises.

The chapter is divided into two main sections. In the first, we will look at the range of conceptions of imagination, address the question of whether 'imagining' can be defined in any useful way, and consider the implications of this for a philosophical understanding of imagination. Despite the important role that is often accorded to the imagination in our mental activities, the topic has been somewhat marginalized in the philosophical literature, particularly (and perhaps surprisingly) in contemporary philosophy of mind. This has led one writer to call imagination the 'missing mystery' of philosophy, and in explaining the approach and themes of the book I will say something about what this mystery is meant to be, and how one might go about 'demystifying' the imagination. In the second main section, we will examine the relationship that imagination has to imagery and supposition, both of which have been seen as closely connected to, and sometimes even identified with, imagination. I will end with a review of the discussion and a preview of what is to come.

The varieties of imaginative experience

What would life be like without imagination? Perhaps, in this very first question, we have found something that is impossible to imagine. Imagination infuses so much of what we do, and so deeply, that to imagine its absence is to imagine not being human. Some people, I am told, think about sex every five minutes. For them, I presume, a sudden loss of imaginative powers would be devastating. Some people (not necessarily the same ones), at certain points in their lives, think about getting married or having a child. They might imagine the sanctity of a white wedding or the horrors of having all their relatives in one place at one time, the patter of tiny feet or the exhaustion of sleepless nights. As they play, children imagine all sorts of things, and their ideas of what they want to be and do when they grow up are fundamental in their development. Most people have ambitions of one kind or another. Imagining being promoted, or seeing something you have done recognized publicly, plays an essential role in motivation. In our idle moments too, or in diverting ourselves amidst tedious tasks, we might imagine winning the lottery or our hero scoring the winning goal in a match or, more sinfully, an obnoxious colleague falling under a bus. When we meet or talk to anyone, whether we are assessing them as potential friends or enemies, lovers or colleagues, for either ourselves or others, we are imagining what they would be like in certain circumstances.

But the imagination is not just involved in thinking of ourselves or other people. When I look at a painting, or read a novel, or hear a piece of music, or taste a wine, I bring my imagination to bear in its appreciation. I imagine other things to compare it with, or simply allow my imagination free flight, making no effort to control the images that spring to mind. Or in creating something myself, I may conjure up an image or images of what I want to realize. Imagination is also involved in the most ordinary experiences. When I go for a walk, I might imagine what it is like to live in a particular house I see, or if it is dark, I might suddenly imagine that there is something following me. In thinking what to cook for dinner, I imagine what I can do with the ingredients I have. In choosing clothes, I imagine what they would go with and the occasions on which I might wear them. In perceiving anything, I might imagine it transformed in some way, coloured differently, radically restructured, or simply moved to another location. And even if I do not deliberately transform it in my mind, previous or anticipated experiences may influence how I perceive it.

Clearly, we talk of imagination across the full range of human experience. Indeed, it may be hard to find an experience in which the imagination is not somehow involved. But if this is so, then does 'imagination' really have a single sense or refer to a single faculty? Can any order at all be brought into the varieties of imaginative experience? What conceptions of imagination might be distinguished? And what philosophical issues arise, or are reflected, in our attempts to do so? We will explore these questions, in a preliminary way, in the first part of this chapter.

Meanings of 'imagination'

A natural starting point is to consider the ways in which 'imagination' and related terms such as 'imagine' and 'image' are used in everyday contexts.

1   Imagine someone asking you to define 'imagination'. What would you say?
2   Can you think of any cases where we would talk of 'imagining' but not of 'images'?
3   Consider the connotations of the term 'imaginary'. What do they suggest as to how the imagination is sometimes regarded?

ACTIVITY

4   What is it for someone to be 'imaginative'? How do the connotations of 'imaginative' compare with those of 'imaginary', and what does this suggest as to our talk of imagination?

5   How would you explain the difference between 'imagination' and 'fantasy' (or 'fancy'), as those terms are used today?

DISCUSSION

1   You may have suggested one or more of various possible definitions. Perhaps you characterized 'imagination' as 'the power to form images'. Alternatively, or additionally, you might have mentioned the capacity to conceive of what is non-existent or to conjure up something new. The definition of 'imagination' in the *Concise Oxford Dictionary* (6th edn) runs as follows: 'Imagining; mental faculty forming images or concepts of external objects not present to the senses; fancy; creative faculty of the mind.' This covers most of what might be thought of in an initial specification, although there is no indication here of the relationship between the various meanings.

2   One such case occurred in posing the first question: 'Imagine someone asking you to define "imagination".' In answering this question, you do not need to conjure up any image in your mind. Perhaps an image of a particular person did go through your mind, but it is not essential. It is certainly not essential in the way in which an image might seem required if you were asked to imagine a hairy monster with six legs. In imagining that I have perfect pitch, or that everyone speaks Gaelic, or that there are parallel universes, what I am doing is conceiving of a possibility. There is a difference, then, between 'imagining' and 'imaging': imagining may involve imaging, but there is a broad sense of 'imagining' in which conjuring up images is not a necessary condition for imagining to occur. This is well brought out in the definition of 'imagination' that Simon Blackburn provides in *The Oxford Dictionary of Philosophy* (1994, 187): 'Most directly, the faculty of reviving or especially creating images in the mind's eye. But more generally, the ability to create and rehearse possible situations, to combine knowledge in unusual ways, or to invent thought experiments.' As we shall see, however, even this more general characterization does not do justice to the full range of meanings of 'imagination' in the philosophical literature.

3   'Imaginary' is contrasted with 'real'. More specifically, what is 'imaginary' may be said to be 'fanciful' or 'illusory'. It is with these senses in mind that

we might talk of 'merely imagining' something, or of something existing 'only in the imagination'. 'Did you really see the knife in the bedroom, or did you only imagine it?' 'Her happiness was just a figment of his imagination.' What these uses suggest is a connection between imagination and fancy or delusion, a connection that we can certainly find in the literature (both philosophical and non-philosophical). When we talk of someone having an 'active imagination', for example, we may well be using the phrase in a derogatory sense. But while important, these uses are only one strand in our complex talk of imagination. Imagining can occur without what is imagined being 'imaginary'. I can imagine something that really happened or that genuinely could happen, and if images are indeed involved, then these may well have been acquired from previous actual experience.

4   If imagining always involved imaging, then someone who is 'imaginative' would be someone who is good at conjuring up images. If what is imagined is always 'imaginary', then someone who is 'imaginative' would be someone who is frequently deluded. But what we normally have in mind in calling someone 'imaginative' is the more general sense of 'imagination' that Blackburn specified. Someone who is imaginative is someone who can think up new possibilities, offer fresh perspectives on what is familiar, make fruitful connections between apparently disparate ideas, elaborate original ways of seeing or doing things, project themselves into unusual situations, and so on. In short, someone who is imaginative is someone who is creative. As far as the connotations of 'imaginative' are concerned, they suggest a more positive view of 'imagination' than do the connotations of 'imaginary'. But taken together, it might be argued, the two sets of connotations indicate the two poles between which our talk of imagination takes place.

5   Nowadays, 'fantasy' has more connotations of unreality or delusion than 'imagination' does, although, as suggested in answer to the third question, 'imagination' can also be used with these connotations. In the *Concise Oxford Dictionary* (6th edn), 'fantasy' is defined as follows: 'Image-inventing faculty, esp. when extravagant or visionary; mental image, daydream; fantastic invention or composition, fantasia; whimsical speculation.' The noun 'fancy' is defined in a similar way. Compare this with the definition of 'imagination' cited above. 'Fancy' is given as one of the meanings of 'imagination', but there is no talk in the latter case of anything 'extravagant', 'whimsical' or 'fantastic'. (The *Concise Oxford*

Dictionary treats 'fantasy' and 'phantasy' as mere variants, but it is sometimes suggested in literary contexts that 'phantasy' indicates a more elevated or visionary power; see Brann 1991, 21.)

Etymologically, 'imagination' derives from the Latin word *imaginatio*, while 'fantasy' and 'fancy' derive from the ancient Greek term *phantasia*. In the works of Plato and Aristotle, *phantasia* meant the power of apprehending or experiencing *phantasmata* ('phantasms'). Arguably, what *phantasma* originally meant was an 'appearance' – an occurrence of something appearing to be such-and-such, as when the sun looks to us as being only a foot across. But even in Aristotle's work, it was also used to mean 'mental image', which is how it was subsequently understood. *Phantasia* came to be translated by *imaginatio* and *phantasma* by *imago* in Latin, preserving the etymological and conceptual connection here, although the original Greek terms were also used in their transliterated form (i.e. employing the Latin rather than Greek alphabet, as I have done here) alongside their Latin correlates. In the seventeenth century, as Latin lost its place as the official language of philosophy, the terms that replaced *phantasia* and *imaginatio* in English were 'fantasy' – or 'fancy' or 'phantasy' – and 'imagination'. In this initial period of English usage, there seems to have been no established distinction between the two terms. In his *Leviathan* of 1651, for example, Hobbes claimed that what 'the Latins call *imagination* ... the Greeks call ... *fancy*' (I, ii). By the end of the eighteenth century, however, the distinction between fantasy and imagination had more or less settled down into its current sense. In his *Dissertations Moral and Critical* of 1783, James Beattie wrote: 'According to the common use of words, Imagination and Fancy are not perfectly synonymous. They are, indeed, names for the same faculty; but the former seems to be applied to the more solemn, and the latter to the more trivial, exertions of it. A witty author is a man of lively Fancy; but a sublime poet is said to possess a vast imagination' (quoted in Engell 1981, 172).

This brief consideration of some of the uses of 'imagination' and related terms illustrates the range of the meanings involved here, and hints at some of the philosophical issues that will concern us in what follows. Does it make sense to talk of a single faculty of imagination? Can 'imagining' be defined? What role do images play in imagination? How does imagining differ from perceiving? What contribution does the imagination make to our thought processes? To what extent does the imagination involve distortion or illusion? What is the relationship between imagination and creativity?

Twelve conceptions of imagination

Can we say anything more systematic about the different ways in which we talk of imagination? In a paper entitled 'Twelve conceptions of imagination' (2003), Leslie Stevenson distinguishes the following meanings of imagination, which I list here (in italics) as he formulates them, together with my own examples to illustrate each one:

1. *The ability to think of something that is not presently perceived, but is, was or will be spatio-temporally real.* In this sense I might imagine how my daughter looks as I speak to her on the phone, how she used to look when she was a baby, or how she will look when I give her the present I have bought her.

2. *The ability to think of whatever one acknowledges as possible in the spatio-temporal world.* In this sense I might imagine how my room will look painted in a different colour.

3. *The liability to think of something which the subject believes to be real, but which is **not** real.* Stevenson talks of 'liability' rather than 'ability' here to indicate that there is some kind of failure in the cognitive process. In this sense I might imagine that there is someone out to get me, or Macbeth imagines that there is a dagger in front of him.

4. *The ability to think of things one conceives of as fictional, as opposed to what one believes to be real, or conceives of as possibly real.* In this sense I might imagine what the characters in a book are like, or imagine the actors in a film or theatre as the characters they portray, aware that the characters are only fictional.

5. *The ability to entertain mental images.* Here I might conjure up an image of a large, black spider or a five-sided geometrical figure.

6. *The ability to think of (conceive of, or represent) anything at all.* Here I might imagine anything from an object before me being transformed in some way to an evil demon systematically deceiving me.

7. *The non-rational operations of the mind, that is, those kinds of mental functioning which are explicable in terms of causes rather than reasons.* Here I

might imagine that smoking is good for me since I associate it with the cool behaviour of those I see smoking in films. It may not be rational, but there is a causal explanation in terms of the association of ideas, upon which advertisers rely so much.

8   *The ability to form beliefs, on the basis of perception, about public objects in three-dimensional space which can exist unperceived, with spatial parts and temporal duration.* Here I might imagine that the whole of something exists when I can only see part of it, or that it continues to exist when I look away.

9   *The sensuous component in the appreciation of works of art or objects of natural beauty without classifying them under concepts or thinking of them as practically useful.* In looking at a painting or hearing a piece of music, for example, I may be stimulated into imagining all sorts of things without conceptualizing it as a representation of anything definite, or seeing it as serving any particular purpose.

10   *The ability to create works of art that encourage such sensuous appreciation.* In composing a piece of music, the composer too may imagine all sorts of things without conceptualizing it in any definite way in the sense, say, of having a message that they want to get across.

11   *The ability to appreciate things that are expressive or revelatory of the meaning of human life.* In contemplating a craggy mountain range at dusk, for example, or a painting by Caspar David Friedrich depicting such a scene, I may imagine how much we are subject to the awesome power of the natural world, and yet ourselves have the conceptual and imaginative power to transcend it all in thought.

12   *The ability to create works of art that express something deep about the meaning of human life, as opposed to the products of mere fantasy.* Michelangelo's Sistine Chapel, Shakespeare's *Hamlet*, Goethe's *Faust*, Beethoven's late string quartets or Wagner's *Ring* cycle might all be offered as examples of this final conception of imagination.

Any attempt at bringing order into discussions of the imagination runs the risk of arbitrariness and distortion, and many alternative divisions are possible. Indeed, Stevenson subdivides some of these conceptions and offers various illustrations, which might be taken to warrant adding to the main list. As a subdivision of the first conception, for example, he identifies 'the ability to think about a particular mental state of another person, whose existence one infers from perceived evidence' (2003, 241), which might be thought to deserve separate recognition. Nor are the conceptions he distinguishes either exhaustive or exclusive, as he admits himself, and there are many interrelationships that are, at best, only implicitly indicated. But the twelve conceptions he distinguishes provide a useful initial framework for locating the philosophical issues.

ACTIVITY

With any division – and particularly with a division into as many as twelve things – there is always the question, 'Why this many?' Why not, in this case, thirteen, or just two with further subdivisions? Looking down the list of the twelve conceptions, are there any ways of simplifying or bringing further order into the division, or any obvious omissions?

DISCUSSION

It seems to me that the twelve conceptions fall naturally into three groups of four. The first four articulate ways in which the imagination is seen as differing from ordinary sense perception. The second four reflect more general conceptions of imagination, in which its relation to thought is stressed more than its relation to sense perception. The final four are concerned with the role of the imagination in aesthetic appreciation and creation. It is hard to think of any omissions, given the generality of the second group of conceptions, and in particular the sixth, 'the ability to think of anything at all'. But you might feel that more specific conceptions deserve to be brought out from under the cover of the ones listed here. For example, the ability to see or make connections, to link what might initially seem disparate things or fields, is also an important conception in both the arts and the sciences – and not least in philosophy.

As far as the first four conceptions are concerned, the contrast with sense perception is fundamental to imagination. In sense perception we have some kind of conscious awareness of something that is actually before us in the spatio-temporal world. Where we are aware of something that is not actually before us in the spatio-temporal world, we speak of 'imagining' it. But this can take several forms. What we imagine can be real (but just not present at the time), merely possible, or even impossible; and where possible or impossible, we can believe it to be such or not. (There is argument over what kind of impossibility is allowed, however. Can you imagine a round square, for example? Or imagine that a banana is a gun? Or imagine being an insect?) This gives us Stevenson's first four conceptions. One or more of these conceptions is involved in every (more complex) conception of imagination that can be found, as we will see in the chapters that follow.

Taken together, the first four conceptions already suggest a certain generality to imagination. Imagination may be said to be involved whenever we think of something not actually present to us. Even when we think of something present to us, i.e. perceive something, that (perceptual) thought may be informed – rationally or non-rationally – by thoughts of other things; so it is a natural move to see the imagination at work in all thought. This gives us the second group of conceptions, numbered 5 to 8 in Stevenson's list. If thinking of something involves having a mental image of it (a view which we will examine shortly), then we have the fifth conception. The sixth is the most general of these conceptions, and the seventh restricts the imagination to the non-rational operations of thought. The eighth makes specific the supposed role of the imagination in perception. Stevenson identifies a source of the fifth conception in Aristotle's work, as already noted above (p.6), and mentions Descartes too in this regard, whose views we explore in the next chapter. All four conceptions he finds illustrated in Hume's philosophy, which we consider in chapter 3, and the eighth in particular is also characteristic of Kant's philosophy, as we will see in chapter 4.

The final four conceptions, numbered 9 to 12, concern the role of the imagination in aesthetic experience, and highlight the creative aspects of imagination. In the eighteenth century, when aesthetics as a discipline itself emerged, a distinction was drawn between the beautiful and the sublime. Flowers and birds were often given as examples of what is beautiful, while towering waterfalls in a thunderstorm and the starry firmament above provide good illustrations of what was seen as sublime. The beautiful gives rise to a kind of calm and comforting pleasure, while the sublime generates a more exhilarating pleasure, but one tinged with pain or fear. If we make use of this distinction, then we could say the following. Imagination is required in both the aesthetic appreciation and artistic creation of what is beautiful, which gives us the ninth and tenth conceptions, and also in both the aesthetic appreciation and artistic creation of what is sublime, which gives us the eleventh and twelfth conceptions. We will consider creativity and the creative imagination in the final two chapters of this book.

A first attempt at defining 'imagining'

So far I have made some preliminary remarks on the meanings of 'imagination' and related terms, and considered one attempt at distinguishing different conceptions of imagination. In a broad sense, 'imagining' means thinking in some way of what is not present to the senses. Imagining may involve, but is not the same as, imaging. In a derogatory sense, 'imagining' may mean 'fantasizing', as suggested by their etymological roots in Latin and Greek, and our use of the term 'imaginary'; in a more appreciative sense, it may mean 'creating', as suggested by our use of the term 'imaginative'. In considering the twelve conceptions of imagination that Stevenson distinguishes, I divided them into three groups of four. The first group, numbered 1 to 4, highlight the point that, in imagining, I am aware of something that is not actually present to the senses. The third conception captures the sense of 'imagining' as 'fantasizing'. In the second group of conceptions, numbered 5 to 8, we have both the conception that imagining is imaging (the fifth conception) as well as further recognition that there may be an element of 'fantasy' or 'delusion' in imagination (the seventh conception). The creative aspects of imagination are explicitly reflected in the third group of conceptions, numbered 9 to 12.

What emerges from this is the possibility of defining 'imagining', in its most basic or core sense, as 'thinking of something that is not present to the senses'. As I have noted, this sense certainly underlies Stevenson's first group of conceptions, which are divided according to whether what is thought is real (but just not present), possible or impossible, and if possible or impossible, whether it is believed to be such or not. We also saw how we might move from the first to the second group of conceptions. One way to think of what is not present to the senses is to conjure up an image of it, which gives the fifth conception. The sixth conception might seem even more general than the core sense. But if it is possible to think of anything regardless of whether it is present to the senses or not, then we might be tempted to identify the heart of any thinking with 'imagining'. (We will return to this shortly.) As far as the example illustrating the seventh conception is concerned, it can certainly be claimed that what I 'imagine' – the goodness of smoking – is unreal, and hence cannot be present to the senses. So too, in my example illustrating the eighth conception, when I imagine that the whole of something exists when I can only see part of it, the part I do not see is not, of course, present to the senses. It is possible to argue, then, that the core sense of 'imagining' just suggested underlies Stevenson's second group of conceptions of imagination as well.

How might this core sense be seen as involved in the third group of conceptions, concerning aesthetic appreciation and creation? In all four conceptions, we have the idea of imagining all sorts of things without fixing on any single definitive conceptualization or representation. So here too we have thinking of things that are not directly present to the senses, things which go beyond what is strictly or literally perceived or created, although the thought of those things may well be triggered by what lies before the senses.

What Stevenson's conceptions suggest, then, is this. If it is possible to identify a core sense of 'imagining', then an obvious candidate is 'thinking of something that is not present to the senses'. Admittedly, this is rather vague and general. But any sense that might be offered as underlying all twelve of Stevenson's conceptions is bound to be vague and general. And there may be virtue in its vagueness. For bearing it in mind may make us less likely to restrict our attention to just a few kinds of case, and more willing to consider the complex relationships that 'imagining' has both to other mental acts and to the wider context in which it occurs. Vague and general though it may be, it is also a sense that has often been articulated and, as we will see, has had a role to play in talking of imagination.

ACTIVITY

Consider the following case. You look out of the window and see a small tree with two branches sticking out from its sides that look like arms and a clump of leaves on top that looks like a head. You know very well that it is a tree, but you 'imagine' it as a person. Is this a counter-example to the claim that imagining is thinking of something that is not present to the senses?

DISCUSSION

In one way, it might seem obviously not. For are you not imagining something – namely, a person – that is not present to the senses? On the other hand, there is certainly something present to the senses that provides a kind of sensory basis for what you imagine. Merely talking of 'thinking of something that is not present to the senses' arguably does not do justice to what is going on here. What you are imagining is that something that *is* present to your senses is something else. So one might feel that some kind of qualification is needed.

What we have here is a case of what is called 'seeing-as'. We see the tree *as* a person, and in this case at least it also seems reasonable to describe what is going on as 'imagining' the tree as a person. We will be exploring seeing-as in chapter 5, when we consider Wittgenstein's remarks on the topic.

Wittgenstein does not talk of 'imagining' in all cases of seeing-as, which we might take to indicate – if we agree with him – that what we have here is a special kind of case. We could still claim, in other words, that the definition of 'imagining' as 'thinking of something that is not present to the senses' captures its core sense, while allowing qualifications or even departures from it in certain cases, which might then be counted as 'non-standard'. But we should keep in mind that such qualifications or departures may be necessary.

Any adequate definition of a term should lay down both necessary and sufficient conditions for its applicability (in all the main kinds of case). If we can handle such cases as imagining a tree as a person, then we might take 'thinking of something that is not present to the senses' as a necessary condition of imagining. If I imagine something, then I am thinking of something that is not present to my senses. Without such thinking, there could be no imagining. But is it a sufficient condition? If I am thinking of something that is not present to the senses, then am I imagining it? The core sense suggested by Stevenson's twelve conceptions is admittedly vague and general. But is it too general?

ACTIVITY

Can you think of (imagine?) any examples of 'thinking of something that is not present to the senses' that you would not describe as imagining?

DISCUSSION

There are various possible counter-examples that might be suggested. Here is one important kind of case. What is involved when you remember something? Are you not thinking of something that is not present to the senses (at that time)? Yet remembering something is not the same as imagining it. What we have, then, is a case of 'thinking of something that is not present to the senses' that would not be described as imagining. Thinking of something that is not present to the senses is not a sufficient condition for imagining.

What is the difference between remembering and imagining something? When we talk of remembering something, we imply that what is remembered actually happened or is true. (We need the clause 'or is true' to cover cases such as remembering a mathematical equation or remembering that I have an appointment tomorrow.) There is no such implication in talk of imagining something. But did I not admit, in illustrating Stevenson's first conception, that I can imagine something that actually happened or is true? We can indeed imagine what actually happened or is true, but when we talk of imagining it, there is nevertheless a recognition that we *could* be wrong (even if we are not). That what we are imagining actually happened or is true is a merely accidental or contingent feature of our imagining, in the following sense. If it had not happened or were not true, then we would still talk of imagining it; whereas if something that we claim to remember had not actually happened or were not true, then we would regard talk of 'remembering' here as illegitimate.

What this suggests, then, is that the definition of 'imagining' as 'thinking of something that is not present to the senses' is inadequate as it stands. While it arguably lays down a necessary condition for imagining, it does not lay down a sufficient condition. The definition is too general, since it includes things – such as remembering – that we would not count as imagining. If what we have said in distinguishing imagining from remembering is right, then in imagining something we are not just thinking of something that is not present to the senses, but also thinking of something that *need not* have actually happened or that *need not* be true. But can more be said about this additional requirement? Or are there alternative or better specifications? One attempt to offer a more restricted definition has been made by Berys Gaut in a paper entitled 'Creativity and imagination' (2003), which is included as Reading 6.

Gaut's analysis of imagination

Berys Gaut's main concern in his paper is to provide an account of the relationship between imagination and creativity, and we will examine this account in detail in the final chapter of this book. But in section 2 he offers an analysis of the notion of imagination, which we will look at here.

ACTIVITY

Read the introduction to Gaut's paper and then section 2, entitled 'Imagination'. You should read the whole section at least once through first, and then consider each paragraph more carefully as you answer the following questions, which are partly intended to guide you through a more detailed reading. The penultimate paragraph, in particular, packs in a number of different issues. You should concentrate, at least initially, on picking out the main point or points.

1   In the first three paragraphs of section 2, Gaut distinguishes four uses of the term 'imagination'. What are these four uses, and how do they relate to what I have already said, and to Stevenson's conceptions?

2   In the fourth and fifth paragraphs, Gaut argues against identifying imagining with imaging. What is his argument? Do you find it convincing?

3   In the sixth paragraph, Gaut presents his basic conception of what he calls (at the beginning of the seventh paragraph) 'propositional imagining'. How does he articulate this conception? Gaut offers several formulations, which he claims are equivalent. Are they equivalent? (There are a number of technical terms used here. You should focus on Gaut's basic conception.)

4   In the seventh paragraph, Gaut explains what he calls 'objectual imagining'. What is this further kind of imagining, and how does Gaut see his account of propositional imagining being extended smoothly to cover it? Is he right that 'imagining some object x is a matter of entertaining the concept of x'?

5   The eighth paragraph is the most difficult of all. Gaut distinguishes a third kind of imagining, which he calls 'experiential imagining', covering both 'sensory imagining' and 'phenomenal imagining'. What are these? Experiential imagining, he says, involves imagery. But since not all imagery implies imagining, what does Gaut suggest is the difference between imagery that is, and imagery that is not, a form of imagining? How does he see the relation between experiential and propositional imagining?

6   In the final paragraph, Gaut considers a final kind of imagining, 'dramatic imagining'. What does he mean by this, and how is it related to the other kinds?

DISCUSSION

1   In the first use that Gaut distinguishes, 'imagining' means 'falsely believing' or 'misperceiving'. This (derogatory) use is related to the sense of 'imagining' as 'fantasizing' mentioned above, reflecting the connotations of 'imaginary', and to Stevenson's third and seventh conceptions. In the second use that Gaut distinguishes, 'imagining' is more or less synonymous with 'creating'. This is the more appreciative sense of 'imagining', reflected in the connotations of 'imaginative', and in the third group of Stevenson's conceptions (numbered 9 to 12). In Gaut's third use, 'imagining' means 'imaging', which is Stevenson's fifth conception. In the first three paragraphs, Gaut does not say exactly what the fourth use is. He merely says what it is not: 'imagining' is here to be distinguished from 'imaging'. The first paragraph also suggests that he sees this as the core sense.

2   Gaut argues that there are cases of imaging – such as we find in memory, dreams and perception – which are not cases of imagining; and conversely, that there are cases of imagining – such as imagining an infinite row of numerals – which are not cases of imaging. We will return to the relationship between imagination and imagery later in this chapter. But with regard to this last example, you might have wanted to object that while no one can form an *accurate* mental image of an infinite row of numerals, they might well have *some* image in mind, such as a row of numerals going off into the distance. So even if having mental images cannot be all there is to imagining, the possibility has not yet been ruled out that imagery may be a necessary condition of imagination.

3   'Propositional imagining' is imagining that something is the case – imagining that p, or 'entertaining the proposition that p', as Gaut puts it. What is meant by 'entertaining' a proposition is thinking of it without commitment to its truth or falsity. Gaut offers two other formulations – thinking of the state of affairs that p, without commitment to the existence of that state of affairs, and thinking of p without 'asserting' that p. Gaut raises a doubt about the latter himself, and one might have doubts also about the appeal to 'states of affairs'. Could there be a 'state of affairs' involving an infinite row of numerals, for example? It is not clear what this might mean. Yet Gaut would presumably admit that we can entertain propositions about infinite rows of numerals. So 'entertaining propositions' is arguably not the same as 'thinking of states of affairs'. (Involved here, again, are questions about whether – or how – we can imagine 'impossible' things. There can be no state of affairs involving round squares, but can we imagine them? Have we not, at least, just entertained a proposition about them? More controversially, it might be argued that there can be no state of affairs in which a human is an insect, since humans and insects are essentially different. But did Kafka not write a story about this? Could we appeal to fictional states of affairs to get round the difficulty? Or does this just cover up the difficulty?) However, Gaut's main point is clear: as he conceives it, imagining that p is thinking of p without commitment to its truth or falsity (without 'alethic' commitment, as he puts it in more technical language).

4   'Objectual imagining' is imagining an object. Gaut suggests that, just as propositional imagining is a matter of entertaining a proposition, so objectual imagining is a matter of entertaining a concept. But what exactly is the relevant concept? Take Gaut's example of a wet cat. Can I not

'entertain' the concept of a wet cat without thinking of any particular cat (real or imagined)? Of course, Gaut defines 'entertaining the concept of x' as 'thinking of x without commitment to the existence (or non-existence) of x', so that by 'concept of x' he means 'concept of a particular x'. Nevertheless, we should still distinguish between imagining a particular wet cat and thinking (without existential commitment) of wet cats in general. And perhaps we might want to go further, and draw a distinction too between imagining a particular wet cat and 'merely' entertaining the concept of that particular wet cat. Imagining, it might be objected, has more of a sensory quality than talk of entertaining concepts does justice to. (In effect, this objection is recognized in what Gaut goes on to say about 'experiential imagining'.)

5 'Experiential imagining' is a richer kind of imagining, imagining with a 'distinctive experiential aspect', as Gaut describes it tautologically. More specifically, he suggests, it covers both sensory imagining and phenomenal imagining. As an example of the former, he gives visually imagining something, and as an example of the latter, imagining what it is like to feel something. In both cases, he says, imagery is involved. But as he argued in the fourth paragraph, imagery does not in itself imply imagining, since imagery can occur in remembering, dreaming and perceiving. So what distinguishes imagery that is, and imagery that is not, a form of imagining? According to Gaut, to have an image is to think of something, and the content of that thought can either be 'asserted' or unasserted'. Having an image is a kind of imagining, he says, when the thought-content is unasserted. (Talking of a thought-content having 'intentional inexistence' is just a technical way of saying that what we think of on a given occasion exists in thought, even if not in reality.) So experiential imagining is like propositional imagining in having an unasserted thought-content. The difference between experiential and propositional imagining, according to Gaut, lies in the way in which the thought-content is presented. In propositional imagining, that content is merely 'entertained'; in experiential imagining, it is visualized or otherwise represented with imagery. In visually imagining a wet cat, for example, I conjure up an image of a wet cat: this is experiential (sensory) imagining. Experiential imagining may well involve propositional and objectual imagining, but imagery is what gives it its experiential character.

6 'Dramatic imagining' is imagining what it is like to be someone else or to be in someone else's position. Gaut sees it as even richer than experiential imagining, but as ultimately reducible to the first three kinds of imagining.

Central to Gaut's account is the idea that mental acts have a 'thought-content' that can be thought of in different ways. The idea is often expressed by saying that mental acts involve the adoption of a certain attitude to a proposition – a 'propositional attitude' – or, in the case of objects, involve thinking of an object under a certain 'mode of presentation'. Take the thought or proposition that Immanuel (my cat) is wet. I can adopt various propositional attitudes to this. I can believe it, I can desire it, I can fear it, or I can imagine it, to mention just four. On Gaut's conception, to imagine it is to think of it without commitment to its truth or falsity. To believe it, on the other hand, as Gaut himself notes, is to think of it *with* commitment to its truth. But in both cases, the 'thought-content' of the propositional attitude is the same – the proposition that Immanuel is wet. The basic idea suggests, too, that there is a kind of bare thinking of this proposition lying at the core of the mental acts, which one might even be tempted to identify *as* 'imagining' in the most general sense possible. (This would give us Stevenson's sixth conception.) Certainly, imagining comes out as a form of thinking, for it involves thinking of a proposition or object (but without alethic or existential commitment, i.e. without commitment to its truth or falsity, or its existence or non-existence, respectively).

The appeal to 'propositions', however, is more controversial than Gaut's account implies. What *are* 'propositions'? I have already raised doubts as to whether they can be construed as 'states of affairs'. Even understanding them simply as 'thought-contents' is problematic. For it has proved notoriously difficult to provide criteria of identity for such contents. Can one really identify one and the same 'thought-content' across the various mental acts? If, as we will see in chapters 4 and 5, there is at least some sense in which imagination plays a role in perception itself, then specifying a 'thought-content' independent of the act of imagining may be more difficult than one might assume. However, let us leave this can of worms for the moment. Let us just accept the tautological point that, when I imagine or think of something, there is something that I am imagining or thinking of. And let us take Gaut's example of a wet cat. There is a whole range of imaginings that might, in some sense, have a particular wet cat, say Immanuel – or the 'state of affairs' in which

Immanuel is wet – as their 'thought-content'. I can imagine that Immanuel is wet, I can imagine a wet Immanuel, I can conjure up an image of a wet Immanuel, I can visually imagine Immanuel as wet, I can imagine Immanuel (who is standing dry before me) as wet, I can imagine what it is like to be as wet as Immanuel, I can imagine (perhaps) what it is like to be wet Immanuel, I can imagine (perhaps) what it is like to be in wet Immanuel's paws, and so on. Obviously, I have set it up this way, but there is clearly something that relates these various imaginings, and the natural thing to say is that they all concern a wet Immanuel, and furthermore involve thinking of a wet Immanuel in some way, a way that does not commit me to taking Immanuel as actually wet. It seems plausible to regard imagining, then, in a wide variety of cases, as thinking of something without alethic or existential commitment. At any rate, this is what Gaut offers as the core sense of 'imagining', and which we can take as constituting his main definition.

ACTIVITY

1. How does Gaut's definition compare with the general definition suggested by Stevenson's twelve conceptions? Are they equivalent? Does one follow from the other?

2. Do any of the examples I gave to illustrate Stevenson's twelve conceptions provide counter-examples to Gaut's definition? If so, how might Gaut respond?

3. I considered possible counter-examples to the general definition in the last section ('A first attempt at defining "imagining"'). Are they also counter-examples to Gaut's definition?

4. Is Gaut's definition an improvement on the general definition?

DISCUSSION

1. In both cases, imagining is defined as a form of thinking. But while on the general definition imagining is thinking of something that is not present to the senses, on Gaut's definition imagining is thinking of something without commitment to its truth or falsity, existence or non-existence. The two are not equivalent, since Gaut's definition does not follow from the general definition. To take the case of objects, if I am thinking of something that is not present to the senses, then it does not follow that I am not committed to its existence or non-existence. (Nor does it follow that I am committed.) However, the general definition does follow from Gaut's definition. For if I am thinking of an object without commitment to its existence or non-existence, then it follows that it cannot be present to the senses, since otherwise, presumably, I would be committed to its

existence. Being acknowledged to exist is part of what is meant by being 'present to the senses', as that phrase is intended to be understood here.

2. Stevenson's very first conception provides a counter-example to Gaut's definition. For in imagining how my daughter looks as I speak to her on the phone, I am certainly committed to her existence. Gaut might reply that I am not committed to the particular way I imagine she looks. Might I not be wrong? But perhaps I do know how she looks, and can imagine it precisely. Stevenson's third conception provides a further counter-example. For when Macbeth imagines that there is a dagger in front of him and reaches out towards it, he is committed (at least at that point) to its existence (even if he is wrong). Gaut might reply here that he has admitted that imagining can sometimes mean 'believing falsely' or 'misperceiving' (this was the first use he distinguished, in the first paragraph of section 2), but that this is not its core sense. But why should we not try to reflect it in our main definition, if we can? Stevenson's fourth, seventh and eighth conceptions provide further counter-examples. In 'imagining' fictional characters, I may be well aware that they are *not* real. In 'imagining' that smoking is good for me, I may actually believe it. And in 'imagining' that the whole of something exists when I can only see a part of it, I am certainly committed to its existence. Perhaps Gaut would see these too as derivative or non-standard senses, but the counter-examples seem to be extensive.

3. The example from the activity on page 12 only adds to the counter-examples to Gaut's definition that I have already mentioned. For in imagining a tree as a person, I may be perfectly aware that no such person exists, i.e. I may well be committed to the non-existence of what I imagine. However, Gaut's definition does suggest an answer to the problem raised in the discussion of the activity on page 13. On Gaut's conception, in imagining something I am not committed to the truth or existence of what I imagine, whereas in remembering something, he would presumably argue, I *am* so committed. So the requisite distinction between imagining and remembering can be drawn.

4. The definition suggested by Stevenson's twelve conceptions was too general in including things that do not count as imagining, such as remembering. In indicating the relevance of issues of truth and existence, Gaut's definition is an improvement. However, the requirement that, in imagining something, I am not alethically or existentially committed seems too strong. It rules out too many cases in which it seems perfectly legitimate to talk of 'imagining'. In all these cases, I can imagine something

while being firmly committed to either its existence or non-existence, truth or falsity. There are too many counter-examples, in other words, for Gaut's definition to be acceptable as it stands, at least if we are trying to capture a basic sense that underlies all the main uses of 'imagine'.

Can a definition be offered that is better than both the general definition and Gaut's definition? What seems to be needed is a definition that is more specific than the general definition, yet less specific than Gaut's definition. Gaut is right that issues of truth and existence are relevant, but they are relevant, I think, in a different way to the one he supposes. At the end of the last section, it was suggested that, in imagining something, I am thinking of something that *need not* be true or existent (in either the past, present or future) in the sense that, were it not true or existent, it would still be legitimate to talk of my 'imagining' it. I may well be alethically or existentially committed myself, but my thinking would still count as imagining even if I were wrong in my alethic or existential commitment. The actual truth or existence of what I am imagining, in other words, is not essential to the imagining itself in the way that it *is* essential to perceiving or remembering by contrast.

If a definition of 'imagining' can be offered at all, then it is something along these lines that I think is needed. But the suggestion will not do as it stands. For we now seem to have lost the distinction between imagining and believing. In believing something, am I not also thinking of something that need not be true or existent, in the sense indicated? So what is the difference between imagining and believing? Gaut characterized this as the difference between thinking of something without alethic or existential commitment and thinking of something with such commitment. But if what I have said is right, then imagining too can occur with alethic or existential commitment. An obvious response is to say that while in the case of believing, I cannot believe something without commitment to its truth or existence, in the case of imagining, I *can* imagine something without such commitment, or indeed with commitment to its falsity or non-existence. This is true, of course. But it does not enable us to distinguish cases of believing something with commitment to its truth or existence from cases of imagining something with commitment to its truth or existence. How can we draw this distinction? Perhaps all we need is a minor refinement to my current suggestion, on the basis of which we can then draw the following contrast. In the case of imagining, if what I imagine were not true or existent, *and I were to realize this*, then it would still be legitimate for me to talk of 'imagining'. But in the case of believing, if what I believe were not true or existent, and I were to realize this, then I could no longer talk of 'believing' it.

This is correct as far as it goes, but it obscures what I think is the crucial point here. Consider the case of Macbeth's imagining that there is a dagger before him, as he feverishly prepares to kill Duncan at the start of Act II of Shakespeare's play. Does he not also, as he reaches out to take it, *believe* that there is a dagger before him? And is this believing not part of his imagining? In the core sense of 'imagine' as Gaut defines it, the answer to this latter question would have to be 'No'. But as we have seen, Gaut does allow that 'imagine' can sometimes mean 'believe falsely'. So his considered answer would presumably be: 'Yes, but not in the core sense of "imagine".' However, a different response is possible which does not force us to distinguish two incompatible senses of 'imagine'. The crucial point, I think, is this. To say that Macbeth 'believes' there is a dagger before him implies that he is committed to the existence of a dagger before him. But to say that he 'imagines' that there is a dagger before him implies not that *he* is not committed to the existence of a dagger before him (though he may be), but that *we* are not committed to its existence in describing him as 'imagining' it. The lack of commitment to the truth or existence of something, in other words, lies not so much on the side of the person who is being described as 'imagining' something, as on the side of the person who is doing the describing. In talking of 'imagining', it is we who are indicating that lack of commitment. Of course, someone can themselves talk of 'imagining' something, as Macbeth in effect goes on to do (after he fails to take hold of the dagger he initially believes to be before him), but this would indicate their own lack of commitment to the truth or existence of what they are thinking of. On this alternative account, then, Gaut is right about the relevance of considerations of truth and existence, but he has brought them in at the wrong place.

The problematic status of the imagination

Let us review the position we have reached. Stevenson's twelve conceptions of imagination suggest that 'imagining' might be defined as 'thinking of something that is not present to the senses'. This definition succeeds in distinguishing imagining from perceiving, but is too general in including such things as remembering. Gaut defines 'imagining', in its core sense, as 'thinking of something without commitment to its truth or falsity, existence or non-existence'. This succeeds in distinguishing imagining from both perceiving and remembering, but is arguably too specific in excluding too many standard cases of imagining (i.e. cases that ought really to be captured in any core sense we specify). Can a better definition be offered? My alternative account might suggest the following possibility. 'Imagining' means thinking of something that is not present to the senses and that may or may not be true or existent, thinking which, in being called 'imagining', indicates a lack of commitment to the truth or existence of what is thought of by the person calling it such.

But in what sense is this a definition, and what are the implications of the suggested alternative account? If talk of 'imagining' says something about the person using the term (namely, that they are not committed to the truth or existence of what is being thought of) and not just about the person doing the thinking, then 'imagining' cannot be taken to denote a specific kind of mental activity or state. The definition, then, does not provide necessary and sufficient conditions for something to *be* imagining, but rather, to the extent that it is correct, explains our use of the term 'imagining'. In describing someone as 'imagining' something, we are indeed describing them as thinking of something, something that is not present to the senses. But at the same time we are evaluating that thinking, in refraining from committing ourselves to the truth or existence of what is being thought of. On some occasions, we may be implying something stronger, that we are committed to the falsity or non-existence of what is being thought of, as when we say that someone is 'merely imagining' something. On other occasions, there may be other implications too. But we might see the definition as capturing what is minimally involved in all the basic uses of the term 'imagining'. However, the key point is that, <u>in using a term such as 'imagining', we are not just referring to some mental activity, but also evaluating that activity in some way</u>. The general idea here – that we must reject the assumption that terms such as 'imagining' get their meaning by simply denoting mental states or processes – is particularly associated with the work of Wittgenstein, whose philosophy we will be exploring in chapter 5. Indeed, it is not too much of an exaggeration to say that this is the governing idea of Wittgenstein's philosophy of mind. Although Wittgenstein does not say as much about 'imagining' and its cognates as he does about other mental terms, and does not himself offer the suggested alternative account, which reflects merely the spirit of his thought, the case of 'imagining' provides a good way to illustrate Wittgenstein's philosophy.

Without saddling Wittgenstein with the suggested alternative account, then, what are the implications of what might nevertheless be called a Wittgensteinian view of imagining? If 'imagining' does not denote a specific kind of mental activity, categorically distinct from forms of thinking such as believing, then talk of 'imagination' – as the faculty responsible for 'imagining' – may be misleading. This might seem disconcerting, but it does offer the beginnings of an explanation of the problematic status that the imagination has had throughout the history of western philosophy. From ancient Greek thought onwards, the imagination has been invoked in describing and explaining certain kinds of unusual or puzzling experiences or phenomena, but it has proved enormously difficult to say just what the imagination is. But if 'imagining' does not denote a specific kind of mental activity, then it is not surprising that it has been hard to say exactly what it is; and if our use of 'imagining' partly expresses an evaluation on our part of a mental activity, then it is not surprising that it should be invoked in trying to account for these experiences or phenomena where we may well be unsure about matters of truth or existence.

In fact, the imagination has been invoked not just in describing and explaining unusual or obviously puzzling experiences or phenomena. In the work of Hume and Kant, for example, the imagination is seen as involved in all forms of perceptual judgement; and in Romanticism, which was heavily influenced by Hume and Kant, we find the imagination glorified as the most important cognitive power. In his essay 'On the imagination' (1817), Coleridge declared: 'The primary IMAGINATION I hold to be the living Power and prime Agent of all human Perception, and as a representation in the finite mind of the eternal act of creation in the infinite I AM' (1983, 304). Wordsworth described the imagination, in Book XIII of *The Prelude*, as 'but another name for absolute strength/And clearest insight, amplitude of mind/And reason in her most exalted mood' (quoted in Wu 1998, 405). But despite the virtually unlimited powers accorded to the imagination, or perhaps because of it, one is hard pressed to find clarification of the nature of the imagination in Romantic writings, and one must look to Hume and Kant for the source of this conception.

Partly in reaction to the excesses of Romanticism, discussion of imagination has been relatively absent in recent philosophy of mind. Sensation and perception, thought and language, content and representation, consciousness and intentionality are all topics that are standardly covered in textbooks, but not imagination. However, there are a few notable exceptions. Eva Brann, for example, in *The World of the Imagination* (1991), makes the most substantial effort to date to explore the imagination in all its relations and ramifications. The imagination, she remarks in her preface, 'appears to pose a problem too deep for proper acknowledgment. It is, so to speak, the *missing mystery* of philosophy' (1991, 3). In referring to this 'missing mystery' later on, with Kant specifically in mind, she writes:

> the imagination emerges as an unacknowledged question mark, always the crux yet rarely the theme of inquiry. It is the osmotic membrane between matter and mind, the antechamber between outside and inside, the free zone between the laws of nature and the requirements of reason. It is, in sum, the pivotal power in which are centered those mediating, elevating, transforming functions that are so indispensable to the cognitive process that philosophers are reluctant to press them very closely.
>
> (1991, 32)

In *The Body in the Mind: The Bodily Basis of Meaning, Imagination, and Reason* (1987), Mark Johnson has also argued against the marginalization of the imagination in contemporary philosophy and cognitive science. His book opens with similarly grandiose claims:

> Without imagination, nothing in the world could be meaningful. Without imagination, we could never make sense of our experience. Without imagination, we could never reason toward knowledge of reality ... It is a shocking fact that none of the theories of meaning and rationality dominant today offer any serious treatment of imagination.
>
> (1987, ix)

In the sixth chapter of his book, Johnson outlines the theory of imagination that he thinks is required, developing Kant's account. It is significant that both Brann and Johnson appeal to Kant in arguing for the importance of the imagination. For the imagination is indeed accorded a central role in Kant's philosophy, and it is natural to see Kant's conception of imagination as the model here.

Despite its importance, however, even Kant described the imagination as a 'hidden art in the depths of the human soul, whose true operations we can divine from nature and lay unveiled before our eyes only with difficulty' (see p.112 below). So Brann might seem right in calling the imagination a 'missing mystery'. But is there really a 'missing mystery' here, in the sense she has in mind? There may be a great deal of philosophical work to do in clarifying our talk of imagination, in understanding the complex ways in which the imagination is invoked, and in explaining the intricate relations between our concepts of perception, imagination, thought, and so on. But if the Wittgensteinian view suggested above is right and 'imagining' does not denote a specific kind of mental activity, then there is nothing that has the astonishing powers attributed to 'imagination', and so, as far as this goes, nothing to explain. There is no problem here that is 'too deep for proper acknowledgment'. Nor is it 'shocking' that current theories of meaning and rationality do not offer any 'serious treatment' of imagination, at least in the sense that Johnson has in mind. It may be regrettable, but it is not clear that the imagination must be accorded pride of place in any such theory. In any case, to use a distinction that Wittgenstein draws, what may be needed is not so much a theory of imagination that 'solves' the mystery of imagination as a conceptual clarification that 'dissolves' it – that demystifies the imagination. We will return to the issue in chapter 5, when we look in more detail at Wittgenstein's philosophy.

Imagery and supposition

Whatever view one takes of whether or how 'imagining' can be defined and whether there is a deep mystery here or not, it remains the case that there are many different conceptions of imagination, which are combined in different ways, sometimes in harmony, sometimes in tension, in the work of individual thinkers. In the four chapters that form Part One, we will explore the work of Descartes, Hume, Kant and Wittgenstein, which together give a good sense of the range of different conceptions, the ways in which the imagination is invoked, and the philosophical issues that arise. However, if there is a single issue that lies at the heart of debates about the imagination, then it is the tension between what might be described broadly as sensory and intellectual conceptions of the imagination. In the rest of this chapter, we will look at two questions that highlight this tension: whether imagery is a form of imagination, and whether supposition is a form of imagination. On the one hand, as reflected in Stevenson's first four conceptions, imagination is conceived in relation to sense perception, the only difference being the presence of the relevant object. In perception, we are aware of something that is present to the senses; in imagination, we are aware of something that is not present to the senses. What relates imagination to perception, it is often thought, is the presence in both of some kind of 'image' of what we are aware of. So imagery is regarded as essential to imagination (see Stevenson's fifth conception). But is this right? We will examine this issue in the next section. On the other hand, imagining is conceived as a kind of thinking. Since, more specifically, it is conceived as thinking of something whose truth or existence is somehow in question (whether on our part or on the part of the person doing the thinking), it has seemed natural to call this type of thinking 'supposing'. So supposition has been seen as a form of imagination. We will look at this issue in the final section of this chapter.

Imagination and imagery

From the very origins of concern with the imagination in the work of the ancient Greeks, the imagination has been associated with imagery. But what is the relationship between imagination and imagery? In chapter 12 of his book, *The Language of Imagination* (1990), Alan White addresses this question and argues that imagination neither implies nor is implied by imagery.

Read the extract from White's book that is included as Reading 1.

ACTIVITY

1   What is White's claim in the first paragraph of the extract? How does he argue for this claim, and how convincing is his argument?

2   What further argument for this claim does he provide in the second paragraph? How convincing is this further argument?

3   What is White's claim in the third paragraph? How does he argue for it, and how convincing is his argument?

4   In the fourth paragraph, White goes on to consider a 'more debatable problem'. What is this problem, and what is White's 'short answer'?

5   In the last three paragraphs, White suggests a number of differences between imagination and imagery. We will look at these in more detail in a moment. But to what specifically is imagining being contrasted?

DISCUSSION

1   White's claim is that imagination does not imply imagery, for which he argues by offering counter-examples. One might have doubts about some of them. In imagining what the neighbours will think, for example, might I not have an image of the neighbours? Having such an image may not

constitute the imagining, but might someone not object that some such image is necessary? But in cases such as imagining an objection (as I have just done), although images *may* be involved, here too it seems implausible to argue that they *must* be. So it seems right to conclude that imagination does not imply imagery, even if it may involve it in particular cases.

2 White's further argument might be formulated as an (attempted) *reductio ad absurdum* of the claim that imagination implies imagery:

 (1) Imagination implies imagery.

 (2) Imagery implies images.

 (3) Images must resemble 'in some copyable way' what they are images of.

 (4) Therefore, we can only imagine what can be 'copied' as an image.

 (5) But we can imagine far more than what can be 'copied' as an image.

 (6) So imagination does not imply imagery.

(1) is the premise that White wants to reject. (2), (3) and (5) are the additional premises, which White accepts, at least here. (In fact, later on in the chapter, White goes on to reject (2) as well, but he does not comment on the implications of this for his earlier argument.) From (1), (2) and (3) he infers (4), but since this is in conflict with (5), he concludes that (1) is false. But as the argument has been formulated, there are clearly other possibilities. Why, in particular, should we accept (3)? Why should images be restricted merely to images of what is 'copyable'? Can we not have images of abstract things? Consider the plates that William Blake prepared for his poems in *Songs of Experience and Innocence* (an example is given in Figure 1). Do these not offer images of things that are not 'copyable' as White seems to understand this? Or consider solving a geometrical problem. Can I not draw exactly how I imagined the problem could be solved? (An example of a geometrical problem is provided in appendix 1, which will be discussed at several points in the chapters that follow.) White's further argument seems unconvincing, then, and adds little to his first argument, although it does reveal an assumption he makes about what 'images' are.

3 Imagination, White has argued, does not imply imagery. In the third paragraph, he argues for the converse: namely, that imagery does not imply imagination. He again proceeds by offering counter-examples. We can have images in dreams and memory, for example, or after-images and

CHAPTER 1 IMAGINATION: THE MISSING MYSTERY OF PHILOSOPHY?

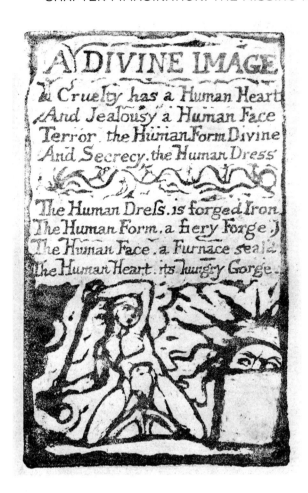

Figure 1 William Blake, *A Divine Image*, from *Songs of Innocence and of Experience, shewing the Two Contrary States of the Human Soul*, 1831–2. By permission of The British Library (C.43.d.25).

The poem here was originally written for Blake's *Songs of Experience* (1794), as the counterpart to 'The divine image' of his earlier *Songs of Innocence* (1789), but it seems not to have been used in any of the copies of the combined *Songs* that Blake produced in his lifetime. The plate that Blake prepared for it was never coloured, and the poem is only known from a print made after Blake's death (see Keynes 1970, 13, 125; Wu 1998, 84). 'The divine image' of the *Songs of Innocence* has five verses, of which the third runs as follows: 'For Mercy has a human heart/ Pity, a human face:/ And Love, the human form divine,/ And Peace, the human dress.' The contrast between this and the poem above is stark, a reaction perhaps to the horrors of the French Revolution. But Blake presumably then felt that it was too extreme, though the plate itself was obviously not destroyed. The poem that actually appeared as the counterpart to 'The divine image' was 'The human abstract', which is far subtler in tone.

As Keynes describes it in his facsimile edition, Blake's plate shows 'Los, the poet and craftsman, forging the Sun, symbol of imagination, into the words of his poem with furious blows of his creative sledge-hammer on the anvil' (1970, 125). The plate may be literally an image of someone hammering something on an anvil, but it clearly represents far more – the way in which our sensitive, imaginative nature can be beaten out of us by hatred and brutality, as revealed in the violence of the French Revolution or the oppression of industrialization, for example. The plate is an image, in other words, of far more than what is merely 'copyable'.

hallucinations, but would not speak of 'imagining' here, he suggests. However, it may be open to us to regard imagination as playing some role in such experiences, although we might agree that the mere having of images does not constitute imagining.

4   As White formulates it, the 'more debatable problem' is whether, when imagery does occur in imagining, it plays an essential role, i.e. whether there are some forms of imagination in which imagery is essential. White wants to argue that there are no such forms, since there are intrinsic differences between imagination and imagery.

5   The contrast that White is drawing seems to be between imagining and the mere having of images. It is worth keeping this in mind in assessing the differences he alleges between imagination and imagery.

In the final three paragraphs of the extract, White seems to be making quite a strong claim: that imagery never plays an essential role in imagination. But is this right? To answer this, let us consider a response to White's arguments that is made by Gregory Currie and Ian Ravenscroft in *Recreative Minds* (2002). In their first chapter, Currie and Ravenscroft distinguish between recreative and creative imagination. By 'recreative imagination' they mean the capacity to recreate in our minds states that are in some sense 'counterparts' to perceptions, beliefs, desires, and so on (2002, 11). In imagining a cat, for example, my imagining is some kind of 'counterpart' to seeing it. The 'creative imagination', on the other hand, is involved in creating something valuable in art, science or practical life, but this is only mentioned in order to be put aside (2002, 9). Their concern is with recreative imagination, and mental imagery, they suggest, is one important kind. In their second chapter, they offer arguments for this view, or more specifically, respond to White's arguments against this view.

ACTIVITY

Read the extract included as Reading 5 ('Is imagery a kind of imagination?'). What are the four arguments that Currie and Ravenscroft find in White's discussion, and what is their response to each one? Do they do justice to White's arguments, and provide a convincing refutation?

DISCUSSION

Let us consider each of the four arguments in turn.

1   According to White's first argument (drawn from the third and fifth paragraphs of Reading 1), imagination is under voluntary control while

imagery is not, or at best under only minimal control. But as Currie and Ravenscroft point out, there are cases of imagination too that are not under voluntary control. So there seems to be no basis here for claiming any essential difference between imagination and imagery.

2   According to the second argument (drawn from the fifth paragraph of Reading 1), imagining, unlike having an image, is something that I do. White does not put it like this himself, but the message is arguably the same. White talks of having imagery, unlike imagining, being an experience. Imagery happens to one; in imagining something, one is active. But as Currie and Ravenscroft remark, imaginings 'can come and go independently of one' in just the way that imagery can. So again, it would seem, there is no basis here for claiming an essential difference.

3   According to the third argument (also drawn from the fifth paragraph of Reading 1), imagery, unlike imagination, 'has an objectivity and independence'. But again, as Currie and Ravenscroft point out, I can be just as surprised by features of what I imagine as I can by features of my images. So they again seem right to reject White's argument.

4   According to the fourth argument (drawn from the sixth paragraph of Reading 1), imagery 'is particular and determinate, whereas imagination can be general and indeterminate', as White puts it himself. This is controversial, as White recognizes in a footnote to the paragraph. Currie and Ravenscroft claim that images can be indeterminate too, just as imagining can be particular, which seems right. So this fourth argument too seems not to establish any essential difference between imagery and imagination.

In the seventh paragraph of Reading 2, White offers a further argument, which Currie and Ravenscroft do not consider. Imagery, White writes, 'does not express anything, whereas imagination does'. Here most of all, perhaps, we can see that what White is concerned to describe are the differences between merely having an image and imagining. Take his example of an image of a sailor on a beach. This could be interpreted as a sailor scrambling ashore, his twin brother crawling backwards into the sea, or any of a host of other things. Imagining that a sailor is scrambling ashore, then, cannot *consist* in having such an image. We can agree with White on this. But it does not follow that having such an image is not an essential part of the imagining, which is the issue at stake as White himself formulates it (in the fourth paragraph of

Reading 1). What turns the mere having of an image into imagining is what we do with that image – the role it plays in our thinking. This is what Currie and Ravenscroft mean when they talk of imagery being a form of imagination. It is acts of producing and using images that constitute one form of imagining, and images are of course essential in this.

If this is right, then we can agree with Currie and Ravenscroft that imagery – or more accurately, using images in our thinking – is one form of imagining. To go back to White's earlier arguments, though, we can agree with White that imagination does not imply imagery, and that imagery does not imply imagination. But this is not to say that there are no forms of imagining in which images play an essential role. As we will see in the next three chapters, Descartes, Hume and Kant all thought that there were forms of imagining in which images were essential. Perhaps they were wrong to focus too exclusively on these forms of imagining, but they were not confused from the outset.

Imagination and supposition

To regard images as playing an essential role in imagining is to conceive of imagination as a sensory power. But as we have seen, imagining can also occur in the absence of imagery, and we might take this to reveal a more intellectual form of imagination. Many philosophers have suggested that this more intellectual form of imagining be construed as *supposing*. On this view, to imagine something, in cases where there may be no imagery involved, is to suppose something. But is it right to identify imagining in such cases with supposing? In the last section we considered White's arguments against the identification of imagination with imagery. In chapter 16 of his book, he also argues against the identification of imagining with supposing.

ACTIVITY

Read the extract from White's book that is included as Reading 2.
1. What is the difference between imagining and supposing that White states in the first two paragraphs of the extract, and what is the conception of each that he offers as the source of this difference?
2. White elaborates on this difference in the final three paragraphs. What does he say, and how convincing do you find his account?

3   As we saw in the last section, in arguing against the identification of imagination with imagery, White offered cases of imagination without imagery and of imagery without imagination. Either drawing on White's discussion in the present extract or thinking up your own examples, can you suggest cases of imagination without supposition and of supposition without imagination?

4   In the case of imagery, White wanted to draw the conclusion that imagery never plays an essential role in imagination. He seems to be suggesting something similar here: that supposition never plays an essential role in imagination. Whether or not this is actually White's view, do you think such a view is right?

DISCUSSION

1   According to White, one can be justified or unjustified in supposing something, but not in imagining something. As he conceives them, to suppose is to hypothesize, whereas to imagine is to think of a possibility.

2   To imagine something, White goes on, is to exercise a power, which some people have to a greater extent than others. This power is a power to 'embroider' in thinking of a possibility, whereas to suppose something is merely to invite consideration of its implications. White is right, I think, that imagining may involve richer thought processes than mere supposing, but I am not convinced that in being asked to imagine something, there may not equally be an invitation to consider its implications.

3   It seems fairly easy to find cases of imagining that could not really be described as 'supposing'. In imagining that the tree in my garden is a person, for example, I am not supposing that it is a person. In imagining that my cat Immanuel is wet, as he stands dry before me, I am not supposing that he is wet. It is perhaps more difficult to find cases of supposing where there is no room for talk of imagining. But here are two kinds of case that might be suggested. In searching for a proof of a complex theorem, a mathematician might suppose that a certain abstract formula holds, in order to see what conclusions can be drawn from it, without 'imagining' that it holds in any normal sense. Or to take one of White's examples, perhaps I can 'suppose' that something terribly evil has happened without being able to 'imagine' it, precisely because it is so terrible.

4   Even if we accept that supposing is not identical with imagining, there seem to be many cases of imagining in which supposing plays an essential role. In imagining how my daughter looks as I speak to her on the phone, I may well be supposing her to look that way. In imagining that there is someone out to get me, I may well be supposing that there is someone out to get me. Perhaps it would be wrong to call these examples cases of hypothesising something, but that would only show that supposing cannot be equated with hypothesizing, as White seems to suggest. However, even if we accept that there are cases of supposing in which there is an invitation to consider the implications of something (which we may or may not wish to call 'hypothesizing'), here too the supposing may play an essential role in acts of imagining. In imagining how my room will look painted in a different colour, I may suppose that it is painted that colour in order to see what follows from it. I may then realize, for example, that the colour of the walls would clash with the colour of the carpet or curtains. In creating imaginative works of fiction, writers may suppose people and things to be thus-and-so, and consider what follows from this. If they set the work in an actual place, populate it with a certain cast of characters, and invent a chronology of events, then they have to think through the implications of all this to tell a coherent story. Indeed, on White's own conception, 'imagining' means thinking of a possibility and 'embroidering' on it. But does this not involve, at least in some cases, *supposing* that this possibility obtains and exploring its consequences?

According to White, in supposing something, I am merely assuming or hypothesizing it, as a preliminary to considering its consequences. But this seems too restricted a conception of supposing. And even if we allow that some cases of supposing involve an invitation to explore the consequences of something, this may still reveal an imaginative act. In finding a mathematical proof or in writing a story, many things may be supposed along the way and their implications thought through, and it seems appropriate to regard this as part of the imaginative process. 'Supposing' and 'imagining' may not be synonymous, just as 'having an image' and 'imagining' are not synonymous, but this is not to say that there no acts of imagining in which supposing plays an essential role, or that supposing itself may not constitute a form of imagining.

'Imagining' covers a wide range of different mental acts and activities, and a number of different things may be involved, depending on the type of case. Imagery and supposition are not the only things that may be involved. Imagining may also involve visualizing, fantasizing, and pretending, for example, all of which have raised further questions in discussions of imagination. But the two issues we have just considered – the relationship that imagination has to imagery and supposition – do illustrate that fundamental tension identified at the beginning of this second main section. Imagery suggests a sensory conception of imagination, while supposition suggests a more intellectual conception. We will see both these conceptions illustrated in the next two chapters when we look at Descartes's and Hume's philosophy. While both Descartes and Hume officially conceive of imagination as imagery, other conceptions of imagination can be found operating implicitly in their thought.

Review and preview

1 We began by considering the meanings of 'imagination' and related terms in everyday contexts, and then looked at the twelve conceptions of imagination that Stevenson distinguishes. This suggested a first definition of 'imagining' – 'thinking of something that is not present to the senses'. This may lay down a necessary condition for imagining, but it does not lay down a sufficient condition, since it fails to exclude such things as remembering. We then examined Gaut's definition of 'imagining' as 'thinking of something without alethic or existential commitment, i.e. without commitment to its truth or falsity, existence or non-existence'. This succeeds in distinguishing imagining from both perceiving and remembering, but excludes many standard cases of imagining. While Gaut is right about the relevance of considerations of truth and existence, he arguably brings them in at the wrong place. In an attempt to formulate a definition that was neither too general nor too specific, the following alternative was suggested. 'Imagining' means thinking of something that is not present to the senses and that may or may not be true or existent, thinking which, in being called 'imagining', indicates a lack of commitment to the truth or existence of what is thought of by the person calling it such. We considered the implications of such a definition and, in particular, the possibility it opens up of demystifying the Romantic conception of imagination.

2   If there is a single issue that underlies debates about the imagination, then it is the tension between sensory and intellectual conceptions. This was brought out by examining the relationship that imagination has to imagery, on the one hand, and to supposition, on the other. Imagination neither implies nor is implied by imagery, it was argued, but this is not to say that there are no forms of imagination in which imagery plays an essential role. So too, it was argued, imagination neither implies nor is implied by supposition, but this is not to say that supposing may not constitute a form of imagining.

3   In the next four chapters we will explore the work of Descartes, Hume, Kant and Wittgenstein. We will see the tension between sensory and intellectual conceptions of imagination in Descartes's and Hume's thought, and will examine and compare the central role that is accorded to the imagination in Hume's and Kant's philosophy. If imagery and imagination find their supreme advocates in Hume and Kant, then Wittgenstein might be regarded as their most acute critic. We will consider Wittgenstein's discussion of imagination and seeing-as in chapter 5.

4   In Part Two (chapters 6 and 7), we will turn to the creative imagination, looking first at how creativity might be defined and whether it can be explained, and then exploring the relationship between creativity and imagination.

Further reading

Stevenson (2003) is a good place to start in clarifying the various conceptions of imagination, but for a fuller exploration, analysing in detail the language of imagination both historically and conceptually, although with many questionable claims, White (1990) can be recommended. Of the other books mentioned in this chapter, Brann (1991) is a superb resource of ideas on the imagination throughout history and in all areas of intellectual life, and Johnson (1987) makes a strong plea for a 'serious treatment' of the imagination, although both books arguably work with too romanticized a conception of imagination. Currie and Ravenscroft (2002) develop a more moderate theory of imagination, drawing upon psychology and cognitive science, and according pride of place to what they call 'recreative imagination'. Engell (1981) approaches the subject from literary criticism rather than philosophy, but offers a rich account of the development of ideas on the creative imagination. Other books that might also be mentioned here are Kearney (1988), which takes a historical journey from ancient times to postmodernism, and Warnock (1976), which offers a lucid and accessible account of Hume and Kant, Coleridge and Wordsworth, and Sartre and Wittgenstein.

Part One
Imagination, perception and thought

CHAPTER 2

Imagination and conception

> [A]s soon as a man reaches what we call the age of discretion he should resolve once and for all to remove from his imagination all traces of the imperfect ideas which have been engraved there up till that time. Then he should begin in earnest to form new ideas, applying all the strength of his intellect so effectively that if he does not bring these ideas to perfection, at least he will not be able to blame the weakness of the senses or the irregularities of nature.
>
> (Descartes, 'The search for truth by means of the natural light', *PW*, vol.2, 406)

In the last chapter we explored some of the different ways in which we talk of the imagination and its activities, and looked, in particular, at the tension between imagining as imaging and imagining as supposing. In this chapter we will see this tension illustrated in the work of René Descartes (1596–1650), whose philosophy lies at the origin of so much of modern thought.

The early modern period has often been characterized as involving a dispute between rationalists and empiricists – between those who privilege the role of reason in the acquisition of knowledge and those who regard knowledge as derived from sense experience. How the imagination was understood in this period reflects the general stance that was taken in this dispute. In the next chapter we will consider the account of the imagination offered by the most important empiricist, David Hume. Here we will focus on Descartes, who is standardly treated as the archetypical rationalist. In his most famous work, the *Meditations on First Philosophy* (1641), Descartes offers a critique of the imagination whose influence has lasted even after the demise of the mind/body dualism in whose context it originated. We will examine this critique in the next section. However, as we will see later in this chapter, Descartes did not always hold the imagination in such apparent disrespect, and even in the *Meditations* it plays a crucial role – albeit in a more intellectual form – in Descartes's reasoning.

In his ground-breaking study of Descartes's conception of imagination, on which I draw in the second main section of this chapter, Dennis Sepper has claimed that 'the philosophy of Descartes, from beginning to end, is an extended reflection on the implications of a dictum first pronounced in Greek antiquity by Aristotle, "There is no thought without phantasms [images]" – no thought without the presence of something in imagination in view of which the power of understanding exercises its activity' (1996, 6). This claim, and the truth of the dictum itself, provides the theme of this chapter.

Descartes's critique of sensory imagination

Descartes's *Meditations on First Philosophy* is perhaps the most famous and widely read work in western philosophy. Its subtitle makes clear its aim: 'in which are demonstrated the existence of God and the distinction between the human soul and the body'. The existence of God was needed in Descartes's system as the ultimate guarantee of the truth of our knowledge, and the distinction between body and soul was intended, on the one hand, to open up the possibility of explaining the world mechanistically, while, on the other hand, ensuring that we have the mental capacities to understand the world. In the First Meditation Descartes raises a series of progressively more radical sceptical doubts, culminating in the supposition of the existence of an evil demon, in order to find what is indubitable. What he comes to feel certain of is his own existence. Even if there is an evil demon deceiving him as much as he can, he (Descartes) must nevertheless exist to be deceived. So, as he concludes at the beginning of the Second Meditation, 'this proposition, *I am, I exist*, is necessarily true whenever it is put forward by me or conceived in my mind' (*PW*, vol.2, 17). It is this argument that becomes abbreviated as '*cogito, ergo sum*' or 'I think, therefore I am'.

Imagination in the Second Meditation

Accepting this argument (to which we will return), the question then is: 'What am I?' All we have from the *cogito* considerations is that I am a thing that thinks (where 'thinking' is understood, though, as involving any form of mental activity: doubting, affirming, willing, perceiving, and so on – see ibid., 19). It is at this point that Descartes considers what else he is, and appeals to his imagination:

> What else am I? I will use my imagination <to see if I am not something more>. I am not that structure of limbs which is called a human body. I am not even some thin vapour which permeates the limbs – a wind, fire, air, breath, or whatever I

depict in my imagination; for these are things which I have supposed to be nothing. Let this supposition stand; for all that I am still something. And yet may it not perhaps be the case that these very things which I am supposing to be nothing, because they are unknown to me, are in reality identical with the 'I' of which I am aware? I do not know, and for the moment I shall not argue the point, since I can make judgements only about things which are known to me. I know that I exist; the question is, what is this 'I' that I know? If the 'I' is understood strictly as we have been taking it, then it is quite certain that knowledge of it does not depend on things of whose existence I am as yet unaware; so it cannot depend on any of the things which I invent in my imagination. And this very word 'invent' shows me my mistake. It would indeed be a case of fictitious invention if I used my imagination to establish that I was something or other; for imagining is simply contemplating the shape or image of a corporeal thing. Yet now I know for certain both that I exist and at the same time that all such images and, in general, everything relating to the nature of body, could be mere dreams <and chimeras>. Once this point has been grasped, to say 'I will use my imagination to get to know more distinctly what I am' would seem to be as silly as saying 'I am now awake, and see some truth; but since my vision is not yet clear enough, I will deliberately fall asleep so that my dreams may provide a truer and clearer representation.' I thus realize that none of the things that the imagination enables me to grasp is at all relevant to this knowledge of myself which I possess, and that the mind must therefore be most carefully diverted from such things if it is to perceive its own nature as distinctly as possible.

(Ibid., 18–19; angle brackets indicate material added in the French translation (1647) of the original Latin version)

ACTIVITY

1. How does Descartes 'use his imagination' in the first four sentences of this passage?
2. According to Descartes, what is wrong with relying on these uses of his imagination?
3. How does the very word 'invent' show Descartes his mistake?
4. What does Descartes mean by 'imagining' in this passage?
5. Why, then, does Descartes think that the imagination should not be used in understanding the nature of the human mind?

DISCUSSION

1. Descartes imagines, first, that he is a human body and, second, that he is some kind of 'vapour' that permeates his body.
2. Descartes is not in a position (at least at this point in the *Meditations*) to *know* that he is anything that he merely imagines.

3   The word 'invent' suggests that what is imagined may be fictitious.
4   'Imagining' simply means 'contemplating the shape or image of a corporeal thing'.
5   As Descartes defines 'imagining', it concerns corporeal things, and according to Descartes, whatever we apprehend of corporeal things can be doubted. So I must ignore anything that my imagination produces if I am to truly understand the nature of mind.

Does this mean that Descartes holds that the imagination is not really part of the mind? We should first distinguish here between the *objects* of imagination and the *faculty* or *power* of imagination. According to Descartes, the objects of imagination cannot be taken to form an essential part of the mind, but this does not imply that the faculty of imagination itself is not part of the mind. On his view, the 'I' who assuredly exists even under the supposition of an evil demon deceiving me is the same 'I' who imagines. As he puts it in the next but one paragraph, 'For even if, as I have supposed, none of the objects of imagination are real, the power of imagination is something which really exists and is part of my thinking' (ibid., 19). To this extent, then, 'I imagine, therefore I am' would also be acceptable as a basis for Descartes's project of securing our knowledge. What is important is not *what* I imagine but *that* I imagine. (We will return to this later in this chapter.) Nevertheless, as we will see, in the Sixth Meditation Descartes does deny that the imagination is an *essential* part of his mind – even if, on occasions, it may be part of his 'thinking', as he puts it in the Second Meditation.

But what precisely does Descartes mean by 'objects of imagination'? Here we should distinguish between images and what those images are images of. 'Objects of imagination' is ambiguous between the two. When Descartes talks of imagining as 'simply contemplating the shape or image of a corporeal thing', this might suggest that the objects of imagination are images. But the remark cited in the previous paragraph suggests that they are what the images are images of, since it is these that can be either real or imaginary. We might agree with Descartes that the objects of imagination, in the latter sense, cannot be an essential part of the mind, but why cannot images themselves be part of the mind? Descartes's answer to this does not become clear until the Sixth Meditation.

The wax example

Further aspects of Descartes's conception of imagination are revealed in his discussion of the wax example. To illustrate the role of the mind in grasping the essence of something, Descartes asks us to consider a piece of wax that has just been taken from the honeycomb. Initially, the wax is cold and hard, and has a particular colour, shape, size and scent. It is then put by the fire, and all the properties by means of which I initially recognized it as a piece of wax alter. It becomes warm and soft, changes colour, shape and size, and loses its scent. But, says Descartes, it is still the same piece of wax. So none of these properties can be what is essential to it. What is its essence, then, and how can I grasp it? Descartes writes:

> Let us concentrate, take away everything which does not belong to the wax, and see what is left: merely something extended, flexible and changeable. But what is meant here by 'flexible' and 'changeable'? Is it what I picture in my imagination: that this piece of wax is capable of changing from a round to a square shape, or from a square shape to a triangular shape? Not at all; for I can grasp that the wax is capable of countless changes of this kind, yet I am unable to run through this immeasurable number of changes in my imagination, from which it follows that it is not the faculty of imagination that gives me my grasp of the wax as flexible and changeable. And what is meant by 'extended'? Is the extension of the wax also unknown? For it increases if the wax melts, increases again if it boils, and is greater still if the heat is increased. I would not be making a correct judgement about the nature of wax unless I believed it capable of being extended in many more different ways than I will ever encompass in my imagination. I must therefore admit that the nature of this piece of wax is in no way revealed by my imagination, but is perceived by the mind alone.
>
> (Ibid., 20–1)

ACTIVITY

1 What does Descartes suggest are the essential properties of the piece of wax?

2 Why does Descartes think that it is not my imagination that enables me to grasp these properties?

3 How would you characterize the conception of imagination that underlies Descartes's argument in this passage?

4 Is Descartes right that the nature of a piece of wax can only be revealed by the mind alone?

> DISCUSSION
>
> 1   A piece of wax, Descartes suggests, is essentially something 'extended [i.e. with spatial dimensions], flexible and changeable'.
> 2   While I can imagine a piece of wax of determinate shape and size, etc. (i.e. with a particular set of non-essential properties), I cannot imagine it as undergoing the innumerable changes that, according to Descartes, I would have to imagine if I were to grasp its properties of flexibility and changeability. So if I do grasp these properties, it cannot be by means of the imagination.
> 3   Descartes seems to regard the imagination as the power of receiving or producing images (understood as a kind of inner picture or representation) of physical things. On his view, it is because I cannot produce or hold in my mind at one time large numbers of such images that I cannot grasp flexibility, changeability and extension by means of imagination.
> 4   We may grant that if imagination merely involves the having of particular images, then this by itself cannot constitute knowledge of properties such as flexibility, changeability or extension. But it does not follow from this that the mind alone is responsible for 'perceiving' these properties. Why should it not require a combination of imagination and (conceptual) understanding? To understand change in something, for example, do I not have to produce, at the very least, images of that thing before and after, by means of which to judge the change?

Clearly, what underlies Descartes's critique of the imagination is the assumption that imagination involves having images – understood as a kind of determinate inner picture or representation of things. (It is tempting to describe them as 'mental' images, but care is needed here. For this might suggest that they are part of the mind, and this is not Descartes's view. We will return to this later.) Grasping a property such as changeability, then, cannot consist in having any one such image. But nor can it consist in having a set of such images. What would make such a set a representation of the *change* in something as opposed to a set of images of different objects? Such a set has to be conceptualized as a temporally ordered series of images of a continuously existing object, subject to some kind of causal process (as Kant was later to argue). All this brings in more than the mere having of images. So to this extent Descartes is right.

But does this mean that I can grasp changeability by the mind alone? This is less clear. According to Descartes, to grasp changeability is to understand that something can be changed in innumerable ways, and since I cannot imagine all these innumerable ways, I cannot grasp changeability by imagination. But while I cannot have a single image that represents changeability, why would I have to imagine *all* these innumerable ways? Is it not enough to imagine *some* of them, albeit with an understanding of their origin and connection? Imagining *some* ways may not be a sufficient condition for grasping changeability, but it might be regarded as a necessary condition. The relation between imagination and conceptual understanding may be more complex and intimate than Descartes seems to allow in the Second Meditation.

Imagination in the Sixth Meditation

Descartes returns to the issue of imagination in the final Meditation. By this point he takes himself to have established not only his own existence but also that of God, and through this to have validated his use of reason. All that is left is to prove the existence of the external world and to complete the argument for the distinction between mind and body. It is in this context that Descartes considers further the difference between imagination and conceptual understanding. Here are the opening three paragraphs of the Sixth Meditation:

> It remains for me to examine whether material things exist. And at least I now know they are capable of existing, in so far as they are the subject-matter of pure mathematics, since I perceive them clearly and distinctly. For there is no doubt that God is capable of creating everything that I am capable of perceiving in this manner; and I have never judged that something could not be made by him except on the grounds that there would be a contradiction in my perceiving it distinctly. The conclusion that material things exist is also suggested by the faculty of imagination, which I am aware of using when I turn my mind to material things. For when I give more attentive consideration to what imagination is, it seems to be nothing else but an application of the cognitive faculty to a body which is intimately present to it, and which therefore exists.
>
> To make this clear, I will first examine the difference between imagination and pure understanding. When I imagine a triangle, for example, I do not merely understand that it is a figure bounded by three lines, but at the same time I also see the three lines with my mind's eye as if they were present before me; and this is what I call imagining. But if I want to think of a chiliagon, although I understand

that it is a figure consisting of a thousand sides just as well as I understand the triangle to be a three-sided figure, I do not in the same way imagine the thousand sides or see them as if they were present before me. It is true that since I am in the habit of imagining something whenever I think of a corporeal thing, I may construct in my mind a confused representation of some figure; but it is clear that this is not a chiliagon. For it differs in no way from the representation I should form if I were thinking of a myriagon, or any figure with very many sides. Moreover, such a representation is useless for recognizing the properties which distinguish a chiliagon from other polygons. But suppose I am dealing with a pentagon: I can of course understand the figure of a pentagon, just as I can the figure of a chiliagon, without the help of the imagination; but I can also imagine a pentagon, by applying my mind's eye to its five sides and the area contained within them. And in doing this I notice quite clearly that imagination requires a peculiar effort of mind which is not required for understanding; this additional effort of mind clearly shows the difference between imagination and pure understanding.

Besides this, I consider that this power of imagining which is in me, differing as it does from the power of understanding, is not a necessary constituent of my own essence, that is, of the essence of my mind. For if I lacked it, I should undoubtedly remain the same individual as I now am; from which it seems to follow that it depends on something distinct from myself. And I can easily understand that, if there does exist some body to which the mind is so joined that it can apply itself to contemplate it, as it were, whenever it pleases, then it might possibly be this very body that enables me to imagine corporeal things. So the difference between this mode of thinking and pure understanding may simply be this: when the mind understands, it in some way turns towards itself and inspects one of the ideas which are within it; but when it imagines, it turns towards the body and looks at something in the body which conforms to an idea understood by the mind or perceived by the senses. I can, as I say, easily understand that this is how imagination comes about, if the body exists; and since there is no other equally suitable way of explaining imagination that comes to mind, I can make a probable conjecture that the body exists. But this is only a probability; and despite a careful and comprehensive investigation, I do not yet see how the distinct idea of corporeal nature which I find in my imagination can provide any basis for a necessary inference that some body exists.

(Ibid., 50–1)

ACTIVITY

1. How does Descartes characterize the imagination in the first paragraph of this passage? What does this suggest as to how the imagination is conceived in its relation to the mind and the body?
2. Taking the case of the triangle, how does Descartes explain the difference between imagination and conception (conceptual understanding)?
3. According to Descartes, can I imagine a chiliagon?
4. What assumption is Descartes here making about the nature of the imagination?
5. What is the example of the pentagon meant to suggest as to the difference between imagination and conception?
6. Why does Descartes think that the power of imagining is not part of the essence of his mind?
7. What is the difference between imagining and conceiving stated in the third paragraph of this passage?

DISCUSSION

1. Imagination, Descartes writes, is 'nothing else but an application of the cognitive faculty to a body which is intimately present to it'. As Descartes conceives it, imagination involves a joint operation of the mind and body, and plays a kind of mediating role. The use of my imagination requires the existence of my body, and is what I become aware of 'when I turn my mind to material things'.
2. When I imagine a triangle, I picture a three-sided figure 'with my mind's eye'. When I conceive of a triangle, I simply understand that it is a three-sided geometrical figure.
3. Strictly speaking, on Descartes's view, I cannot imagine a chiliagon. If I try to do so, then I may imagine something, but there would be no difference between what I imagine in this case and what I imagine when I try to imagine some other many-sided figure. The image I conjure up is simply too confused to count as an image of any particular many-sided figure.
4. Descartes is assuming that imagining consists in having an image of something before the 'mind's eye'. What it is an image of (if anything) depends on how clear the image is.
5. I can both conceive of a pentagon, understanding that it is a five-sided figure, and imagine a pentagon, forming an image of it. But in the latter case, I have to run my 'mind's eye' over the image to apprehend that it does

indeed have five sides. The extra mental effort that this requires shows the difference between imagination and conception, according to Descartes.
6 On Descartes's view, I would still be me, even if I lacked the power of imagination altogether, and thus this power cannot be part of my essence – that is, part of my essence as a mind or soul.
7 In imagining, I am 'inspecting' something in the body (i.e. an image in the brain); in conceiving, I am 'inspecting' something in the mind.

This passage makes clear that Descartes conceives the imagination as a sensory faculty dependent on the body and, in particular, on the presence of bodily or corporeal images, in just the same way as sensory perception is supposed to be. So let us call it 'sensory imagination'. According to Descartes, what happens in sensory imagination is that my 'mind's eye' contemplates images in the body, i.e. brain images. However, this suggests that we ought to distinguish sensory imagination from mere 'corporeal imagination', which is simply the corporeal faculty of having or processing images in the brain. Descartes often marks this distinction himself by using the Latin term *imaginatio* for the former and the Greek term *phantasia* (in its Latin transliteration) for the latter (see *PW*, vol.1, 41, n.2). Sensory imagination thus depends on corporeal imagination, according to Descartes, which is why he denies that (sensory) imagination is part of the essence of the mind. On this conception, too, we can see how the ambiguity I noted on page 43 arises. For while it might be natural to take 'object of imagination' to mean *what* is imagined – i.e. what the relevant image is an image of – it could also mean the image itself, which is what the 'mind's eye' looks at in acts of imagining.

Images and ideas

The difference that Descartes describes in the third paragraph of the Sixth Meditation suggests that a distinction should be drawn between images and ideas: images are involved in imagination, ideas (or concepts) in conception. Although Descartes is not always consistent in his terminology (as the passage cited at the very beginning of this chapter shows), this distinction is made explicit elsewhere. When the *Meditations* was first published in 1641, it appeared together with a series of objections by various of Descartes's contemporaries and Descartes's replies to them, generally known as the

'Objections and Replies'. In the third set of objections, Thomas Hobbes (1588–1679) criticizes Descartes's argument for the existence of God on the grounds that his underlying assumption – that we have an idea of God within us – is false. In his reply, Descartes points out that while we may have no image of God, as a depiction of a material thing in the corporeal imagination, we certainly have an idea of God. He notes that by 'idea' he means 'whatever is immediately perceived by the mind' (*PW*, vol.2, 127), and it is in this sense that we have an idea of God when we conceive of God as an all-perfect being. As he remarks in response to Pierre Gassendi (1592–1655), the author of the fifth set of objections, in which similar criticisms are made, 'You are confusing understanding with imagination, and are supposing that we imagine God to be like some enormous man, just as if someone who had never seen an elephant were to imagine it was like some enormous tick, which, I agree, would be extremely foolish' (ibid., 252).

In other places, Descartes talks of both ideas of the imagination and ideas of the mind, but even here his considered position seems to be that ideas and images are not the same. In his reply to the second set of objections, compiled by Marin Mersenne (1588–1648), he defines 'idea' as follows:

> *Idea*. I understand this term to mean the form of any given thought, immediate perception of which makes me aware of the thought. Hence, whenever I express something in words, and understand what I am saying, this very fact makes it certain that there is within me an idea of what is signified by the words in question. Thus it is not only the images depicted in the imagination which I call 'ideas'. Indeed, in so far as these images are in the corporeal imagination, that is, are depicted in some part of the brain, I do not call them 'ideas' at all; I call them 'ideas' only in so far as they give form to the mind itself, when it is directed towards that part of the brain.
>
> (Ibid., 113)

In a letter to Mersenne written at the time that the objections and replies were being put together, Descartes remarks that 'whatever we conceive without an image is an idea of the pure mind, and whatever we conceive with an image is an idea of the imagination' (*PW*, vol.3, 186).

ACTIVITY

Does this last remark conflict with what Descartes says in defining 'idea'? Are 'ideas of the imagination' images?

It is tempting to interpret Descartes as holding that ideas of the imagination are images. But this is not his considered view. An idea of the imagination is 'whatever we conceive *with* an image', and this is consistent with what he says in defining 'idea'. Images are corporeal, while ideas are mental. So ideas of the imagination can be regarded as what are generated in the mind when I direct my attention to the images that are produced in my brain. Ideas of imagination, on Descartes's view, are the mental correlates of images.

We might grant with Descartes that there is a distinction between ideas (or concepts) and images, and that there are many things that we can only conceive and not imagine – 'imagine' in the sense of forming some determinate image. But does this mean that conception provides the only genuine source of knowledge, and that imagination is not merely dispensable but strictly to be avoided? Even if we accept that the imagination simply involves receiving and producing images, there may be a closer connection between imagination and conception than Descartes allows. There seem to be many concepts our grasp of which is manifested in the images that we can either recognize or form of the objects that fall under them. Could I really be said to grasp the concept of a triangle, for example, if I were unable to conjure up or recognize images of triangles? Although I may be unable in practice to recognize a chiliagon if one appears in front of me, I can do so in principle given time and resources. (In the case of a drawn figure on paper, for example, I may need a magnifying glass to see the individual sides and a pen to mark, say, every tenth side.) And even if we insist that actual images are irrelevant in the case of conceiving of a chiliagon, the ability to do so presupposes the ability to conceive of simpler polygons such as squares and pentagons, which may well be argued to require imagination.

Of course, Descartes is right that conceiving of a square does not consist in having an image of a square, but then nor does it consist in having an idea – if this is seen as something 'in' the mind that the mind 'immediately perceives'. If conceptual understanding is an ability (as Kant and Wittgenstein, for example, were later to argue) rather than the simple possession or 'perception' of a mental entity, then this ability may well involve or require the ability to recognize and form images. Again, we can agree with Descartes that there are no obvious images involved in conceiving, say, of God or of abstract objects such as numbers. But here too the ability to form some kind of image might well be required. In any case, the ability to form images of things is not all that is involved in what we call 'imagination'. As we will see, even in Descartes's thought a different conception of imagination can be found in play.

Descartes's use of intellectual imagination

Descartes did not always hold the imagination in the disregard suggested by his arguments in the *Meditations*, and even here he arguably continues to value at least one form of imagination. In recent years, there has been a growing interest in Descartes's conception of imagination. A landmark study is Dennis Sepper's *Descartes's Imagination*, which appeared in 1996, and this was followed by Peter Schouls's *Descartes and the Possibility of Science* (2000). Sepper focuses on Descartes's conception of imagination in his early writings and, in particular, in his *Rules for the Direction of the Mind*. Schouls argues that the views expressed in the *Rules*, and the role played by an intellectual form of imagination, continue into his later work.

Descartes's *Rules for the Direction of the Mind*

'Rules for the Direction of the Mind' is the standard translation of the title of Descartes's most important early work, the *Regulae ad directionem ingenii*, which was written in the 1620s, abandoned unfinished in 1628, and only published posthumously in 1684. But according to Sepper, neither 'mind' nor the French term *esprit* accurately captures what Descartes means by the Latin term *ingenium*, which is better translated as 'native human endowment' or 'native intelligence' (1996, 84, 94). More specifically, Sepper suggests, *ingenium* refers to 'the general faculty of forming and acting upon images' (1996, 84). If this is right, then concern with the imagination lies at the very heart of Descartes's early work.

The aim of the *Rules* is, as Rule One puts it, 'to direct the mind [*ingenium*] with a view to forming true and sound judgements about whatever comes before it' (*PW*, vol.1, 9). Rule Twelve sums up Descartes's recommendations in the first eleven rules, and is the key rule as far as his conception of the relationship between mind and imagination is concerned. Identifying the four faculties taken as involved in knowledge, its advice is 'to make use of all the aids which intellect, imagination, sense-perception, and memory afford' (ibid., 39). Descartes writes: 'It is of course only the intellect that is capable of perceiving the truth, but it has to be assisted by imagination [*imaginatio*], sense-perception and memory if we are not to omit anything which lies within our power' (ibid.). Although, as in his later work, Descartes emphasizes the intellect here, what is notable is the recognition of the importance of the imagination. According to Descartes, however, underlying all four faculties is a single cognitive power, which, 'when it forms new ideas in the corporeal imagination [*phantasia*], or concentrates on those already formed, the proper term for it is 'native intelligence' [*ingenium*]' (ibid., 42). *Ingenium* is thus indeed seen as the power of operating on ideas of the imagination, either forming new ones or examining existing ones.

Descartes's *Rules* had been intended to have three parts, each with twelve rules. Only the first part is complete, and the third part is missing altogether. The first set of twelve rules is concerned with what Descartes calls 'simple propositions', and the incomplete second set with 'perfectly understood problems'. The third set was to have dealt with 'imperfectly understood problems'. (Ibid., 7, 50–1.) Good examples of 'perfectly understood problems' are geometrical problems, such as those found in Euclid's *Elements*. On Descartes's view, it is in problem-solving that the imagination is most crucially involved, employed, in particular, in the construction of figures. This is made explicit in Rule Fourteen: 'The problem should be re-expressed in terms of the real extension of bodies and should be pictured in our imagination entirely by means of bare figures. Thus it will be perceived much more distinctly by our intellect' (ibid., 56). In elaborating on this rule, Descartes goes on:

> If, moreover, we are to make use of the imagination as an aid we should note that whenever we deduce something unknown from something already known, it does not follow that we are discovering some new kind of entity, but merely that we are extending our entire knowledge of the topic in question to the point where we perceive that the thing we are looking for participates in this way or that way in the nature of the things given in the statement of the problem. For example, if someone is blind from birth, we should not expect to be able by force of argument to get him to have true ideas of colours just like the ones we have, derived as they are from the senses. But if someone at some time has seen the primary colours, though not the secondary or mixed colours, then by means of a deduction of sorts it is possible for him to form images even of those he has not seen, in virtue of their similarity to those he has seen.
>
> (Ibid., 56–7)

54   IMAGINATION AND CREATIVITY

ACTIVITY   What is Descartes's main point in this passage?

DISCUSSION   In making use of the imagination in problem-solving, we are not discovering (or inventing) something entirely new, but coming to understand the relation of something to things that we already know. (It is significant that Descartes's language here echoes Euclid's language in the *Elements*. For Euclid's aim was indeed to show how something could be constructed from the things given in the statement of the problem. See appendix 1.)

The example that Descartes gives is particularly interesting, and we will return to it in the next chapter when we consider Hume's problem of the missing shade of blue. Our concern here is with the role that figures or diagrams play in problem-solving, for it is by means of these that we can abstract from the particularities of something and allow the relations in which it stands to be exhibited and investigated. The success of such a method depends on the analogies or proportionalities between the figures and the figured, and the assumption that these proportionalities obtain was central to Descartes's early thought. According to Descartes, there was an underlying harmony in the world, and it was by 'figuring out' the proportionalities that we could come to understand the world (see Sepper 1996, 41). Significantly, Descartes's earliest surviving work is on music, and what his *Compendium musicae* sets out to show is how both rhythm and tonal relationships can be represented geometrically. The case of tone is illustrated in Figure 2, which shows how the tonal relationships of consonance – when two notes sound in harmony – can be represented by the proportionalities of a line. (Think of the sounds you hear when a string is plucked when held at different points along its length.)

Figure 2 Descartes's division of a line by successive bisectioning gives rise to ratios of the principal consonances. Point *C* bisects *AB*; *D* bisects *CB*; *E* bisects *CD*; and *F* bisects *CE*. *AC* produces the octave above *AB*; *AC* and *AD* yield a fifth; *AD* and *AB* produce a fourth; *AC* and *AE* yield a major third. These proportions are based on the numbers 2, 3, and 5 or their multiples; the process of bisection makes this visually comprehensible. All the relationships dependent on the last bisection at *F* lead to dissonances. As a result of this technique of division, all the consonances are simply imaged by a single line. (Figure and description are reproduced from Sepper 1996, 43.)

The case of music suggested to Descartes the possibility of a general theory of proportionality, which he came to call a *mathesis universalis*, a kind of universal mathematics encompassing algebra, arithmetic and geometry, by means of which everything could in principle be represented, investigated and understood. Just as we can work out the distance from A to B in the actual world by using a map in which the scale is known, so too, in general, problems can be solved by working out the relationships in an appropriate figure or symbolic representation.

If imagination is understood as the power of producing and operating with figures and images, then it clearly has a central place in our cognitive activities, and Descartes's *Rules* can indeed be seen as concerned with directing its use. But if this is so, then how did Descartes apparently come to downgrade the imagination in his later work? The answer is that he did not so much repudiate his earlier view as qualify it, in thinking through its implications. The most obvious problem that confronts his earlier view is the justification of his central assumption that the world contains underlying proportionalities. How do we know that such a principle of proportionality is true? What Descartes found himself forced to admit (as a condition of scientific understanding) was the necessary truth of certain fundamental laws ultimately grounded in the existence of God. As its subtitle indicates (see p.41 above), one of the aims of the *Meditations* was to provide the proof that was needed here.

Thinking through the presuppositions of the use of figures in problem-solving, then, leads one into metaphysics, and in metaphysics images seem to have far less of a role to play. Indeed, given the abstract nature of the concepts involved, they may actually be misleading. As Descartes remarked in a letter to Mersenne written at the time that he was working on the *Meditations*, 'The imagination, which is the part of the mind that most helps mathematics, is more of a hindrance than a help in metaphysical speculation' (*PW*, vol.3, 141). The idea of God is just one example of an idea the grasp of which may be confused if we attempt to conjure up images. Nevertheless, the fact that Descartes continued to value the imagination in mathematics suggests that, on his later view, he sought only to limit its use, not to repudiate it altogether. However, as we will see, even in his own metaphysics Descartes underestimated the role that imagination – in some sense – still plays.

Intellectual imagination in the *Meditations*

In his later work, Descartes seems to understand the imagination as an essentially sensory power – the power to apprehend corporeal images. Although he does not use the term 'intellectual imagination', both Sepper and Schouls have argued that the term is required to make sense of Descartes's views. As Schouls has put it, 'Descartes constantly and consciously used the power which this phrase might have named' (2000, 62). To see this, we need only consider the short First Meditation.

As I noted earlier, in the First Meditation Descartes raises a series of progressively more radical sceptical doubts. Why should I trust my senses, given that they often deceive me? How do I know that I am not dreaming? And most radically of all, how can I be sure that I am not being misled about everything by some all-powerful evil demon? Descartes draws the conclusion (at the beginning of the Second Meditation) that even under this most radical scenario, he (Descartes) must still exist to be deceived; and it is this line of reasoning that came to be encapsulated in the famous statement, 'I think, therefore I am'. But it is significant that this statement does not appear in the *Meditations* itself (although it does appear in part IV of his earlier *Discourse on the Method* and in section 7 of part I of his later *Principles of Philosophy*). For the statement should be seen only as an abbreviation of a complex train of reasoning, and not as a principle that can simply be laid down and immediately understood and assented to independently of any context. 'I think, therefore I am' seems obviously true, for anything that thinks must exist. But as Descartes himself emphasized, it is not to be understood as a deduction (with an implicit general assumption), for at this point in the *Meditations* he cannot rely on the truth that '*Everything* that thinks exists' (see *PW*, vol.2, 100). Interpreted properly, the statement might be expanded as follows: 'Even on the most radical sceptical supposition that there is an evil demon deceiving me, I have to exist to be deceived, so I can be certain that I do exist.' Without this supposition, there would be no argument at all. The statement gains its meaning from the background supposition.

ACTIVITY

Given this view of Descartes's *cogito* reasoning, how might the imagination be seen as involved?

> **DISCUSSION**
>
> What the First Meditation asks us to do is engage in a series of thought experiments, *imagining* possible scenarios in order to see what follows. The imagination might thus be seen as playing an essential role in Descartes's reasoning: without its use, there would simply be no *cogito* argument.

It may be impossible or potentially confusing to conjure up an *image* of an evil demon, but we can *suppose* that there is such a being. It is in this sense of 'imagination', for which the term 'intellectual imagination' is indeed appropriate, that the imagination is still required in Descartes's metaphysics. As Sepper puts it, 'the entire First Meditation is an exercise in imagination punctuated by insights of intellect into what the exercise reveals' (1996, 255). He notes that Descartes himself reportedly called works of the imagination 'meditation', reserving the term 'contemplation' for works of the understanding, a distinction that has roots in medieval discussions of our cognitive powers (1996, 256–8). Schouls summarizes the point as follows: 'Without the use of intellectual imagination, there would have been no cogito-experience, no proof of God's existence, no validation of reason – that is, no foundations for systematic knowledge could have been put in place' (2000, 103–4). For Descartes, he concludes, 'truth is reached through fiction' – the fiction of the evil demon deliberately invoked by the imagination (2000, 106).

In understanding Descartes's philosophy, then, we should distinguish between sensory imagination and intellectual imagination. Descartes's critique of the imagination in the *Meditations* applies only to sensory imagination; we might agree that knowledge cannot consist merely in the having or apprehending of corporeal images – and this is most obviously so in the case of metaphysics. But this is not to say that there is no role for the imagination to play in generating hypotheses and suppositions, and indeed Descartes himself makes essential use of what is appropriately called 'intellectual imagination'.

Review and preview

1. Descartes is often seen as the archetypical rationalist, a mark of which is his critique of imagination in the Second and Sixth Meditations. But this critique is directed at the use of sensory imagination, taken as involving the apprehension of corporeal images. We can agree that more is needed

for conceptual understanding, but this is not to say that images are not needed at all.

2 Descartes's critique of sensory imagination does not imply that the imagination (in some form or other) plays no role in his thought. In his early work the imagination (with a sensory dimension) was accorded a central place in our cognitive activities, particularly in its use in problem-solving. Even in the *Meditations* itself, the imagination – in a more intellectual form – is employed in raising sceptical doubts, without which there would be no *cogito* argument. Perhaps a better abbreviation of the latter would have been, 'I imagine an evil demon, therefore I am'.

3 Does thought require images? Given Descartes's distinction between images and ideas, the answer on his later view is 'No'. But although there is a difference between imagining (in the sense of apprehending images) and conceiving, they may not be as independent as Descartes makes out. This is not to say that there is no distinction. In the next chapter we will consider an empiricist view which collapses together images and ideas, which arguably gives rise to greater problems. The relationship between imagining and conceiving seems to be more complex than either Descartes or the empiricist suggests; and in chapter 4 we will turn to Kant's attempt to offer a more sophisticated account which reconciles the two positions. On Kant's view, genuine thought requires images or sensory representations, but there are rules that govern their interpretation and transformation in our cognitive activities, and our knowledge of these rules is not itself constituted by the having of images. So while conception is different from imagination, it nevertheless presupposes it.

Further reading

The works of Descartes cited in this chapter are all translated in the three-volume Cambridge edition by Cottingham and others (*PW*). There are brief accounts of Descartes's views on imagination in Brann (1991, part I, chapter 3, section A), Cottingham (1993, entries under 'images' and 'imagination') and White (1990, chapter 3). For general introductions to Descartes's views on the mind, which include discussion of the imagination, Cottingham (1986, chapter 5), Sorell (1983) and Wilkinson (1999, chapters 1–2; 2000, chapter 2) can be recommended. The two best books on Descartes and the imagination, referred to above, are Sepper (1996) and Schouls (2000). Sepper only discusses the *Meditations* in his final chapter, but he offers a thorough reading of Descartes's early writings.

CHAPTER 3

Imagination and perception

> Nothing is more free than the imagination of man; and though it cannot exceed that original stock of ideas furnished by the internal and external senses, it has unlimited power of mixing, compounding, separating, and dividing these ideas, in all the varieties of fiction and vision.
>
> (Hume, *An Enquiry concerning Human Understanding*, section 5, part 2, 47)

In the last chapter we examined Descartes's views on the imagination. Descartes is often taken as the original modern rationalist, and in the *Meditations* he does indeed criticize the (sensory) imagination, arguing that concepts are what are important in understanding rather than images. In this chapter we will consider the views of the eighteenth-century empiricist David Hume (1711–76). Hume is sceptical of the power of reason to acquire knowledge, and sees all knowledge as based on sense experience. But if the role of reason is limited, and given that sense experience on its own does not generate the kind of knowledge we take ourselves to have, then there must be some other faculty of the mind to perform the necessary cognitive functions. According to Hume, this faculty is the imagination.

The early modern period, and in particular the emergence of British empiricism, has often been characterized as inaugurating an 'epistemological turn' in philosophy. Central to this is the emphasis placed on the role of 'ideas' in human cognitive activities. We will look at this 'way of ideas' in the first main section of this chapter, before exploring the role of the imagination in Hume's philosophy in the second main section.

The way of ideas

The new form of philosophy that developed in the seventeenth century has often been called the 'way of ideas'. Although characteristic of empiricism, this too can be traced back to Descartes. As we saw in chapter 2, Descartes defines an 'idea' as 'whatever is immediately perceived by the mind'. But for Descartes there was a distinction between ideas and images, which suggests that while the 'way of ideas' might be appropriate in understanding conception, the 'way of images' is required to understand (sensory) imagination. What happens in the empiricist tradition is that the distinction between ideas and images is elided, and the 'way of ideas' comes to signify the approach to all mental activities.

Ideas in Locke

The centrality of the way of ideas can be first seen in the work of John Locke (1632–1704). In introducing his main philosophical treatise, *An Essay concerning Human Understanding* (first published in 1690), Locke writes:

> before I proceed on to what I have thought on this Subject, I must here in the Entrance beg pardon of my Reader, for the frequent use of the Word *Idea*, which he will find in the following Treatise. It being that Term, which, I think, serves best to stand for whatsoever is the Object of the Understanding when a Man thinks, I have used it to express whatever is meant by *Phantasm*, *Notion*, *Species*, or whatever it is, which the Mind can be employ'd about in thinking; and I could not avoid frequently using it.
>
> I presume it will be easily granted me, that there are such *Ideas* in Men's Minds; every one is conscious of them in himself, and Men's Words and Actions will satisfy him, that they are in others.
>
> (*Essay*, I, i, 8)

ACTIVITY

1. How does Locke define 'idea'?
2. How does this definition compare with Descartes's definition just cited?
3. What terms does Locke offer as meaning the same as 'idea'? What does this suggest as to his conception of ideas?
4. Would Locke endorse the (Aristotelian) thesis that all thought requires images (phantasms)?
5. What are the three assumptions that Locke states in the second paragraph? What do they reveal as to how he conceives ideas?
6. Is Locke right that these assumptions are 'easily granted'?

DISCUSSION

1. Locke defines 'idea' as 'whatsoever is the Object of the Understanding when a Man thinks'.

2   The intention is arguably the same, although they are worded differently. Locke's definition of 'idea' as just given might be thought to leave open whether things in the world can be 'ideas', insofar as they are 'Objects of the Understanding', whereas Descartes's definition states that only the 'immediate' objects of thought are ideas, i.e. ideas are purely mental. (Recall the ambiguity of 'objects of imagination' noted on p.43.) But what Locke goes on to say suggests that he does share Descartes's conception.

3   As Locke understands the terms, 'idea' means the same as 'phantasm', 'notion' or 'species'. All these terms were used in medieval Aristotelian discussions. For our purposes here, 'phantasm' is the most significant, for it suggests that 'ideas' are indeed construed as mental entities. (There are differences between the earlier uses of the terms, which Locke is ignoring here, partly because he rejects Aristotelianism. His definition amounts to a revisionary simplification: 'idea' is now to be understood as the generic term for 'whatever it is, which the Mind can be employ'd about in thinking'.)

4   Yes. Indeed, Locke seems to hold the stronger thesis that images – or ideas – are the very objects of thought (and not just required, among other possible things).

5   Locke's first two assumptions, that our minds do indeed contain ideas and that we are all conscious of them in ourselves, confirm that ideas are construed by Locke as mental entities. The third assumption, that we know that other people have ideas by what they say and do, indicates recognition of the problem that the first two assumptions raise. For if knowledge consists in having ideas and these are private mental entities, then how can I really know whether anyone else has a mental life, since their ideas cannot be mine? Locke's third assumption is intended to forestall this objection.

6   As I have just suggested, the assumptions are far from unproblematic. What is it for ideas to be 'in' the mind? In what sense are they 'objects' of understanding? What is it to be 'conscious' of them? Do ideas only exist when we are aware of them? Can we not have 'unconscious' ideas? How can we genuinely solve the so-called 'problem of other minds'? Is objective knowledge possible on Locke's assumptions? It is not our task to answer these questions on behalf of Locke, but they do serve to indicate the problems that confront the way of ideas.

Locke shares with Descartes, then, the fundamental assumption that the objects of thought are ideas, understood as private mental entities which we perceive in ourselves when we exercise our cognitive faculties. But unlike Descartes, who distinguishes ideas from images, Locke seems to collapse the two together, treating 'idea' and 'phantasm' or 'image' as synonymous. This elision is characteristic of British empiricism, as is the fundamental Cartesian/Lockean assumption (that the objects of thought are ideas). Locke's most important immediate successor was George Berkeley (1685–1753). This is how the main part of his key work, *A Treatise Concerning the Principles of Human Knowledge* (1710), opens:

> It is evident to anyone who takes a survey of the objects of human knowledge, that they are either ideas actually imprinted on the senses, or else such as are perceived by attending to the passions and operations of the mind, or lastly ideas formed by help of memory and imagination, either compounding, dividing, or barely representing those originally perceived in the aforesaid ways.
>
> (*Principles*, I, 1)

'Idea' is clearly also being used here as the generic term for whatever is the 'object of human knowledge'. Note, too, Berkeley's conception of imagination – understood as responsible for the 'compounding' and 'dividing' of ideas initially received by the senses. This is equally a feature of British empiricism, and was central to Hume's philosophy.

Hume's distinction between ideas and impressions

The way of ideas that was introduced by Descartes and Locke reached its apotheosis in the philosophy of David Hume, whose first main work, *A Treatise of Human Nature*, was published in 1739–40. Book I is entitled 'Of the Understanding', and although its arguments were later reworked – more succinctly – into his *Enquiry concerning Human Understanding* (the first edition of which appeared in 1748), we will focus on the former here. The *Enquiry* is one of the most elegantly written works in the history of philosophy, but the *Treatise* reveals Hume's empiricist assumptions and their implications more clearly. I have mentioned that the elision of Descartes's distinction between ideas and images was characteristic of the way of ideas in British empiricism. But Hume does distinguish between ideas and impressions. Indeed, it is with this distinction that the *Treatise* opens:

All the perceptions of the human mind resolve themselves into two distinct kinds, which I shall call IMPRESSIONS and IDEAS. The difference betwixt these consists in the degrees of force and liveliness, with which they strike upon the mind, and make their way into our thought or consciousness. Those perceptions, which enter with most force and violence, we may name *impressions*; and under this name I comprehend all our sensations, passions and emotions, as they make their first appearance in the soul. By *ideas* I mean the faint images of these in thinking and reasoning; such as, for instance, are all the perceptions excited by the present discourse, excepting only, those which arise from the sight and touch, and excepting the immediate pleasure or uneasiness it may occasion. I believe it will not be very necessary to employ many words in explaining this distinction. Every one of himself will readily perceive the difference betwixt feeling and thinking. The common degrees of these are easily distinguished; tho' it is not impossible but in particular instances they may very nearly approach to each other. Thus in sleep, in a fever, in madness, or in any very violent emotions of soul, our ideas may approach to our impressions: As on the other hand it sometimes happens, that our impressions are so faint and low, that we cannot distinguish them from our ideas. But notwithstanding this near resemblance in a few instances, they are in general so very different, that no-one can make a scruple to rank them under distinct heads, and assign to each a peculiar name to mark the difference.

(*Treatise*, I, i, 1)

ACTIVITY

1 How does Hume characterize the difference between impressions and ideas?
2 What is the relationship between ideas and impressions?
3 What objection does Hume consider to his distinction?
4 How does he respond?
5 Does Hume's distinction between ideas and impressions correspond to Descartes's distinction between ideas and images (see pp.49–52 above)?

DISCUSSION

1 Impressions and ideas differ in the degrees of 'force and liveliness' with which they strike the mind, impressions being the more forceful.
2 Ideas are faint images of impressions.
3 Sometimes, as in a fever, our ideas can seem as lively as our impressions; and sometimes our impressions can seem as faint as our ideas.
4 Hume admits that there may be 'near resemblances' in some cases, but maintains that the distinction still holds in general.

5   There is some correspondence, to the extent that Humean impressions, like Cartesian images, have their source in (bodily) sensation, and Humean ideas, like Cartesian ideas, are what are involved in thinking and reasoning. But for Hume the distinction is only a matter of degree, not of kind; and he does himself describe ideas as 'images'.

For Hume, then, both impressions and ideas might be regarded as a form of image. 'Perception' is the generic term that Hume uses to cover both impressions and ideas. Like both Locke's and Berkeley's 'ideas', perceptions are construed as the sole 'objects of the understanding', which suggests that they are essentially mental entities (the source of impressions in sensation notwithstanding, the bodily basis of which Hume raises some sceptical doubts about, as we will see). Locke had written: 'To ask, *at what time a Man has first any* Ideas, is to ask, when he begins to perceive; having *Ideas*, and Perception being the same thing' (*Essay*, II, i, 9). Berkeley too had equated having ideas with perceiving. Hume is very much part of the empiricist tradition, then, in classifying all types of 'ideas' or 'perceptions' or 'images' as essentially the same.

The missing shade of blue

Having divided perceptions into impressions and ideas, Hume goes on to make a second division into simple and complex perceptions, which applies to both impressions and ideas. Simple perceptions are 'such as admit of no distinction nor separation', and complex perceptions are composed of simple perceptions (*Treatise*, I, i, 1). He then formulates a general principle that is central to his empiricism: 'That all our simple ideas in their appearance are deriv'd from simple impressions, which are correspondent to them, and which they exactly represent' (ibid.). While a complex idea, such as the idea of a New Jerusalem, 'whose pavement is gold and walls are rubies' (ibid.), need not correspond to anything real, and hence to a corresponding complex impression, every simple idea must be derived from a corresponding simple impression, i.e. have its source in empirical sensation. According to Hume, all knowledge is based on sense experience, and there is no room in his system for simple ideas to come from any other source.

Hume gives a number of examples to illustrate the truth of this principle. I cannot have an idea of scarlet without having seen something scarlet, or an idea of the taste of a pineapple without having tasted a pineapple (ibid.). Hume considers an objection to this, however, which has come to be known as the problem of the missing shade of blue.

> There is however one contradictory phænomenon, which may prove, that 'tis not absolutely impossible for ideas to go before their correspondent impressions. I believe it will readily be allow'd, that the several distinct ideas of colours, which enter by the eyes, or those of sounds, which are convey'd by the hearing, are really different from each other, tho' at the same time resembling. Now if this be true of different colours, it must be no less so of the different shades of the same colour, that each of them produces a distinct idea, independent of the rest. For if this shou'd be deny'd, 'tis possible, by the continual gradation of shades, to run a colour insensibly into what is most remote from it; and if you will not allow any of the means to be different, you cannot without absurdity deny the extremes to be the same. Suppose therefore a person to have enjoyed his sight for thirty years, and to have become perfectly well acquainted with colours of all kinds, excepting one particular shade of blue, for instance, which it never has been his fortune to meet with. Let all the different shades of that colour, except that single one, be plac'd before him, descending gradually from the deepest to the lightest; 'tis plain, that he will perceive a blank, where that shade is wanting, and will be sensible, that there is a greater distance in that place betwixt the contiguous colours, than in any other. Now I ask, whether 'tis possible for him, from his own imagination, to supply this deficiency, and raise up to himself the idea of that particular shade, tho' it had never been conveyed to him by his senses? I believe there are few but will be of opinion that he can; and this may serve as a proof, that the simple ideas are not always derived from the correspondent impressions; tho' the instance is so particular and singular, that 'tis scarce worth our observing, and does not merit that for it alone we should alter our general maxim.
>
> (Ibid.)

ACTIVITY

1 According to Hume's general empiricist principle, all simple ideas derive from corresponding simple impressions. What is the counter-example to this principle that Hume considers in this passage?

2 What assumption is made here about the nature and individuation of shades of colour?

3 Is the counter-example a genuine one?

4 Do you agree with Hume that 'the instance is so particular and singular, that 'tis scarce worth our observing'?

5   What does this passage tell us about the role of the imagination, on Hume's view?

DISCUSSION

1   Hume asks us to suppose that a spectrum of all the shades of colour is laid out with a gap where a particular shade of blue should be. Hume grants to his objector that someone could conjure up an idea of the missing shade of blue without ever having had the corresponding simple impression.

2   Shades of colour are assumed to be both simple and what we might call 'minimally distinct'. No shade of colour can be decomposed into simpler elements, and shades are individuated at the finest level according to barely noticeable differences. In other words, starting from one shade on the spectrum, the next shade is that for which there is a barely noticeable difference from the first. Were there to be a shade in between, we would be unable to notice any difference between it and one or other of the neighbouring shades. Our perceptual capacities thus determine the individuation of shades of colour.

3   On Hume's assumptions, yes. We would have here a case of someone acquiring a simple idea without ever having had the corresponding simple impression, although they are assumed to have had very similar impressions.

4   One question would be: how far can the thought experiment be extended? If a neighbouring shade of blue were also missing, could I conjure up this too? What if three shades were missing, or four, or every shade between, say, the darkest and lightest shades of blue? Could we generate ideas of all the colours from ideas of just the primary colours, as Descartes suggested in his *Rules* (see p.53 above)? Could there be similar counter-examples in the case of sounds or tastes? (Lurking in the background here are problems about the 'simplicity' of ideas and impressions, to which we will return shortly.)

5   The passage suggests that one function of the imagination is to conjure up ideas of things of which we have had no experience, i.e. of which we have never had the corresponding impression.

Hume's discussion of this counter-example is repeated verbatim in the *Enquiry* (section 2), which might suggest that he saw no insuperable problem here. Barry Stroud has commented that 'Hume tended to leave out of the *Enquiry* anything he saw as a real difficulty in writing the *Treatise*' (1977, 33).

(This is one reason why the *Treatise* is the work to consider if we want to explore his underlying assumptions.) We can grant that if all the shades were laid out along a spectrum with one shade missing, then we would notice the gap. But merely noticing a gap is not the same as conjuring up an idea of what is missing. Or if we want to talk of 'having an idea' of the missing shade, then why should we not construe this as simply consisting in having the capacity to notice the gap, or to recognize the shade should we ever come across it? What seems to be driving Hume to admit that we are able to conjure up an idea – as some kind of mental image – of the missing shade is his underlying (Aristotelian) assumption that thought requires ideas or images. If we were not able to conjure up such an idea, then how could we think about there being a missing shade? Since we can recognize a gap, must there not be some sense in which we can generate the relevant idea? Hume presumably felt that he could concede this without undermining his empiricism, since recognizing a gap presupposes having impressions of the neighbouring shades. So the counter-example may well have seemed to pose no serious threat to his 'general maxim'.

Pictorial versus descriptional conceptions

Hume's discussion suggests that he does conceive ideas, at least here, as some kind of mental image, and with this goes the corresponding conception of the imagination – as what is responsible for conjuring up and dealing with these images. But as we saw in the last chapter in discussing Descartes's use of 'intellectual imagination', there are other conceptions of imagination. Indeed, intellectual imagination is precisely what Hume himself employs – and relies on us employing – in raising the problem of the missing shade of blue. Although Hume uses the word 'suppose' in setting up the thought experiment, if what I said in chapter 1 ('Imagination and supposition') is right, then this may signal the start of an imaginative process just as much as if he had used the word 'imagine'. Here we seem to have a good example of supposing as a form of imagining. But do we actually have to conjure up *images* of each of the colours in order to understand the thought experiment? I was not aware of doing this myself. And if this is so, then perhaps we can give a different account of having ideas than forming mental images.

How might such an account run? Perhaps we might turn, at this point, to the so-called 'imagery debate' in recent cognitive psychology, which has been characterized as the debate between 'picture' and 'descriptional' theories (Tye

1991, chapters 3–4; Tye 1994), or between 'analogue' and 'propositional' theories (Hamlyn 1994, 365). On the one hand, an image is construed as some kind of mental picture, as an inner analogue of what it is (or purports to be) an image of. This does seem to be the view embodied in seventeenth-century British empiricism and Hume's official conception. On the other hand, an image is construed as some kind of description, encoded linguistically or propositionally. If we can talk at all of having an 'image' of the missing shade of blue, then the latter construal seems to be the more plausible. We can grant that, in recognizing the gap in the spectrum as laid out before me, I know that there is a missing shade of blue here, and so in some sense have an 'idea' of it. But I do not have a mental picture of it, at least in the sense in which arguably, and certainly on Hume's view, I have a mental picture of the other shades of blue. So how do I represent it to myself? Perhaps I *describe* it to myself as 'the shade that is between this shade and that shade'. Certainly, I can offer some kind of description of it, and to this extent I can be said to have an 'idea' of it. Of course, in describing it as 'between this shade and that shade', I am presupposing the ideas of these other two shades, for which a different account may be needed. But it does show that there are other conceptions of ideas than simply the official empiricist one.

Now whatever the legitimacy or merits of descriptional theories of *images*, I do think that one can talk of 'pictorial' and 'descriptional' conceptions of *imagining*. As argued in chapter 1, there seem to be forms of imagining in which images play an essential role, and forms of imagining in which suppositions play an essential role. Whether or not images should be construed pictorially, pictorial conceptions have certainly been prevalent in the history of philosophy. But in the case of suppositions, only descriptional conceptions of imagining look capable of doing them justice, since suppositions do indeed seem to require linguistic or conceptual articulation. When Hume asks us to suppose that there is a spectrum of colours with a missing shade of blue laid before someone, for example, he gives a description, or in broader terms tells a story, which we understand in imagining the situation ourselves. Although Hume does not recognize this conception explicitly himself, we can see it as implicit in his work, in just the same way as we saw an intellectual conception of imagination implicit in Descartes's work. What I have here called 'pictorial' and 'descriptional' conceptions of imagining is just a further illustration of the opposition between sensory and intellectual conceptions that underlies debates about the imagination.

Hume's empire of the imagination

In the final paragraph of his 'Abstract' to the *Treatise* (published in 1740), Hume famously summarizes what he takes to be his most important contribution to philosophy:

> Thro' this whole book, there are great pretensions to new discoveries in philosophy; but if any thing can intitle the author to so glorious a name as that of an *inventor*, 'tis the use he makes of the principle of the association of ideas, which enters into most of his philosophy. Our imagination has a great authority over our ideas; and there are no ideas that are different from each other, which it cannot separate, and join, and compose into all the varieties of fiction. But notwithstanding the empire of the imagination, there is a secret tie or union among particular ideas, which causes the mind to conjoin them more frequently together, and makes the one, upon its appearance, introduce the other. Hence arises what we call the *apropos* of discourse: hence the connection of writing: and hence that thread, or chain of thought, which a man naturally supports even in the loosest *reverie*. These principles of association are reduced to three, *viz. Resemblance*; a picture naturally makes us think of the man it was drawn for. *Contiguity*; when *St. Dennis* is mentioned, the idea of *Paris* naturally occurs. *Causation*; when we think of the son, we are apt to carry our attention to the father. 'Twill be easy to conceive of what vast consequence these principles must be in the science of human nature, if we consider, that so far as regards the mind, these are the only links that bind the parts of the universe together, or connect us with any person or object exterior to ourselves. For as it is by means of thought only that any thing operates upon our passions, and as these are the only ties of our thoughts, they are really *to us* the cement of the universe, and all the operations of the mind must, in a great measure, depend on them.
>
> (*Treatise*, 661–2)

Hume identifies his associationism – his use of principles of association – as the key to his philosophy. We will explore Hume's appeal to these principles, and consider just how extensive he saw the 'empire of the imagination' which is governed by these principles, in the rest of this chapter.

The liberty of the imagination

ACTIVITY

Consider the case in which I have experienced the two shades of blue between which the missing shade of blue lies. On Hume's assumptions, why can I not combine the ideas I have of these two shades to form the idea of the missing shade, in the way that I can mix two paints to form a paint with an intermediate colour?

DISCUSSION

In the case of mixing paints, a new colour can be produced because the paints are broken down into smaller parts which are then recombined in the mixing process. So the paints are not themselves 'simple'. But our ideas of shades of colours, according to Hume, are paradigms of 'simple' ideas. So they cannot be blended in this way to form new simple ideas.

Hume's official position is clear: we form new ideas by dividing and combining ideas we already have. But this leaves it mysterious as to how we manage to conjure up the simple idea of the missing shade of blue. Hume understands the process of decomposition and recomposition of ideas mereologically, that is, in whole-part terms, where wholes are simply sums of their parts and any part can exist independently. So the only new ideas that can be generated are (mereologically) complex ideas. I can form the idea of a unicorn, for example, by decomposing the idea of a rhinoceros into the idea of a horn and the idea of a hornless rhinoceros, and then combining the idea of a horn with the idea of a horse. Since ideas are discrete mental entities (capable of existing independently of other ideas), on Hume's view, some of our ideas must therefore be simple ideas. This is confirmed by experience itself, according to Hume. As he puts it in the *Treatise*, 'the imagination reaches a *minimum*, and may raise up to itself an idea, of which it cannot conceive any sub-division, and which cannot be diminished without a total annihilation' (I, ii, 1). Out of these simple ideas all other ideas are formed, and these simple ideas originate from the simple impressions of which they are copies (at least normally). The model here is one of epistemological atomism: the simple impressions and ideas are the atoms out of which all cognitive content is built. There is no room in this model for a simple idea to be generated from two other simple ideas.

So although Hume grants to the imagination the mysterious – one might almost say divine – power to create new simple ideas *ex nihilo* in certain cases, his official position is that the imagination is just responsible for the reproduction, division and combination of existing impressions and ideas. It is this that he calls the 'liberty of the imagination' – the ability to 'transpose and change' our ideas (*Treatise*, I, i, 3). The fables we come across in literature, he writes, demonstrate this liberty:

> Nature there is totally confounded, and nothing mentioned but winged horses, fiery dragons, and monstrous giants. Nor will this liberty of the fancy appear strange, when we consider, that all our ideas are copy'd from our impressions, and that there are not any two impressions which are perfectly inseparable. Not to mention, that this is an evident consequence of the division of ideas into simple and complex. Where-ever the imagination perceives a difference among ideas, it can easily produce a separation.
>
> (Ibid.)

It is significant that Hume treats 'imagination' and 'fancy' here as synonymous, for the 'liberty' of the imagination precisely consists in its ability to separate existing complex ideas and recombine their parts in weird and wonderful ways.

The principles of association

If our imagination is at liberty to combine ideas in whatever way takes our fancy, then what distinguishes its proper use from its improper use? Hume addresses this question in the fourth section of the *Treatise*:

> As all simple ideas may be separated by the imagination, and may be united again in what form it pleases, nothing wou'd be more unaccountable than the operations of that faculty, were it not guided by some universal principles, which render it, in some measure, uniform with itself in all times and places. Were ideas entirely loose and unconnected, chance alone wou'd join them; and 'tis impossible the same simple ideas should fall regularly into complex ones (as they commonly do) without some bond of union among them, some associating quality, by which one idea naturally introduces another.
>
> (I, i, 4)

He goes on to identify three principles of association based on the relations of resemblance, contiguity in time or place, and cause and effect. It is these principles that the imagination uses to link ideas together. The imagination runs naturally, according to Hume, from one idea of something to an idea of something that resembles it, to an idea of something near it in time or place, or to an idea of something that is its cause or effect.

> Look back at the paragraph from the 'Abstract' to the *Treatise* cited on page 70. What are the examples that Hume gives to illustrate each principle?
>
> ACTIVITY
>
> DISCUSSION
>
> Hume's first example illustrates the operation of the principle of resemblance. According to Hume, when I see a portrait, i.e. acquire an idea (or impression) of a picture of a person, I immediately think of that person, i.e. conjure up the further idea of that person. To the extent that the picture *resembles* the person, my mind moves easily from the idea of the one to the idea of the other. Hume's second example illustrates the operation of the principle of contiguity. On hearing the name 'St. Dennis', and hence conjuring up the idea of the church by that name, I think of Paris, i.e. conjure up the further idea of Paris. My idea of St. Dennis is of a church which is *in* Paris, which makes me naturally think of the broader surroundings in which it is located. Hume's third example illustrates the operation of the principle of causation. When I think of someone, I may also be led to think of their father, understood as a cause of their existence. Once again, according to Hume, my mind is led naturally from the idea of one thing to the idea of another thing, which in this case is its cause or effect. In all three cases, then, I am led to *associate* one idea with another idea on the basis of a relation of either resemblance, contiguity or causation.

Most of the rest of Book I of the *Treatise* consists in showing how these principles of association operate in the various areas of human thought. We will look here at just two examples: our use of general terms and our belief in the existence of an external world.

Abstract ideas

One fundamental question for the way of ideas, which had been raised by both Locke and Berkeley, is this: since ideas are particular, how can there be abstract or general ideas, ideas that embody our understanding of abstract or general terms? ('Abstract' and 'general' were treated as synonymous here.) I am said to have a 'general idea' of a cat, for example, when I know in general what cats are – when I can recognize cats when I see them, and so on. But if all I ever have are particular ideas of cats – i.e. mental images of particular cats – then how can there be such a thing as a general idea of a cat? In the section of the *Treatise* entitled 'Of abstract ideas', Hume endorses Berkeley's answer, which he reports as follows: 'all general ideas are nothing but particular ones, annexed to a certain term, which gives them a more extensive signification, and makes them recall upon occasion other individuals, which are similar to them' (I, i, 7). In elaborating on this answer, Hume appeals to the work of the imagination:

> When we have found a resemblance among several objects, that often occur to us, we apply the same name to all of them, whatever differences we may observe in the degrees of their quantity and quality, and whatever other differences may appear among them. After we have acquired a custom of this kind, the hearing of that name revives the idea of one of these objects, and makes the imagination conceive it with all its particular circumstances and proportions. But as the same word is suppos'd to have been frequently applied to other individuals, that are different in many respects from that idea, which is immediately present to the mind; the word not being able to revive the idea of all these individuals, only touches the soul, if I may be allow'd so to speak, and revives that custom, which we have acquir'd by surveying them. They are not really and in fact present to the mind, but only in power; nor do we draw them all out distinctly in the imagination, but keep ourselves in a readiness to survey any of them, as we may be prompted by a present design or necessity. The word raises up an individual idea, along with a certain custom; and that custom produces any other individual one, for which we may have occasion.
>
> (Ibid.)

ACTIVITY

1. What is the principle of association involved here?
2. How do we learn to use general terms, according to Hume?
3. The imagination is accorded two functions in this passage. What are they?
4. What does Hume mean by 'custom'?
5. In one sentence, how would you describe the relationship between the use of the relevant principle of association and the roles of custom and imagination? (You might take this as a request for a one-sentence summary of the passage.)

DISCUSSION

1. The principle of association is the one based on resemblance.
2. We notice a resemblance between certain objects, to which we then apply the same term.
3. The imagination is involved, first, in conjuring up the idea of a particular object to which a general term applies, on our hearing the term, and, second, in generating – when needed – ideas of other objects to which the term applies.

4   By 'custom' Hume means, broadly, a habit of doing the same thing on different occasions, such as applying the same term to the same objects whenever we come across them.
5   The custom of associating particular ideas with one another, on the basis of resemblance, establishes a readiness of the imagination to supply a series of ideas of objects to which a given general term applies.

According to Hume, then, our general or abstract idea of a cat, say, is in truth nothing but an idea of a particular cat which is 'annexed' to the word 'cat' in such a way (through 'custom') as to enable us to conjure up other ideas of particular cats. The function of conjuring up these ideas is assigned to the imagination. What this means is that the imagination, in Hume's philosophy, has a fundamental role to play in perceptual recognition itself – in our application of general terms to the objects of perception. To appreciate this, consider the account that Hume would offer of how we recognize a cat as a cat, i.e. how we come to apply the term 'cat' to a particular cat that we see in front of us. When I first see the cat I acquire a particular idea (impression) of that cat. My imagination then conjures up similar ideas (according to Hume's first principle of association, based on the relation of resemblance), and sooner or later I conjure up the particular idea (or one of the particular ideas) 'annexed' to the word 'cat'. Since I know that this latter idea is an idea of a cat, and can discern the resemblance between this idea and my original idea (impression), I 'conclude' that my original idea is also an idea of a cat. In other words, I recognize that the thing before me is a cat. This might seem like a lengthy process, but the more 'accustomed' I am to cats, the faster this may occur. When fully 'accustomed', my recognition may be almost instantaneous. But even then, on Hume's account, the imagination is still playing a role in conjuring up the relevant ideas.

Can any deeper explanation be provided of this custom of associating ideas or this readiness of the imagination to supply appropriate ideas or images? Hume's answer is 'No'; all we can do is show that it happens, in accordance with the principles he has identified: 'To explain the ultimate causes of our mental actions is impossible. 'Tis sufficient, if we can give any satisfactory account of them from experience and analogy' (ibid.). 'Nothing is more admirable,' he writes, 'than the readiness, with which the imagination suggests its ideas, and presents them at the very instant, in which they become necessary or useful.' This is just a fortunate fact of human life. The ideas we have are collected, he goes on, 'by a kind of magical faculty of the soul, which, tho' it be always most perfect in the greatest geniuses, and is properly what we call a genius, is however inexplicable by the utmost efforts of human understanding'. (Ibid.)

The problem of the external world

According to Hume, all thinking involves the apprehension of 'perceptions' – either impressions or ideas, conceived as discrete mental entities whose existence depends on the mind. In experiencing what I take to be an object in the external world, all I am directly aware of, on Hume's view, is a stream of constantly changing sense-impressions. But if this is so, then how can we know that the world really does contain objects that persist through time and exist independently of us? Hume tackles this question in the section of the *Treatise* entitled 'Of scepticism with regard to the senses' (I, iv, 2, 187–218). This section is both long (over 30 pages) and complex, and a full discussion would take us into the most problematic areas of Hume's philosophy. My aim here is just to bring out the role that Hume sees the imagination as playing in our belief in the external world.

As Hume characterizes it, there are two questions to be answered here: 'Why we attribute a CONTINU'D existence to objects, even when they are not present to the senses; and why we suppose them to have an existence DISTINCT from the mind and perception' (ibid., 188). These two questions are different, but he takes it that an answer to one is at the same time an answer to the other. 'For if the objects of our senses continue to exist, even when they are not perceiv'd, their existence is of course independent of and distinct from the perception; and *vice versa*, if their existence be independent of the perception and distinct from it, they must continue to exist, even tho' they be not perceiv'd' (ibid.). It is not clear that distinctness implies continuity. (Why should God not create objects that exist only when we are having corresponding perceptions?) But we can accept that continuity implies distinctness, and concentrate on continuity here.

According to Hume, the three possible sources of our belief in the continued and distinct existence of external objects are the senses, reason and imagination. But as I have just noted, as far as our senses are concerned, as Hume puts it, 'they convey to us nothing but a single perception, and never give us the least intimation of any thing beyond' (ibid., 189). But nor can reason be the source: 'we can attribute a distinct continu'd existence to objects without ever consulting REASON, or weighing our opinions by any philosophical principles' (ibid., 193). Children, peasants and 'the greatest part of mankind' believe in external objects, comments Hume, but do not do so as a result of reasoning (ibid.). So that leaves the imagination. How does the imagination provide the belief?

External objects exhibit a certain constancy and coherence, so we must look to explain corresponding constancy and coherence in our impressions (ibid., 194–5). It is at this point that Hume appeals to a feature of the imagination that he had noted in an earlier section of the *Treatise* (I, ii, 4):

> I have already observ'd, in examining the foundation of mathematics, that the imagination, when set into any train of thinking, is apt to continue, even when its object fails it, and like a galley put in motion by the oars, carries on its course without any new impulse. This I have assign'd for the reason, why, after considering several loose standards of equality, and correcting them by each other, we proceed to imagine so correct and exact a standard of that relation, as is not liable to the least error or variation. The same principle makes us easily entertain this opinion of the continu'd existence of body. Objects have a certain coherence even as they appear to our senses; but this coherence is much greater and more uniform, if we suppose the objects to have a continu'd existence; and as the mind is once in the train of observing an uniformity among objects, it naturally continues, till it renders the uniformity as compleat as possible. The simple supposition of their continu'd existence suffices for this purpose, and gives us a notion of a much greater regularity among objects, than what they have when we look no farther than our senses.
>
> (*Treatise*, I, iv, 2, 198)

ACTIVITY

1. What is the principle that Hume suggests helps explain our belief in the continued existence of external objects?

2. Hume's reference to his earlier appeal to the principle is cryptic (and that appeal is not much clearer in the earlier section itself). Recalling the problem of the missing shade of blue, how might the principle be illustrated in the case of our experience of shades of colour?

3. What does Hume's use of 'imagine' in the second sentence and of 'suppose' and 'supposition' in the fourth and final sentences suggest as to the conception of imagination that is now in play?

4 What is the difference, then, between the role of the imagination in the case of the missing shade of blue and its role in the case of our belief in the continued existence of external objects?

DISCUSSION

1 The imagination is apt to continue a train of thinking even when the original sensory basis or impulse fails.
2 Here is the most obvious suggestion. Let us assume that we have before us a series of objects showing the spectrum of shades of colour that begins, say, with a deep red and breaks off at a certain shade of blue. We run our eye along these objects and when we get to the last shade of blue we continue thinking of the next shade in the spectrum – and perhaps the next one and the next one – even though there is no longer anything of that shade. The imagination simply conjures up what is missing. This seems consistent with what Hume says in the first sentence of the passage. But the second sentence suggests that he has something else in mind. A better illustration might therefore be the following. We experience a number of different shades of colour on a number of occasions, and make various loose assessments of similarity and difference. We begin to acquire a sense that there is a regular pattern underlying our experience – some 'correct and exact ... standard' by means of which every shade can be related to one another in a uniform progression. We are thus led to suppose that there is some complete spectrum of colours – or objects exemplifying those colours – external to us. (Indeed, Hume illustrated this use of the imagination himself in setting up his thought experiment concerning the missing shade of blue.)
3 Hume's use of 'imagine' and 'suppose' suggests that he has in mind a more intellectual use of the imagination – hypothesizing the existence of something to make better sense of our experience.
4 In the case of the missing shade of blue, the imagination is involved in actually conjuring up the idea or image of the missing shade. In the case of our belief in the continued existence of external things, such as our belief in a series of objects showing the colour spectrum, the imagination is involved in *supposing* that they exist – without necessarily having to conjure up any additional images.

We have here a further illustration of the tension between sensory and intellectual conceptions of the imagination – between the image-forming and hypothesizing roles that the imagination is taken to play. In the case of the missing shade of blue as well as in the case of abstract ideas, the role of the imagination lies in conjuring up appropriate ideas or images. In the case of our belief in an external world, it might initially look as if this is also what Hume is appealing to – the imagination's capacity to make additions to a series of impressions to give it greater uniformity. Increasing uniformity is indeed the aim, but this is achieved by supposing the existence of something that underwrites this uniformity.

As Hume himself recognizes, however, merely appealing to the principle identified in this passage does not explain how this supposition is made. In the rest of the section, by focusing on the constancy rather than coherence of our impressions, Hume fills out his account. Let us assume that we are looking at a single object and have a series of impressions of that object – a set of mental snapshots, as it were, punctuated by blinks of the eye. These impressions are so alike that we are inclined to treat them as the same impression. Hume writes: 'Nothing is more apt to make us mistake one idea for another, than any relation betwixt them, which associates them together in the imagination, and makes it pass with facility from one to the other' (ibid., 202). In this case it is the principle of association based on resemblance that is responsible for the imagination's activity and, in particular, for the confusion of similarity with identity. As Hume puts it, 'The smooth passage of the imagination along the ideas of the resembling perceptions makes us ascribe to them a perfect identity' (ibid., 205).

But this only gets us to the supposition of the continued existence of our perceptions, not to the continued and distinct existence of objects in the world. What induces us to take this second step? It is at this point that reason plays a role. According to Hume, we know that our impressions are actually different, however similar they may be, and only exist when consciously apprehended by the mind. So we know that the supposition of the continued existence of our perceptions is merely a fiction. What we have, then, is a conflict between our imagination and reason. Our imagination tempts us into believing in the continued existence of our perceptions, but reason tells us that all we ever have is a series of resembling perceptions. How can we reconcile this conflict? Hume writes:

> In order to set ourselves at ease in this particular, we contrive a new hypothesis, which seems to comprehend both these principles of reason and imagination. This hypothesis is the philosophical one of the double existence of perceptions

and objects; which pleases our reason, in allowing, that our dependent perceptions are interrupted and different; and at the same time is agreeable to the imagination, in attributing a continu'd existence to something else, which we call *objects*. This philosophical system, therefore, is the monstrous offspring of two principles, which are contrary to each other, which are both at once embrac'd by the mind, and which are unable mutually to destroy each other.

(Ibid., 215)

According to Hume, then, what gives rise to our belief in the external world is the desire to avoid the conflict between reason and imagination. We attempt to both have our cake and eat it by supposing what Hume calls the 'double existence' of perceptions and objects: that what exists are not only ideas but also what those ideas are ideas of. But which faculty of the mind is responsible for this supposition? Hume never explicitly says. It cannot be reason, on Hume's view, because reason tells us that all we ever have is a series of resembling but discrete perceptions. Yet Hume also denies that the imagination is responsible. He says little more than that this would be contrary to the 'original tendency' of the imagination (ibid., 212). According to his associationism, all that the imagination can generate, from a given stock of ideas, are further ideas associated with them on the basis of resemblance, contiguity or causation – although, as we have just seen, he also allows that the imagination produces the supposition of their continued existence. But he presumably felt that while the imagination can generate further ideas, it cannot generate the external objects that supposedly also exist – and hence cannot produce the supposition itself.

It would obviously be most natural to attribute the supposition of double existence to the work of the imagination, especially since the supposition of the continued existence of our perceptions is attributed to the imagination, and both suppositions are fictions, according to Hume. At the end of the section, Hume admits that he feels uneasy at the sceptical impasse he has reached. But for our purposes, what is of most interest is Hume's reluctance to ascribe the supposition of double existence to the imagination. Hume has implicitly admitted a more intellectual form of imagination in the supposition of the continued existence of our perceptions, although he attempts to account for this in terms of his empiricist principles of association. The supposition of double existence illustrates further the important role that the intellectual imagination plays in our mental life, but Hume has left himself little room to accommodate this in his system.

Review and preview

1. Central to British empiricism in the seventeenth and eighteenth centuries was the 'way of ideas'. Descartes's definition of an 'idea' as 'whatever is immediately perceived by the mind' was endorsed, but the distinction that he had drawn between idea and image was elided. On the empiricist view, all mental activities involve operations on ideas. Hume's philosophy represents the culmination of the way of ideas. Although a distinction was drawn between ideas and impressions, both were called 'perceptions' and regarded as a form of mental image. The assumption that ideas are mental images comes out clearly in Hume's discussion of the problem of the missing shade of blue, which he cannot be said to have solved satisfactorily, however.

2. On Hume's official view, the imagination is the faculty that is responsible for the reproduction, division and combination of impressions and ideas, and it was the power to do this that Hume termed the 'liberty of the imagination', forming his 'empire of the imagination'. Hume's discussion of abstract ideas shows the centrality that he accorded to our image-forming ability. But this power of the imagination to form images was seen as governed by principles of association, such as that based on the relation of resemblance. It is the mind's natural tendency to associate ideas that gives rise, on Hume's view, to certain (mistaken) beliefs, such as the belief in the continued existence of perceptions. This belief in turn, according to Hume, in its conflict with reason, gives rise to our belief in an external world. This suggests that there is a further, more intellectual conception of imagination operating implicitly in Hume's philosophy, just as it does in Descartes's philosophy (as we saw in the last chapter). On this conception, imagination involves supposition, which consists not in the formation of images but in the generation of hypotheses.

3. Although the imagination, on Hume's view, is not directly involved in the reception of impressions, which occurs in sensation, it is very much involved in our taking what we perceive as a perception of something external to us. It is also involved in our use and understanding of general terms. As we will see in the next chapter, for Kant the imagination plays an even deeper role in our cognitive activities than it does for Hume. Kant finds a place in his system not only for a Humean form of 'empirical' imagination but also for what he calls 'transcendental' imagination.

4 In Hume's philosophy, the imagination is creative in two senses: first, in the liberty it has to 'transpose and change' our ideas, as Hume puts it, and, second, in its generation of suppositions. For Hume, 'imagining' has strong connotations of conjuring up fictions, as indeed is suggested by his frequent use of 'imagination' and 'fancy' as synonyms.

Further reading

Brief accounts of empiricist conceptions of imagination can be found in Brann (1991, part I, chapter 3) and White (1990, chapters 4–6). Locke's main work is his *Essay*, and Berkeley's main work is his *Principles*. Hume's two most important works are his *Treatise*, Book I of which we focused upon here, and his later *Enquiry*, which may be the better place to start, although the *Treatise* is more revealing of Hume's underlying assumptions.

For further discussion of the topics addressed in this chapter, Pears (1990), Stroud (1977), Warnock (1976) and Yolton (1984) can be recommended. Pears focuses on Book I of the *Treatise*, examining Hume's theory of mind in chapters 1–4, and his problems with sense-perception in chapters 10–11. Stroud covers the full range of Hume's philosophy, but chapter 2 is concerned with Hume's theory of ideas, and chapter 5 with the problem of the external world. Warnock provides a lucid account of both Hume and Kant on imagination and perception in part 1 of her book. Yolton discusses the 'way of ideas' from Descartes to Hume. Chapter 9 is entitled 'Hume on imagination: a magical faculty of the soul', and chapter 10 'Hume's ideas'.

A brief account of the imagery debate is given by Tye (1994). Hamlyn (1994), in the same volume, mentions the debate too, but his topic is 'imagination' rather than 'imagery'. Tye (1991) offers a much fuller account.

CHAPTER 4

Imagination and synthesis

> ... the power of imagination represents not just one faculty among others, but rather their mediating center.
>
> (Martin Heidegger, *Kant and the Problem of Metaphysics*, 124)

In this chapter we will be concerned with the ideas of Immanuel Kant (1724–1804) as presented in the first of his three great *Critiques*, the *Critique of Pure Reason* (*CPR*). Kant is *the* philosopher of the imagination. He is also, arguably, the most important philosopher in the modern period. His philosophy represents the culmination of the Enlightenment movement, and at the same time points the way forward to later developments from Romanticism onwards. Kant's works are notoriously difficult to comprehend and have inspired a whole range of reactions and interpretations. But there is, I think, a broad consensus on the basic thrust of Kant's philosophy, and our first aim will be to get as clear as possible about his governing motivation. The main aim of this chapter is to explore Kant's view of the role that the imagination plays in human experience. But this is not distinct from the first aim. Exploring Kant's conception of imagination provides an excellent way of appreciating the heart of his philosophy, with regard to both his positive views and his powerful critique of earlier rationalism and empiricism. Kant's *Critique* is long (over 700 pages in the original editions), but we will concentrate on just two chapters: the chapter on the so-called 'transcendental deduction', which is without doubt the core of the work, and the short chapter on 'schematism', which is also important – though more controversially. Admittedly, these are as tough to understand as anything in the history of philosophy, but the rewards more than make up for the effort in doing so, and as I hope will be seen, clear sense can indeed be made of their essential message (even if not of all their details).

This chapter has three main sections. In the first, after an initial explanation of Kant's governing motivation, we will look at Kant's main account of the imagination in the first edition of the *Critique*. In the second edition the emphasis shifts away from the reproductive, empirical imagination; and in the second main section, we will explore his conception of the productive, transcendental imagination. We will end by examining the role of the imagination in the process that Kant calls 'schematism'.

Kant and the reproductive imagination

Kant saw himself as reconciling the two competing traditions of rationalism and empiricism. The rationalist privileges the role of reason and understanding in the acquisition of knowledge, and Descartes is often taken as the first of the modern rationalists – although, as we have seen, his work is also a source of the empiricist 'way of ideas'. The empiricist regards knowledge as entirely based on sense experience, and this is certainly Hume's position. According to Kant, however, knowledge requires both understanding and sense experience. Kant sums up his position in what is perhaps his most famous claim, 'Thoughts without content are empty, intuitions without concepts are blind' (*CPR*, A51/B75). We will look first at what Kant means by this, before considering how the imagination comes into play, on Kant's account, in bringing together understanding and sense experience.

Intuitions and concepts

Kant's *Critique of Pure Reason* was first published in 1781, and a second, revised edition appeared in 1787. In a number of places there are significant differences, and most modern editions, while based on the second edition, note the original formulations and, where an entire section has been changed, give the whole of the first version as well. We will come to an important difference, as far as Kant's treatment of the imagination is concerned, in due course. (References to the *Critique* are standardly given in the form 'Ax/By', where 'A' and 'B' indicate the first and second editions, respectively, and 'x' and 'y' give the relevant page numbers of the original editions, which are also given in the margins of modern editions.)

The *Critique* divides, very unequally, into what Kant calls the 'Transcendental Doctrine of Elements' and the 'Transcendental Doctrine of Method'. The former divides, even more unequally, into the 'Transcendental Aesthetic' and the 'Transcendental Logic'. (For details of the structure of Kant's *Critique*, in so far as it concerns us, see appendix 2.) Let us begin with the opening of the 'Transcendental Logic':

> Our cognition arises from two fundamental sources in the mind, the first of which is the reception of representations (the receptivity of impressions), the second the faculty for cognizing an object by means of these representations (spontaneity of concepts); through the former an object is **given** to us, through the latter it is **thought** in relation to that representation (as a mere determination of the mind). Intuition and concepts therefore constitute the elements of all our cognition, so that neither concepts without intuition corresponding to them in some way nor intuition without concepts can yield a cognition. Both are either pure or empirical. **Empirical**, if sensation (which presupposes the actual presence of the object) is contained therein; but **pure** if no sensation is mixed into the representation. One can call the latter the matter of sensible cognition. Thus pure intuition contains merely the form under which something is intuited, and pure concept only the form of thinking of an object in general. Only pure intuitions or concepts alone are possible *a priori*, empirical ones only *a posteriori*.
>
> If we will call the **receptivity** of our mind to receive representations insofar as it is affected in some way **sensibility**, then on the contrary the faculty for bringing forth representations itself, or the **spontaneity** of cognition, is the **understanding**. It comes along with our nature that **intuition** can never be other than **sensible**, i.e., that it contains only the way in which we are affected by objects. The faculty for **thinking** of objects of sensible intuition, on the contrary, is the **understanding**. Neither of these properties is to be preferred to the other. Without sensibility no object would be given to us, and without understanding none would be thought. Thoughts without content are empty, intuitions without concepts are blind. It is thus just as necessary to make the mind's concepts sensible (i.e., to add an object to them in intuition) as it is to make its intuitions understandable (i.e., to bring them under concepts). Further, these two faculties or capacities cannot exchange their functions. The understanding is not capable of intuiting anything, and the senses are not capable of thinking anything. Only from their unification can cognition arise.
>
> (*CPR*, A50–1/B74–5; note that Kant used bold type for emphasis, and the Cambridge edition quoted here has followed his practice)

ACTIVITY

1. What are the two mental faculties whose joint operation gives rise to cognition (i.e. knowledge), according to Kant, and how are they characterized?
2. What is Kant's distinction between the empirical and the pure?

DISCUSSION

1. The two faculties are sensibility and understanding. Sensibility is responsible for (passively) receiving what Kant calls 'intuitions', which are basically raw sense impressions, and understanding is responsible for (spontaneously, i.e. freely and actively) applying concepts. The objects of our experience are *given* to us in sensibility and *thought* through conceptual understanding; both are required for us to have genuine knowledge. (The German term that has come to be translated as 'intuition' in the context of Kant's philosophy is *Anschauung*, from the verb *anschauen*, which means 'to look at'. The other German term to note here is *Vorstellung*, which is rendered as 'representation', although it also has the more everyday sense of 'idea'. As a first approximation, 'intuitions' are Humean impressions and 'representations' are Humean ideas. We will see why this is only a first approximation shortly.)

2. Something is 'empirical' if it has a sensory element, and is 'pure' if it does not. As Kant understands it, this cuts across the distinction between intuition and concept. Both intuitions and concepts can be 'pure' – when they have to do with form rather than (sensory) content.

According to Kant, when we receive intuitions in sensibility we impose upon them a spatial-temporal form, and we apprehend space and time in 'pure intuition'. (This was the topic of the earlier 'Transcendental Aesthetic', and the basic idea, strange as it might initially sound, is that space and time are in some sense functions of the way we represent the world. That the world 'in itself' does not have the three spatial dimensions that we experience it to have, and that events do not occur in an absolute framework of time that is independent of us, are more familiar to us now in the light of modern physics. But we will not go into this further here. The key point is just that the spatial-temporal organization of the world as we experience it is something that *we* impose, according to Kant. Space and time, as Kant puts it, are the 'pure forms of intuition'.) Kant also talks of pure intuitions or concepts as *a priori*. Roughly speaking, something is *a priori* if it is *prior* to experience, i.e. if it is a *precondition* of experience; something is *a posteriori* if it is dependent on a particular experience. According to Kant, if we did not bring spatial-temporal order into the world, then we could have no experience, so space and time are preconditions of experience. But so too, Kant goes on to argue, if we did not conceptualize the world in certain fundamental ways, then we could have no experience.

Kant's critique of the way of ideas

Kant's emphasis on the co-operation of sensibility and understanding cannot be overestimated. Its significance can be brought out by comparing his approach with the empiricist 'way of ideas'. According to the way of ideas in its Humean version, we start with simple impressions, and show how everything else is generated from them. Memory copies these impressions into ideas, and imagination reproduces, divides and recombines these ideas into other ideas – impressions and ideas being the sole 'objects of our understanding'. But if, on Hume's view, all we perceive are our impressions and ideas, then how can we know that there is an external world? As we saw in chapter 3, for Hume our belief in the continued and distinct existence of objects was a mistaken result of a conflict between imagination and reason. For Descartes, too, there was a similar problem in justifying the existence of an external world, and it was only by appealing to God that he was able to offer an answer. But if his arguments for the existence of God turn out to be unsound, then we are left in no less a sceptical quandary.

Kant turns the issue on its head. The fact that such extreme scepticism is an inevitable consequence of the way of ideas shows the falsity of that way, and Kant responds to (Cartesian/Humean) scepticism by undermining the very picture on which it depends. According to Kant, and this is his governing motivation, we start with human experience as it actually is and consider what that *presupposes*. To start with impressions and ideas, conceived as free-floating atoms of knowledge tied together only by loose empirical principles of association, as Hume does, is already to go wrong. Experience is always experience *of* something *by* someone. It presupposes both a world and a consciousness that is aware of that world. If experience involves both sensibility and understanding, then there must be both something 'outside us' to give rise to the intuitions we receive and a unity of consciousness to guarantee the coherence of the concepts we apply. This unity of consciousness Kant rather grandly calls the 'transcendental unity of apperception'. Kant uses 'apperception' and 'consciousness' more or less as synonyms, and what he means by 'transcendental' is whatever functions as a necessary *precondition* of experience – without which experience is not even possible for us as finite human beings. ('Transcendental' is distinguished from 'transcendent'. If 'transcendental' means what necessarily preconditions or limits our experience, i.e. what lies *at* the limits of experience, then 'transcendent' indicates what is *beyond* the limits of experience, about which we can know nothing, according to Kant. See A296/B352.) Kant's 'Transcendental Aesthetic' had been concerned with the necessary preconditions of human experience with respect to the faculty of sensibility, his conclusion being that such experience has to take a spatial-temporal form. His 'Transcendental Logic' is concerned with the necessary preconditions of human experience with respect to the faculty of understanding.

The Transcendental Deduction

The chapter of Kant's *Critique* entitled 'On the deduction of the pure concepts of the understanding' contains one of the most important and controversial arguments in the history of philosophy – Kant's so-called 'Transcendental Deduction'. It is also the chapter that gave Kant himself the most trouble. He completely rewrote it for the second edition, and there are significant differences. Kant sets out in this chapter to demonstrate the necessary applicability of certain fundamental concepts to our experience. Kant had identified these fundamental concepts – which he called 'categories' – in an earlier argument usually referred to as the 'Metaphysical Deduction', based on the logical forms of judgements. For example, a judgement such as 'This cat is friendly' is a singular, affirmative, categorical and assertoric judgement, and our understanding of such a judgement presupposes that we have a grasp of the relevant logical forms. ('This cat is friendly' is 'singular' as opposed to 'particular' or 'universal' because it concerns a single cat rather than some cats or all cats. It is 'affirmative' as opposed to 'negative' or 'infinite' because it ascribes friendliness rather than denying it or ascribing unfriendliness. It is 'categorical' as opposed to 'hypothetical' or 'disjunctive' because it affirms something unconditionally and without alternatives. It is 'assertoric' as opposed to 'problematic' or 'apodictic' because it affirms what is actually rather than possibly or necessarily the case. As this suggests, Kant distinguishes twelve logical forms, arranged in four groups of three, but the full details need not concern us here.) Our grasp of these forms is logically prior to our grasp of whatever empirical concepts are involved – in this case, the concepts of *cat* and *friendly*. Without a (prior) grasp of the logical forms, we could not make or understand any judgement about the world. Corresponding to each of the twelve logical forms is a category or 'pure concept'. Corresponding to the four forms involved in the judgement that 'This cat is friendly', for example, are the four categories of unity, reality, substance and existence. What Kant attempts to show in the Transcendental Deduction is that the categories or pure concepts are necessarily implicated in any experience that a human being can have.

Kant's project seems well motivated. Consider again the judgement that 'This cat is friendly', which I might make in experiencing a cat leaping on to my lap. To make any such judgement, it seems reasonable to suppose, I must have the ability to identify what I see before me as a cat – as a single thing that has a continued and distinct existence outside me. If this is right, then any such judgement I make presupposes a grasp of the concepts of unity, reality, substance and existence. But does this mean that the cat itself must exist? Can I not have experiences *as if* there is a cat before me even when there is not? Might I not be hallucinating? Can I not make judgements about cats even if there are no cats present, or about unicorns even if there are no unicorns anywhere? But even in these cases, must I not have had some acquaintance with animals and other external objects to be able to make such judgements? How much can we say *in general* must be true for human experience to be possible? Human experience would be possible even if cats did not exist. But what if there were no objects at all that existed for long enough to provide some stability and coherence to our mental lives? If this were true, Kant argues, then human experience would not be possible. But since human experience *is* possible, since we have it, then certain general conditions, such as the existence of an external world, must obtain. Kant has often been accused of trying to establish too much in his Transcendental Deduction; and it is controversial just how much he does succeed in establishing. Our main concern here, however, is with the role that the imagination plays in human experience, on Kant's view.

The synthesis of apprehension in intuition

Experience may require both intuitions (sensory impressions) and concepts, but it does not arise simply from the application of concepts to intuitions. Those intuitions have to be synthesized or put together in some way for concepts to be applicable to them. By 'synthesis' in its most general sense, Kant writes, 'I understand the action of putting different representations together with each other and comprehending their manifoldness [i.e. multiplicity] in one cognition' (A77/B103). Shortly after this remark comes his first mention of the imagination:

> The first thing that must be given to us *a priori* for the cognition of all objects is the **manifold** of pure intuition; the **synthesis** of this manifold by means of the imagination is the second thing, but it still does not yield cognition. The concepts that give this pure synthesis **unity**, and that consist solely in the representation of this necessary synthetic unity, are the third thing necessary for cognition of an object that comes before us, and they depend on the understanding.
>
> (*CPR*, A78–9/B104)

What underlies this account is the traditional division of the mental faculties into sensation, imagination and understanding. Sensation supplies us with a manifold of intuitions, i.e. a mass of sensory impressions; the imagination synthesizes them into a whole; and the understanding supplies the concepts that enable this whole to be conceptualized as a coherent unity. The German term that is translated here as 'imagination' is *Einbildungskraft*, which literally means the 'power to form into one (in one's mind)'. Kant occasionally uses just *Einbildung*, which refers more to the mere having rather than power of imagination – in the sense in which we might talk of *having* imagination (*Einbildung*) rather than of *using our power of* imagination (*Einbildungskraft*). But *Einbildungskraft* is his main term. Other German words that are often also translated as 'imagination' are *Phantasie*, which has the sense of 'fancy' or 'fantasy', and *Vorstellungskraft* (or even just *Vorstellung*), which has the broader and more neutral sense of 'power to form ideas or representations' (or 'ideation'). So it is significant that Kant chose the word *Einbildungskraft*, which suggests an active role of synthesis.

In fact, as Kant elaborates it in the first edition version of the Transcendental Deduction, synthesis is involved at all three levels. These levels he calls the synthesis of apprehension in intuition, the synthesis of reproduction in imagination (*Einbildung*), and the synthesis of recognition in a concept. What happens at the first level is that the manifold of sensory data that enters through our senses is 'run through and [taken] together', as Kant puts it (A99). Consider again my experience of seeing a cat. I have a set of impressions of that cat – of its face, its tail, its fur, its colour, etc. – and must bring these together in my overall intuition of the cat. This is the synthesis of apprehension. We will look at the second and third levels of synthesis in the next two sections.

The synthesis of reproduction in imagination

The second level of synthesis involves the imagination. Here is the whole of the subsection entitled 'On the synthesis of reproduction in the imagination':

> It is, to be sure, a merely empirical law in accordance with which representations that have often followed or accompanied one another are finally associated with each other and thereby placed in a connection in accordance with which, even without the presence of the object, one of these representations brings about a transition of the mind to the other in accordance with a constant rule. This law of reproduction, however, presupposes that the appearances themselves are actually subject to such a rule, and that in the manifold of their representations an accompaniment or succession takes place according to certain rules; for without that our empirical imagination would never get to do anything suitable to its capacity, and would thus remain hidden in the interior of the mind, like a dead and to us unknown faculty. If cinnabar were now red, now black, now light, now heavy, if a human being were now changed into this animal shape, now into that one, if on the longest day the land were covered now with fruits, now with ice and snow, then my empirical imagination would never even get the opportunity to think of heavy cinnabar on the occasion of the representation of the colour red; or if a certain word were attributed now to this thing, now to that, or if one and the same thing were sometimes called this, sometimes that, without the governance of a certain rule to which the appearances are already subjected in themselves, then no empirical synthesis of reproduction could take place.
>
> There must therefore be something that itself makes possible this reproduction of the appearances by being the *a priori* ground of a necessary synthetic unity of them. One soon comes upon this if one recalls that appearances are not things in themselves, but rather the mere play of our representations, which in the end come down to determinations of the inner sense. Now if we can demonstrate that even our purest *a priori* intuitions provide no cognition except insofar as they contain the sort of combination of the manifold that makes possible a thoroughgoing synthesis of reproduction, then this synthesis of the imagination would be grounded even prior to all experience on *a priori* principles, and one must assume a pure transcendental synthesis of this power, which grounds even the possibility of all experience (as that which the reproducibility of the appearances necessarily presupposes). Now it is obvious that if I draw a line in thought, or think of the time from one noon to the next, or even want to represent a certain number to myself, I must necessarily first grasp one of these manifold representations after another in my thoughts. But if I were always to lose the preceding representations (the first parts of the line, the preceding parts of time, or the successively represented units) from my thoughts and not reproduce them when I proceed to

the following ones, then no whole representation and none of the previously mentioned thoughts, not even the purest and most fundamental representations of space and time, could ever arise.

The synthesis of apprehension is therefore inseparably combined with the synthesis of reproduction. And since the former constitutes the transcendental ground of the possibility of all cognition in general (not only of empirical cognition, but also of pure *a priori* cognition), the reproductive synthesis of the imagination belongs among the transcendental actions of the mind, and with respect to this we will also call this faculty the transcendental faculty of the imagination.

(*CPR*, A100–2)

ACTIVITY

1. Although Kant mentions no names, it is Hume to whom he is alluding in the first sentence of this passage. What aspect of Hume's philosophy is he referring to? (Look back at pp.72–3.)

2. In the second sentence, Kant offers a criticism of Hume's view. What is this criticism?

3. What are the thought experiments that Kant offers in the third sentence meant to show?

4. What is Kant's argument in the first three sentences of the second paragraph? (You need not worry too much about the second sentence, which raises issues – about Kant's 'transcendental idealism' – that we will leave aside here.)

5. What is the point of the examples that Kant gives in the last two sentences of the second paragraph?

6. What does Kant mean by saying, in the third paragraph, that the reproductive synthesis of the imagination belongs among the transcendental actions of the mind?

DISCUSSION

1. Kant is alluding to Hume's conception of the (empirical) imagination. On Hume's view, the mind becomes accustomed, through repeated experience, of running from one idea to another in accordance with the principles of association.

2. According to Kant, the operations of the (empirical) imagination in accordance with the principles of association presuppose a more fundamental rule which makes such operations possible.

3   If things were always changing in the way suggested in Kant's thought experiments, then the empirical association of ideas could never even get started. So if the latter does occur, as Hume himself allows, then there must be more underlying stability and coherence to the world than Hume is able to account for.

4   The empirical reproduction of ideas in accordance with the principles of association presupposes a more fundamental power in us, which makes possible the empirical imagination. (Kant is not at his most succinct in the third sentence, and I am not simplifying too much in saying what I have just said.)

5   To engage in any genuine process of thought, I must keep in mind or reproduce what I have earlier thought in continuing to think.

6   What Kant means by the 'transcendental' actions of the mind are those actions that are necessary conditions of – i.e. that are presupposed by – my everyday (empirical) actions. Since the ability to reproduce ideas is the condition of associating ideas, it is thus to be counted as a transcendental ability.

This passage provides a good illustration of Kant's governing motivation. We start with experience as it actually is and consider what this presupposes. We know our experience exhibits a certain pattern and regularity, and we must consider what makes this possible. The world itself must have a corresponding stability and order, but equally our minds must have a certain character to experience the world in the way we do. Our focus here is on the latter.

Consider once again the example of the cat. What is required for me to experience it leaping on my lap? I might have a series of impressions of the cat from the time I saw it walk through the door to the time I see it settled comfortably on my lap. At each point in time the mass of sensory impressions I receive must be synthesized into a single complex intuition, but in order to experience the whole event, I must also be able to collect together these various complex intuitions in one temporal sequence. So my ability to have such an experience presupposes that I can reproduce earlier intuitions alongside my current intuition.

Take a second example, which Edmund Husserl (1859–1938) was later to give in his discussion of the phenomenology of time-consciousness (1990, 30).

Consider the experience of hearing a simple melody. According to the way of ideas, all we receive is a series of aural impressions of musical notes, one after another. But merely receiving a series of notes does not constitute hearing a melody. In experiencing a melody, I retain the previous notes *as* I listen. Indeed, Husserl emphasizes the involvement too of *anticipating* the notes to come, so that experiencing something like a melody has a complex 'retentional' and 'protentional' structure that a naive empiricist account fails to recognize. To appreciate this, think of the difference between hearing a piece of music for the first time – where it might just seem like a series of noises going nowhere – and hearing it again when it has become familiar. Although the actual reproduction of past intuitions (and the anticipation of future ones) illustrates the workings of the empirical imagination, the underlying power to do this Kant attributes to what he calls the transcendental faculty of the imagination.

The synthesis of recognition in a concept

The third level of synthesis involves conceptualization. As Kant puts it in opening the subsection entitled 'On the synthesis of recognition in a concept', 'Without consciousness that that which we think is the very same as what we thought a moment before, all reproduction in the series of representations would be in vain' (A103). Reproduction may be necessary for human experience, in other words, but it is not sufficient; conceptualization too is required. If I was not aware that what I saw was a cat the whole time, then I could have no experience of a cat leaping on to my lap. The intuitions I apprehend and reproduce must be united in the concept of a cat. This is the synthesis of recognition in a concept.

Just as the empirical association of ideas presupposes the transcendental faculty of the imagination, however, so too the empirical application of a concept such as that of a cat presupposes a transcendental condition. This condition is the unity of consciousness mentioned above (p.87) – what Kant calls the 'transcendental unity of apperception'. Conceptualization requires both a unity in what is being conceptualized and a unity in what is doing the conceptualizing; otherwise the whole process would fall apart. The transcendental unity of apperception comes to play the central role in the second edition version of the Transcendental Deduction, where Kant talks of the 'I think' that must be able to accompany all my representations (B131).

Imagination as mediation

The conception of imagination that emerges from this account can be summarized thus. Experience – of the kind that human beings have – involves sensibility, imagination and understanding, and a synthesis operates at each level. The manifold of intuitions (i.e. mass of impressions) we receive through the senses must be apprehended in a single complex intuition; previous intuitions must be reproduced in imagination; and the synthesized intuitions must be conceptualized by the understanding. On this account, the imagination mediates between sensibility and understanding: understanding requires imagination, which in turn requires sensibility.

We started with what seemed to be a dichotomy in Kant's philosophy: between sensibility and understanding, intuitions and concepts. But when we look at exactly how each contributes to experience, we see that the imagination is necessarily involved. The impressions delivered by our senses are of no use unless they can be controlled and reproduced by the imagination, and understanding can only get to work on intuitions that have already been synthesized by the imagination. As Kant had said in first mentioning the imagination, what are brought under concepts are not representations themselves but the '**synthesis** of representations' (A78/B104; see p.90 above).

Kant concludes his discussion of the imagination in the first edition version of the Transcendental Deduction as follows:

> We therefore have a pure imagination, as a fundamental faculty of the human soul, that grounds all cognition *a priori*. By its means we bring into combination the manifold of intuition on the one side and the condition of the necessary unity of apperception on the other. Both extremes, namely sensibility and understanding, must necessarily be connected by means of this transcendental function of the imagination, since otherwise the former would to be sure yield appearances but no objects of an empirical cognition, hence there would be no experience.
>
> (*CPR*, A124)

Without imagination, there would be no human experience, because there would be nothing to bring together sensibility and understanding.

Hume and Kant on imagination in perception

Let us draw out the implications of Kant's conception of imagination in the first edition version of the Transcendental Deduction by taking the example of experiencing a cat leaping on to my lap, and comparing the accounts that Hume and Kant would give of our perceptual experience. Let us start with the following remark that Kant makes in a footnote to his account:

> No psychologist has yet thought that the imagination is a necessary ingredient of perception itself. This is so partly because this faculty has been limited to reproduction, and partly because it has been believed that the senses do not merely afford us impressions but also put them together, and produce images of objects, for which without doubt something more than the receptivity of impressions is required, namely a function of the synthesis of them.
>
> (*CPR*, A120)

ACTIVITY

1 Kant gives two reasons why 'psychologists' have not regarded the imagination as a necessary ingredient of perception itself. What are these two reasons?

2 In referring to the 'psychologist', Kant particularly has in mind the associationist – someone like Hume who seeks to explain the operations of the mind through the association of ideas. In the light of the previous chapter, does Kant give a fair representation of Hume's conception of imagination?

DISCUSSION

1 According to Kant, the 'psychologist' restricts the role of the imagination to the mere reproduction of impressions and ideas. Furthermore, although it is granted that sensory impressions need to be put together somehow, this is regarded as performed by sensibility itself and not imagination. So the imagination is given no role to play in perception itself.

2 Hume does regard sensory impressions as put together in sensibility, and he does attribute to the imagination the role of reproducing impressions and ideas. But this is not all. He also sees the imagination as responsible for the division and recombination of ideas in new ways, although we may grant that this does not mean the imagination is an 'ingredient' in perception itself. More importantly, however, Kant does no justice here to Hume's view of the role that imagination plays in our belief in an external world. In perception, we at least believe that there is something

'out there', and since imagination contributes to the formation of that belief, according to Hume, it would seem to have a role in perception itself.

ACTIVITY

Consider the example of seeing a cat as it walks through the door and leaps on to my lap.

1. Look back at pages 76–80, on Hume's solution to the problem of the external world. How do I come to attribute a 'continued and distinct existence' to the cat, on Hume's account? How does Hume see the imagination as involved in this process?
2. How is the imagination a 'necessary ingredient' in my perception of the cat, on Kant's account?
3. What are the main similarities and differences between Hume's and Kant's accounts?
4. What would you say are the main difficulties in each account?

DISCUSSION

1. On Hume's account, I have a series of discrete impressions ('perceptions') of the cat, which resemble one another so closely that I am tempted into believing that they are identical, i.e. that the cat has 'continued existence'. Yet I know (through reason) that those impressions are different, so I posit an external object that itself has continued existence: I come to believe too that the cat has 'distinct existence'. The imagination is involved in both these beliefs, first, in my confusing similarity with identity, encouraged by the 'smooth passage of the imagination along the ideas', as Hume puts it, and second, albeit in a more intellectual sense, in positing the external object.
2. On Kant's account, the imagination is involved in the second stage of 'synthesis' – in bringing the temporally ordered series of my impressions of the cat together in experiencing it as the same cat. This temporally ordered series *presupposes* the existence of the cat: it could not be temporally ordered in the coherent way it is if there was no cat responsible for the series of impressions.
3. On both Hume's and Kant's accounts, the imagination plays a role in reproducing past impressions (as ideas) to be associated (Hume) or synthesized (Kant) with present impressions to constitute the perceptual experience. We can also take them to agree that the problem here concerns the relation between a series of impressions and belief in an external object

that underwrites that series. But whereas Hume thinks that such a belief is false, Kant regards it as true. For Hume, in other words, the imagination generates something imaginary, while, for Kant, its activities are somehow constitutive of reality as we experience it.

4   The main difficulty in Hume's account, I would say, is the extreme scepticism in which he seems to have landed himself. As I remarked earlier in this chapter ('Kant's critique of the way of ideas'), according to Kant, Hume goes wrong at the very first step – in assuming that impressions ('perceptions') are discrete mental images, which can only be bound together by weak principles of association. Given this assumption, it is not surprising that he cannot get from there to justified belief in an external world. For Kant, on the other hand, belief in an external world is *constitutive* of perceptual experience. Even a single, supposedly 'simple' perception of an object such as a cat is actually complex, with presuppositions to be revealed. This governing conception of Kant's, however, is hard to articulate, and the main question that arises is just what Kant attempts to answer in the *Critique* as a whole: what exactly *is* constitutive of perceptual experience, and how is this to be shown? But there is also the more specific question: how is the *imagination* involved in the constitutive process?

Let us focus here on the more specific question, concerning the role of the imagination in the constitutive process. The position we have reached so far is this. According to Kant, the association of ideas, which was basic for Hume, presupposes a more fundamental cognitive power – the power to reproduce past ideas alongside present ones in constituting perceptual experience. This power is attributed to the imagination. Since having this power is a necessary condition of associating ideas, Kant terms it 'transcendental'. But is this the only role that the imagination plays in constituting experience? As we will now see, as Kant thinks through the presuppositions of experience further, he gradually comes to realize that this is not the only power of imagination that we have, and stops calling this merely reproductive power 'transcendental'. There are other, more fundamental, 'productive' powers, and he reserves the term 'transcendental' for these.

Kant and the productive imagination

In the first edition version of the Transcendental Deduction, it is the reproductive work of the imagination that is highlighted. In the passages we have considered so far, Kant talks of this reproductive work as being among the transcendental actions of the mind (A102). Later on in the first edition version, however, he offers a rather different view. In two places, he talks of the *productive* imagination, seen as distinct from the reproductive imagination (A118, A123). It is only the former that is transcendental; the latter is merely empirical. This suggests that Kant's ideas were on the move even during the writing of the first edition. The distinction is made explicit in the second edition version of the Transcendental Deduction, although much less is said about the imagination in this second version.

The productive and reproductive imagination

The distinction between the productive and reproductive imagination is first drawn in the first edition version of the Transcendental Deduction. After explaining the need to ground the empirical association of ideas on something transcendental, Kant writes:

> The imagination is therefore also a faculty of a synthesis *a priori*, on account of which we give it the name of productive imagination, and, insofar as its aim in regard to all the manifold of appearance is nothing further than the necessary unity in their synthesis, this can be called the transcendental function of the imagination.
>
> (*CPR*, A123)

This seems to contradict what Kant had said earlier in calling the reproductive work of the imagination transcendental (A103). But we might take it as representing Kant's considered view. On this view, the reproductive imagination associates ideas and is empirical, but this is grounded on the productive imagination, which is transcendental.

Imagination as an active power

The second edition version of the Transcendental Deduction (B129–69) is several pages longer than the first edition version (A95–130), but the imagination is only discussed in one of its 13 subsections. There is no mention of the threefold synthesis of the first edition – of apprehension, reproduction and recognition. Instead, Kant distinguishes between figurative and intellectual synthesis – although, as a first approximation, one can think of intellectual synthesis as the synthesis of recognition in a concept (i.e. as conceptualization) and figurative synthesis as the synthesis that operates at the pre-conceptual level, which is where the imagination is still seen as operating. Kant himself calls figurative synthesis the 'transcendental synthesis of the imagination'. Here is the key passage. It is not an easy passage to understand: the second sentence, in particular, is obscure. But its main point can, I think, be extracted.

> ***Imagination*** is the faculty for representing in intuition an object even **without its presence**. Now since all of our intuition is sensible, the imagination, on account of the subjective condition under which alone it can give a corresponding intuition to the concepts of understanding, belongs to **sensibility**; but insofar as its synthesis is still an exercise of spontaneity, which is determining and not, like sense, merely determinable, and can thus determine the form of sense *a priori* in accordance with the unity of apperception, the imagination is to this extent a faculty for determining the sensibility *a priori*, and its synthesis of intuitions, **in accordance with the categories**, must be the transcendental synthesis of the **imagination**, which is an effect of the understanding on sensibility and its first application (and at the same time the ground of all others) to objects of the intuition that is possible for us. As figurative, it is distinct from the intellectual synthesis without any imagination merely through the understanding. Now insofar as the imagination is spontaneity, I also occasionally call it the **productive** imagination, and thereby distinguish it from the **reproductive** imagination, whose synthesis is subject solely to empirical laws, namely those of association, and that therefore contributes nothing to the explanation of the possibility of cognition *a priori*, and on that account belongs not in transcendental philosophy but in psychology.
>
> (*CPR*, B151–2; I have continued to use the Cambridge translation here, but have modified slightly the translation of the first sentence)

ACTIVITY

1 How does Kant define 'imagination' in this passage? How does it compare with the general definition of 'imagining' suggested by Stevenson's twelve conceptions of imagination (see p.11 above)?

2 The second sentence again illustrates Kant at his most verbose. How would you summarize its point? (Don't worry if it baffles you on a first – or

even second or third – reading. Just see if you can state what the two aspects of the imagination are that Kant seems to be describing.)

3 Recall my discussion of Gaut's analysis of imagination in chapter 1 (pp.14–22) and, in particular, what I said in answer to the fourth question of the first activity in that section (pp.16–17). Take the example of imagining a wet cat. A distinction might be drawn here between conjuring up some kind of sensory image of a wet cat and 'entertaining' the concept of a wet cat. Which of these do you think illustrates better the conception of imagination that Kant seems to be articulating in the first two sentences of this passage? How might this example be used to illustrate Kant's point in the second sentence?

4 How does Kant characterize the productive imagination? What do you think Kant means in giving this characterization?

5 The final sentence offers an implicit criticism of his earlier view. What is this criticism?

6 In the light of all this, what feature of the imagination would you say Kant is now recognizing that leads him to modify his earlier view?

DISCUSSION

1 Stevenson's twelve conceptions suggested the general definition of 'imagining' as 'thinking of something that is not present to the senses'. Kant's definition of 'imagination' as 'the faculty for representing in intuition an object even without its presence' suggests something similar; but unlike the general definition, Kant's definition allows that the imagination can be involved in thinking of something that *is* present to the senses. In characterizing imagining as representing *in intuition*, Kant also stresses its sensory aspect, which is not captured in the general definition (which is more general in this respect). This aspect is made clear in the rest of the passage.

2 Here is my attempt at summarizing Kant's main point. The imagination belongs, on the one hand, to sensibility since it involves intuitions, and, on the other hand, to understanding since it plays an active role in conceptualization (i.e. in synthesizing those intuitions in accordance with the categories).

3 Imagining a wet cat, on the conception of imagination that I think Kant is articulating here, is more like conjuring up a sensory image of a wet cat than merely 'entertaining' the concept of a wet cat. As just noted, imagining is representing *in intuition*, by which Kant means that it takes

some sensory form. But it does not consist simply in having a sensory image of a wet cat; that image (or synthesis of intuitions, in Kant's terminology) must also be apprehended or conceptualized *as* a wet cat. So imagining has both a sensory and an intellectual aspect, which is the main point I have suggested Kant is making in the second sentence.

4   The productive imagination is characterized as involving spontaneity. What is meant by 'spontaneity' is indicated in the second sentence: spontaneity is exhibited in 'determining' sensibility in our conceptual activities. The contrast that Kant is drawing here, I think, is between the passive and active functions of the mind. In sensation and perception, we passively receive sensory impressions (intuitions, in Kant's terminology). In imagination, we actively generate sensory images (which Kant also calls 'intuitions') ourselves. Imagination is like sensibility in involving intuitions (sensory impressions or images), but like understanding in operating freely or spontaneously (within the constraints of the categories, which govern what is thinkable). Imagination, in other words, is subject to the will to an extent that sensory perception is not. (Compare what was said on pp.30–1 above about the imagination being subject to the will). As I read the passage, then, it is this feature that Kant is describing in talking of 'spontaneity'.

5   The final sentence makes clear that Kant now sees the reproductive imagination as purely empirical – operating in accordance with the principles of association – and as such a matter for psychology, not philosophy. Philosophy is concerned with the transcendental grounds of human experience, i.e. with its necessary preconditions. He now realizes that there are deeper presuppositions, which he wants to capture in talking of the productive imagination.

6   What Kant now recognizes, I think, is the active role of imagination. The first edition version of the Transcendental Deduction stressed the importance of the reproductive imagination, but Kant now sees that there is a more fundamental power presupposed in our conceptual activities, which he also accords to the imagination – the productive imagination.

In the second edition version of the Transcendental Deduction, then, Kant moves even further away from Hume. For Hume, the association of ideas is indeed an empirical process, without any further grounding. But why do we associate these ideas in this way rather than those ideas in that way? Hume's answer is that this is just the way the mind works, but Kant thinks that there is far more to be said philosophically. We associate ideas for particular purposes in our freely chosen, conceptual activities. For Hume, the association of ideas is something that just happens to us, whereas for Kant it is governed by deeper and active cognitive processes and projects, which it is the aim of 'transcendental' philosophy to articulate.

Except for one final comment, which I will pick up later in this chapter, this is all that Kant says about the imagination in the second edition version of the Transcendental Deduction. We need to look elsewhere for further elucidation of his conception of imagination.

Imagination as the hidden root of sensibility and understanding

Kant's two versions of the Transcendental Deduction illustrate very well the central theme of this book – the problematic status of the imagination between sensibility and understanding. In the first edition version, Kant seems to regard the imagination as intermediate between the two – almost as a third faculty mediating between them. In the second edition version, the original dichotomy between sensibility and understanding is restored and reinforced, but with the imagination now seen as playing some deeper role in their interaction. If the second represents Kant's considered position, then what exactly *is* this role?

In his book, *Kant and the Problem of Metaphysics*, which was first published in 1929, Martin Heidegger (1889–1976) argues that the transcendental imagination was central to Kant's philosophy. Heidegger recognizes the differences between the two editions of the *Critique*, but he takes seriously Kant's remark in the 'Introduction' that 'there are two stems of human cognition, which may perhaps arise from a common but to us unknown root, namely, **sensibility** and **understanding**' (A15/B29). This root, Heidegger suggests (in section 27 of his book), is the transcendental imagination. There are a number of things driving Heidegger's suggestion, not least the concern to reconcile some of the dualisms in Kant's philosophy. Heidegger argues (in section 29), for example, that the transcendental power of the imagination provides an 'original unity of receptivity and spontaneity'. Heidegger's interpretation of Kant, however, is as much about his own philosophy as it is about Kant's. So rather than pursue this here, let me follow up on Heidegger's central claim independently. That the transcendental imagination may be the root of the two stems of sensibility and understanding is a suggestive idea, and it might be illustrated, first, in Kant's account of geometrical methodology and, second, in his discussion of schematism.

Philosophical and mathematical methodology

Although Kant's discussion of methodology is tucked away at the back of the *Critique*, in the 'Transcendental Doctrine of Method', in many ways it holds the key to his philosophy. Kant opens the first section of chapter 1 with the claim that 'Mathematics gives the most resplendent example of pure reason happily expanding itself without assistance from experience' (A712/B740). We might see this as asserting the creative power of mathematics, a power that can be exercised simply by drawing on the resources of the mind and, in particular, the imagination. Although the imagination is only mentioned once in this section, its role is clear. Mathematical cognition involves the construction of concepts, and to construct a concept, Kant writes, 'means to exhibit *a priori* the intuition corresponding to it' (i.e. to provide some kind of sensory representation of it in our mind). This can be done, he goes on, 'either through mere imagination, in pure intuition, or on paper, in empirical intuition, but in both cases completely *a priori*, without having had to borrow the pattern for it from any experience' (A713/B741). Given that empirical intuition is itself grounded in the work of the imagination, as Kant had argued in the Transcendental Deduction, the imagination is clearly crucial in mathematics.

Kant's main concern in this section is to distinguish philosophical method from mathematical method. He takes the example of a simple geometrical problem to illustrate the difference:

> Give a philosopher the concept of a triangle, and let him try to find out in his way how the sum of its angles might be related to a right angle. He has nothing but the concept of a figure enclosed by three straight lines, and in it the concept of equally many angles. Now he may reflect on this concept as long as he wants, yet he will never produce anything new. He can analyze and make distinct the concept of a straight line, or of an angle, or of the number three, but he will not come upon any other properties that do not already lie in these concepts. But now let the geometer take up this question. He begins at once to construct a triangle. Since he knows that two right angles together are exactly equal to all of the adjacent angles that can be drawn at one point on a straight line, he extends one side of his

triangle, and obtains two adjacent angles that together are equal to two right ones. Now he divides the external one of these angles by drawing a line parallel to the opposite side of the triangle, and sees that here there arises an external adjacent angle which is equal to an internal one, etc. In such a way, through a chain of inferences that is always guided by intuition, he arrives at a fully illuminating and at the same time general solution of the question.

(*CPR*, A716–17/B744–5)

ACTIVITY

The example is in fact taken from Euclid's *Elements*, where it is solved in Book I (Proposition 32). According to Kant, why is it only the geometer and not the philosopher who can solve this problem?

DISCUSSION

Kant's point is that no amount of conceptual analysis, which he assumes is what the philosopher (of a rationalist disposition) pursues, will solve the problem. It is only by actually constructing the triangle and then extending the figure in appropriate ways that success can be achieved.

According to Kant, mere conceptual analysis does not generate genuine knowledge. Knowledge can be gained through mathematics, but only by employing the imagination in constructing the relevant figures. This need not involve actual diagrams; imagined diagrams will suffice. It is in this sense that mathematics can expand 'without assistance from experience'. But if imagination is required, then the need for constructions suggests that creativity too is involved.

Creativity in Euclidean geometry

The example that Kant gives – showing that the sum of the angles of a triangle is equal to two right angles – is too simple to see how creativity is involved in geometrical problem-solving. A richer example is provided in appendix 1.

ACTIVITY

Read appendix 1 (pp.214–19). It is suggested there that 'construction' has two senses. What are these two senses? With which sense is creativity associated?

DISCUSSION

In the first sense, 'construction' just means the exhibiting (drawing or imagining) of a geometrical figure. It is in this sense that Kant talks of the 'construction' of a concept. In the second sense, 'construction' means the generating of new lines, the auxiliary lines that are needed to solve the geometrical problem. It is here that creativity is involved.

Transcendental imagination in Euclidean geometry

Given this distinction between two senses of 'construction', it is tempting to line it up both with the distinction between the reproductive and productive imagination and with the distinction between the empirical and transcendental imagination. This would suggest that the source of creativity lies in the productive or transcendental imagination. What does such a suggestion mean?

Construction in Euclidean geometry proceeds in accordance with the first three postulates (as noted in appendix 1): drawing a line between any two points, extending a line, and drawing a circle (or segment of a circle) with any given centre and radius. But these postulates themselves presuppose that the operations can be carried out – in the inner (Euclidean) space of our imagination, if not in the actual world. So geometry itself (and indeed, figurative art in general) depends on something more fundamental – the ability we have to draw figures in our imagination. If 'transcendental' means whatever functions as a condition of experience (see p.87 above), then this ability is rightly attributed to the 'transcendental' imagination.

I mentioned above (p.100) that Kant talks of 'figurative synthesis', which he calls the 'transcendental synthesis of the imagination'. Kant comments on this as follows: 'We also always perceive this in ourselves. We cannot think of a line without **drawing** it in thought, we cannot think of a circle without **describing** it, we cannot represent the three dimensions of space at all without **placing** three lines perpendicular to each other at the same point ...' (B154). Since all these acts of thinking are basic, so too is the transcendental imagination. Our very representation of space depends on the transcendental imagination. Later in the *Critique*, Kant writes that 'I cannot represent to myself any line, no matter how small it may be, without drawing it in thought, i.e., successively generating all its parts from one point, and thereby first sketching this intuition ... On this successive synthesis of the productive imagination, in the generation of shapes, is grounded the mathematics of extension (geometry) with its axioms' (A162–3/B203–4). Our recognition of the axioms and postulates in Euclidean geometry is often taken as basic, but this recognition itself depends on our ability to draw lines.

Underlying all geometrical constructions, then, is the productive, transcendental imagination. It is 'transcendental' in the sense that it is a condition for spatial-temporal experience, and it is 'productive' in the sense that it generates geometrical figures. If 'creative' is understood as synonymous with 'productive', then we might also talk of the transcendental imagination as 'creative'. But this is a relatively weak sense of 'creative'. As we have seen, some constructions play a more crucial role in geometrical problem-solving than others. So while a necessary condition, the use of transcendental imagination is not a sufficient condition for creativity in the richer sense illustrated in appendix 1.

The mental rotation of three-dimensional figures

Even accepting the explanation I have given, talk of 'transcendental' imagination may still sound esoteric and other-worldly. So it may be helpful here to cite some recent work in cognitive psychology that can be used to illustrate Kant's conception. Empirical findings cannot be used to *demonstrate* Kant's philosophy (even if they are universally accepted), since, as I have said, Kant's concern is with what the empirical *presupposes*. But it is possible to suggest ways in which something 'transcendental' can indeed be seen as presupposed in the empirical.

In 1971 Roger Shepard and Nancy Metzler published a paper in *Science* called 'Mental rotation of three-dimensional figures', reporting on experiments they had done to investigate people's ability to transform images. The experiments seem to have acquired canonical status in cognitive psychology, and are frequently referred to (for example, Rollins 1989, 18–20; Tye 1991, 56–8). Subjects were shown a series of pairs of images of three-dimensional figures, such as those in Figure 3, and asked if the members of each pair were congruent or not.

1 Consider the three pairs of images in Figure 3 (overleaf). In each case, are the two figures congruent, i.e. do they have the same shape?

2 What did you do to find the answer?

ACTIVITY

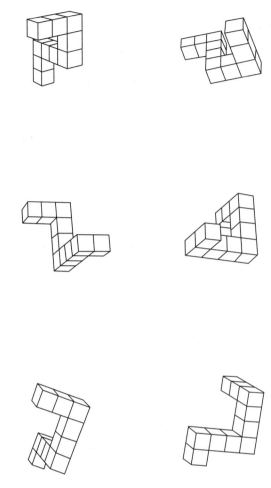

Figure 3 Taken from R.N. Shepard and N. Metzler, 'Mental rotation of three-dimensional figures', *Science*, 171 (1971), pp.701–3 © AAAS.

3   Which case took you the shortest time to find the answer, and which the longest?

DISCUSSION

1   The figures in each of the first two cases are congruent; the figures in the third case are not. (Overall, in the actual experiments, the right answer was given in 95 per cent of the cases.)

2   You may have done it differently yourself, but when the subjects of the experiment were asked how they did it, they reported that they imagined the figures rotated to see if one could be superimposed on the other.

3   In the cases where congruence obtained, the time taken to answer was found to be directly proportional to the amount of rotation required to superimpose one figure on to the other. So you probably found that it took longer to find the answer in the second case than in the first. Things are less straightforward in negative cases, since one may well try out different possible rotations before being satisfied that the two figures are not congruent; but this will typically take longer than establishing congruence in comparable positive cases.

The high success rate might be taken to suggest that we all have the same ability to transform images in our imagination. But the success rate itself is of less significance than what goes on in finding the answers. For in working out which figures are congruent, it does seem that we imagine the figures rotated, and this presupposes, as Kant pointed out, an underlying ability that we all have to carry out geometrical operations in the inner space of our imagination. As Kant recognized, too, such operations take time, so it is not surprising that the greater the rotation required for superimposition, the greater the time taken to find the answer.

The experiments are often cited to demonstrate that we can transform *mental* images, where these are understood pictorially. Perhaps we can indeed look at the figures, close our eyes and then imagine one of our mental pictures being rotated and superimposed on another. But this seems quite difficult. When I worked out the answers, it was the image on the page that I imagined rotated. Nevertheless, the important point is that there is something I am doing 'in my imagination', which is a condition of finding the answers, and it was this sort of thing that Kant had in mind in talking of the 'transcendental' imagination. As we will see, however, geometrical operations do not exhaust the work of the transcendental imagination.

Images and schemata

The chapter entitled 'On the schematism of the pure concepts of the understanding' (A137–47/B176–87) is one of the shortest in Kant's *Critique*, but its brevity is not an indication of its lack of importance. Kant's discussion complements the Transcendental Deduction, with the imagination once again taking centre stage. In this respect it is significant that the schematism chapter underwent little change from the first to the second editions, surviving the radical rewriting of the Transcendental Deduction. It is this chapter that we will consider here.

The art of judgement

As I noted earlier, the 'Transcendental Logic' forms the bulk of Kant's *Critique of Pure Reason*. This divides into the 'Transcendental Analytic', concerned with the legitimate use of human understanding, and the 'Transcendental Dialectic', concerned with its illegitimate use. We will not be looking at the latter here. The former divides in turn into two books, the 'Analytic of Concepts' and the 'Analytic of Principles'. The aim of Book I is to establish the role of concepts – and in particular, the categories – in our experience; and the Transcendental Deduction forms its heart. The aim of Book II, of which the schematism chapter is the first chapter, is to establish certain principles governing the application of concepts to intuitions. (Again, for details of the structure of Kant's *Critique*, see appendix 2.)

In introducing Book II, Kant makes some general remarks about judgement. Judgement, according to Kant, consists in applying a concept to an object – or subsuming an object under a concept, as it is also put. In judging that what is before me is a cat, for example, I am applying the concept *cat* to the object I see in front of me. It is thus in judgement that sensibility and understanding are brought together in articulating the experiences we have as conscious human beings. But how does judgement occur? We have already seen that the imagination is taken – at least in the first edition of the *Critique* – as what mediates between sensibility and understanding. So the obvious suggestion is that judgement is the work of the imagination. But judgement involves more than the synthesis of intuitions, which is what Kant attributes to the reproductive imagination, and dismisses anyway in the second edition as merely empirical. And as far as the productive imagination is concerned, this may have a role in generating the spatial-temporality of experience (as we have just seen illustrated in discussing geometrical construction), but how is it involved in the application of concepts?

The schematism of understanding

The problem of how we can make judgements, i.e. subsume intuitions or objects under concepts, seems particularly acute in the case of the pure concepts or categories. How, for example, can we apply the abstract concept of substance to the everyday objects that we experience through our senses? How can what is sensory be combined with what is intellectual? This is the problem that Kant addresses in the schematism chapter. According to Kant, what must be found is some 'third thing' that is homogeneous both with sensible intuitions and with intellectual concepts. This mediating entity, he states, is the 'transcendental schema'. A 'schema' might be characterized metaphorically as a way of bringing a concept down to earth – encapsulating what is required if the concept is to have application in spatial-temporal experience. Kant writes: 'We will call this formal and pure condition of the sensibility, to which the use of the concept of the understanding is restricted, the **schema** of this concept of the understanding, and we will call the procedure of the understanding with these schemata the **schematism** of the pure understanding' (A140/B179).

Talk of the imagination enters in elaborating this appeal to schemata:

> The schema is in itself always only a product of the imagination; but since the synthesis of the latter has as its aim no individual intuition but rather only the unity in the determination of sensibility, the schema is to be distinguished from an image. Thus, if I place five points in a row, ..., this is an image of the number five. On the contrary, if I only think a number in general, which could be five or a hundred, this thinking is more the representation of a method for representing a multitude (e.g., a thousand) in accordance with a certain concept than the image itself, which in this case I could survey and compare with the concept only with difficulty. Now this representation of a general procedure of the imagination for providing a concept with its image is what I call the schema for this concept.

> In fact it is not images of objects but schemata that ground our pure sensible concepts. No image of a triangle would ever be adequate to the concept of it. For it would not attain the generality of the concept, which makes this valid for all triangles, right or acute, etc., but would always be limited to one part of this sphere. The schema of the triangle can never exist anywhere except in thought, and signifies a rule of the synthesis of the imagination with regard to pure shapes in space. Even less does an object of experience or an image of it ever reach the empirical concept, rather the latter is always related immediately to the schema of the imagination, as a rule for the determination of our intuition in accordance

with a certain general concept. The concept of a dog signifies a rule in accordance with which my imagination can specify the shape of a four-footed animal in general, without being restricted to any single particular shape that experience offers me or any possible image that I can exhibit *in concreto*. This schematism of our understanding with regard to appearances and their mere form is a hidden art in the depths of the human soul, whose true operations we can divine from nature and lay unveiled before our eyes only with difficulty. We can say only this much: the **image** is a product of the empirical faculty of productive imagination, the **schema** of sensible concepts (such as figures in space) is a product and as it were a monogram of pure *a priori* imagination, through which and in accordance with which the images first become possible, but which must be connected with the concept, to which they are in themselves never fully congruent, always only by means of the schema that they designate. The schema of a pure concept of the understanding, on the contrary, is something that can never be brought to an image at all, but is rather only the pure synthesis, in accord with a rule of unity according to concepts in general, which the category expresses, and is a transcendental product of the imagination, which concerns the determination of the inner sense in general, in accordance with conditions of its form (time) in regard to all representations, insofar as these are to be connected together *a priori* in one concept in accord with the unity of apperception.

(*CPR*, A140–2/B179–81)

ACTIVITY

1 What is Kant's distinction between an image and a schema, in the case of sensible concepts? (Kant offers a number of slightly different characterizations of 'schema', but the message seems to be the same.)

2 Why does Kant think that schemata rather than images 'ground our pure sensible concepts'?

3 What role does the imagination play in schematism?

4 Does Kant think that schematism can be explained?

5 What is the difference between the schema of a sensible concept and the schema of a pure concept?

DISCUSSION

1 An image is a particular sensory representation of something; a schema is (a representation of) a method for generating images appropriate to a given sensible concept. To have an image of a dog, for example, is one thing; to know how to produce a series of images of dogs is quite another.

2 Since an image is only ever a particular representation, it can never reflect the generality of a concept. A schema, on the other hand, as a rule for

generating the images appropriate to a concept, does have the requisite generality.

3 The imagination is responsible for schematization. Not only are the particular images generated in the imagination, but the schemata themselves are also seen as products of the imagination.

4 Not really. Kant remarks that schematism is 'a hidden art in the depths of the human soul', which can only be revealed 'with difficulty'. (Recall how Hume had said something similar about the (empirical) imagination, describing it as a 'magical faculty of the soul' (see p.76 above), which Kant had implicitly criticized (see p.92 above). Kant, it seems, has only pushed the magic down one level from the empirical to the transcendental.)

5 The schema of a sensible concept is a rule for generating images; the schema of a pure concept is a more abstract rule, which does not involve generating images.

How, then, do schemata mediate between intuitions and concepts? Take Kant's example of a triangle. What is it to make judgements about triangles – to attain and articulate genuine knowledge of triangles? Let us assume that we understand that a triangle is a three-sided geometrical figure, i.e. that we recognize its definition. For a rationalist such as Descartes, this would be to grasp the 'idea' of triangle (see p.51 above); and we might agree that, in a minimal sense, we grasp the 'concept' of a triangle. But as we saw above (pp.104–5), this is not enough to be able to prove things about triangles; it cannot lead to genuine mathematical knowledge. What I need to do is generate an image of a triangle. For an empiricist such as Hume, having an image is all that knowledge consists in. But as Hume himself recognized, this underdetermines the beliefs that we at least normally take ourselves to have, such as the belief in an external world (see pp.76–80 above). Hume was led to dismiss such beliefs as illusory products of the imagination (in its conflict with reason). But the problem is with the underlying empiricist assumption. Knowledge does not consist in having images, although images may be necessary for thought. I may need to construct a triangle in order to prove, say, that the sum of the angles of a triangle is 180 degrees, but what I prove is not just true of the particular triangle I draw. What gives my proof the requisite generality is the operations I perform. What is important in geometry is not the individual diagrams but the operations – the rules for constructing the diagrams or, in Kant's terms, the schemata of geometrical concepts. These operations or schemata mediate between the images and concepts by being the rules for producing the images appropriate to a given concept.

We can now see how Kant could claim to have reconciled rationalism and empiricism in a grand synthesis. Having geometrical knowledge does not consist simply in recognizing the relevant definitions and theorems, nor in having appropriate images. More fundamentally, it involves being able to produce those images in accordance with the definitions, seeing the definitions as capturing what is in common to a set of images, appreciating what constructions are required for proving a given theorem, recognizing the legitimacy of the steps in a proof, and so on. Underlying all this is our ability to generate lines and transform figures; and this is where the (transcendental) imagination is involved, connecting understanding and sensibility.

Transcendental schemata

Not all schemata are rules for producing images, however. Kant's primary concern in the schematism chapter is with the schematism of the pure concepts or categories. Since these concepts are the most abstract of all, there are no images appropriate to them. But these too can be brought down to earth by specifying how they apply to the spatial-temporal world. I will take just one example here, the category of substance, to illustrate the basic idea. As Kant writes, at the purely formal or logical level, 'substance' signifies 'nothing more than a something that can be thought as a subject (without being a predicate of something else)' (A147/B186). But as applied to the empirical world, it signifies 'the persistence of the real in time, i.e., the representation of the real as a substratum of empirical time-determination in general, which therefore endures while everything else changes' (A144/B183). When we talk of substances in everyday life, in other words, what we mean are things that remain essentially the same over a period of time. We may conjure up images of a piece of wax in different states, for example, but in thinking of it as a substance, what we are doing is recognizing that it has an underlying identity or nature that remains constant. We have no image of this underlying nature, but this is not to say that there is no such nature or that we cannot think about it (as Descartes had pointed out).

Empirical schemata

Although the motivation of the schematism chapter was to show how the categories or pure concepts are applicable to the spatial-temporal world, its implications are general. For even in the case of empirical concepts, the question arises as to how they apply to objects or intuitions in making judgements. Kant himself gives an example of an empirical concept in illustrating the generality of his conception of schematism. I may understand that a dog is a four-footed animal of genus *Canis*, and so in a minimal sense grasp the concept of a dog, but to apply this concept in articulating genuine knowledge, I must grasp its schema. This schema is, as Kant puts it, 'a rule in accordance with which my imagination can specify the shape of a four-footed animal in general, without being restricted to any single particular shape that experience offers me or any possible image that I can exhibit *in concreto*' (A141/B180). In this passage, Kant seems to identify the concept itself with this rule, and hence by implication with its schema. He does indeed think of concepts generally as rules – rules for ordering our intuitions. However, in the previous sentence, he writes that the concept is 'related immediately' to the schema, which suggests that there is still a difference between concept and schema. So we might distinguish between grasp of the concept in the minimal sense just indicated, and grasp of the concept in its full-blown, schematized sense. I cannot make judgements about dogs, conceptualizing actual experience, without being able to schematize in the way Kant describes.

What are the roles of the empirical and transcendental imagination here? In the passage quoted above, Kant writes that while the image is a product of the 'empirical faculty of productive imagination', the schema is a product of 'pure *a priori* imagination' (i.e. transcendental imagination). This suggests that the distinction between the empirical and transcendental imagination does not neatly line up with the distinction between the reproductive and productive imagination. Rather, productive imagination itself has both an empirical and a transcendental use. In its empirical use, the productive imagination produces (new) images appropriate to a given concept; in its transcendental use, it delineates the shape of such images in general, i.e. it provides the method or rule (schema) for generating such images.

In our use of empirical concepts too, then, the imagination is deeply involved, responsible for producing both images and schemata. Experiencing a dog, or knowing what a dog is, does not simply consist in having either an image of a dog or some Cartesian 'idea' of a dog. It involves the ability to generate and recognize images of dogs. It is in this way that images and ideas, or intuitions and concepts, are brought together. The importance of the schematism chapter lies not just in the mediating role accorded to the imagination, however, but also in the emphasis placed on our imaginative activities. Kant may have focused on the production of images, understood as mental representations, which suggests that Kant never entirely freed himself from a basically Cartesian or internalist approach. But the crucial move was to recognize the role of *operations* such as drawing lines and delineating shapes. It is only one step from here to rule-governed behaviour more generally – from internal to external activities. As we will see in the next chapter, this is the step that Wittgenstein makes.

Hume and Kant on abstract ideas

In considering the role of imagination in perception (pp.96–8 above), Hume's and Kant's views on our ascription of 'continued and distinct existence' to objects were compared. In a paper entitled 'Imagination and perception' (first published in 1971), Peter Strawson has suggested that, at least on Hume's and Kant's accounts, there are two dimensions to the role of imagination in perception. He writes: 'In one dimension, (a), it connects perceptions of different objects of the same kind; in the other dimension, (b), it connects different perceptions of the same object of a given kind. It is the instrument of our perceptual appreciation both of kind-identity and of individual-identity, both of concept-identity and of object-identity' (1974, § 2, 46–7). In the example of seeing a cat, I recognize that it is indeed a cat (similar to other cats), and believe that it continues to be that cat, as a distinct individual, throughout the time that I observe it (and even when there are gaps in my observation). It has an identity both as a cat and as the particular object it is; and the imagination is involved in my recognition of both aspects. We have considered the operation of the connecting power of imagination in its second dimension – in connecting different perceptions of the same object of a given kind. Let us now compare the views of Hume and Kant on the operation of the connecting power of the imagination in its first dimension – in connecting perceptions of different objects of the same kind, which enables us to recognize something as the kind of thing it is.

ACTIVITY

1 Look back at the section on 'Abstract ideas' in the last chapter (pp.73–6 above). How does Hume see the imagination as involved in our recognition of a cat as a cat?

2 In the light of his account of schematism, how does Kant see the imagination as involved in our recognition of a cat as a cat?

3 What are the main similarities and differences between Hume's and Kant's accounts?

4 What would you say are the main difficulties in each account?

DISCUSSION

1 Here is how I expounded Hume's account. When I first see the cat I acquire a particular impression of the cat. My imagination is then involved in conjuring up ideas that resemble this impression until I reach an idea that is 'annexed' to the word 'cat'. Given the resemblance, I 'conclude' that my original impression is an impression of a cat, i.e. I recognize that what is before me is a cat.

2 To be able to recognize a cat as a cat, i.e. to apply the concept *cat* on a particular occasion, on Kant's view, I must grasp the schema of the concept: that is, I must grasp the rule for generating images of a cat. The imagination is responsible for the production not only of these images but also of the schema itself. As to how I then recognize the cat, presumably Kant thinks that I simply realize that my impression (image) of the cat accords with the schema of the concept *cat*, the precise mechanism being 'a hidden art in the depths of the human soul'.

3 Unlike in the case of individual-identity, the similarities between Hume's and Kant's views here are perhaps more striking than the differences. According to both Hume and Kant, the imagination is responsible for generating ideas or images of objects of the relevant kind, our ability to do this being a precondition for conceptual recognition. Both Hume and Kant also see this ability as mysterious – attributed to a 'magical faculty' or 'hidden art'. The main difference is that whereas Hume's account involves images and words, Kant's account involves images, concepts and schemata.

4 Given the similarity in their accounts, the main difficulty seems to me to be the same. How do I manage to call up the right images or schema with which to compare my present impression, in order to judge that what I see is a cat? Perhaps the particular cat I am presently seeing is more similar to some other type of animal than to my paradigm image or images of a cat (as

generated by the relevant schema). Is it satisfactory just to appeal to a 'magical faculty' or a 'hidden art'? Can more not be said, whether empirically or philosophically?

In both Hume's and Kant's accounts of perceptual judgement, ideas or images play a crucial role, and this makes it natural to see the imagination as involved. The imagination is responsible for conjuring up these images and allowing the relevant connections to be made. But do I really have *actual* images of other cats in my mind when I recognize the cat before me as a cat? Perhaps I must have the *ability* to generate such images (as a result of 'custom' or in accord with the relevant schema) as a precondition of recognizing the cat as a cat. But that is different from saying that the images must be actually present in my mind in order to make a perceptual judgement. But if we say that only the *ability* to generate images is required and not the images themselves, then can we really talk of imagination as involved in perception?

Actual and non-actual perceptions

Let us return to the earlier example of hearing a melody (pp.93–4). In experiencing what I hear as a melody and not just as a series of notes, I must in some sense recall the previous notes and anticipate the notes to come. But do I actually hear these past or future notes? Clearly not, or else my head would be full of a cacophony of noise. Yet more is involved than just the *ability* to hear these notes: I must be aware of them in some sense. What seems required, then, is to distinguish between actual and 'non-actual' perceptions. I do not actually hear the past or future notes, but they are somehow present 'non-actually'.

This is just the distinction that Strawson draws, in 'Imagination and perception', in explaining Kant's claim that 'imagination is a necessary ingredient of perception itself' (in the footnote cited on p.96 above). As I have noted, Strawson suggests that the connecting power of the imagination operates in two dimensions: in connecting perceptions of different objects of the same kind, and in connecting different perceptions of the same object of a given kind. In both cases, he argues, what is connected is my current actual perception to other, past or possible, 'non-actual' perceptions. Consider, for example, what is involved when I see a cat as a 'continuing and distinct' object.

I must in some sense recall past perceptions and anticipate possible future perceptions. In experiencing it as lying on my lap, I must know how it got there (otherwise I will be shocked rather than relaxed), and I must know how to push it away if I want (otherwise I might be equally worried). So too, in the case of simply recognizing a cat as a cat, I recognize it as one of a kind – that is, as being similar to other cats that I have seen or could see. Even an apparently 'simple' or 'momentary' perception is informed by all sorts of other thoughts or 'non-actual' perceptions.

Here is the key paragraph of Strawson's paper:

> It seems, then, not too much to say that the actual occurrent perception of an enduring object as an object of a certain kind, or as a particular object of that kind, is, as it were, soaked with or animated by, or infused with – the metaphors are *à choix* – the thought of other past or possible perceptions of the same object. Let us speak of past and merely possible perceptions alike as 'non-actual' perceptions. Now the imagination, in one of its aspects ... is the image-producing faculty, the faculty, we may say, of producing actual representatives (in the shape of images) of non-actual perceptions. I have argued that an actual perception of the kind we are concerned with owes its character essentially to that internal link, of which we find it so difficult to give any but a metaphorical description, with other past or possible, but in any case non-actual, perceptions. Non-actual perceptions are in a sense represented in, alive in, the present perception; just as they are represented, by images, in the image-producing activity of the imagination. May we not, then, find a kinship between the capacity for this latter kind of exercise of the imagination and the capacity which is exercised in actual perception of the kind we are concerned with? Kant, at least, is prepared to register his sense of such a kinship by extending the title of 'imagination' to cover both capacities; by speaking of imagination as 'a necessary ingredient of perception itself'.
>
> (1974, § 2, 53–4)

ACTIVITY

1 How does Strawson describe the relation between a present perception and the relevant 'non-actual' perceptions?

2 In what sense, then, is the imagination involved in perception, as Strawson interprets Kant?

3 How convincing do you find the explanation suggested here of Kant's claim that imagination is 'a necessary ingredient of perception itself'?

DISCUSSION

1   Strawson describes the relation in a number of ways, all of them more or less metaphorical. He talks of the present perception as being 'soaked with or animated by, or infused with' the non-actual perceptions, and of the latter as being 'alive' in the present perception. He also speaks, though, of there being an 'internal link' between the actual and non-actual perceptions. Strawson takes the idea of an 'internal link' from Wittgenstein's philosophy. Since we will be considering Wittgenstein's philosophy in the next chapter, however, I will postpone elucidation of this idea until then.

2   In one of its core senses (or functions), the imagination is responsible for generating actual images. What is responsible for involving non-actual perceptions? (They are not generated as actual images, of course, but are implicated in some way.) It seems natural to attribute this to the imagination too, which is what Strawson suggests Kant does, 'extending the title of "imagination" to cover both capacities'. So the imagination is involved in perception, as Strawson interprets Kant, in doing whatever it is that enables non-actual perceptions to be 'alive' in a present perception.

3   As Strawson admits himself, he makes use of metaphors in explaining Kant's claim. So the role of the imagination might still seem mysterious. What is it for a present perception to be 'soaked with or animated by, or infused with' non-actual perceptions? What exactly is an 'internal link'? Nevertheless, Strawson offers a nice diagnosis of why Kant may have been led to appeal to the imagination here. Recall Kant's own definition of imagination as 'the faculty for representing in intuition an object even without its presence' (see p.100 above). For if there is some sense in which non-actual perceptions are 'alive' in a present perception, then is it not natural to regard the imagination as responsible?

Let me summarize the position that has now been reached in our exploration of Kant's conception of imagination. The governing motivation of Kant's *Critique of Pure Reason* was to uncover the presuppositions of human experience. What he realized was that there was far more to perception than meets the eye, so to speak, and he set as the task of 'transcendental' philosophy to articulate these presuppositions. He made an initial attempt in the first edition version of the Transcendental Deduction, but soon recognized that there were deeper powers than the reproductive power of imagination he had identified in his critique of associationism. Image-forming, of the kind involved in human experience, presupposes more fundamental abilities – in geometry, and in figurative activities in general, and in the very application of concepts. In the latter case, Kant was led to emphasize the role of schemata rather than images – schemata being rules for the direction of the imagination, rules that are constrained by the relevant concepts. Perhaps his move away from images to schemata explains why he was led to say less about the role of the imagination in the second edition version of the Transcendental Deduction. But in another way, it might be argued that the imagination is still involved, albeit in a more mysterious way, as what supplies those 'non-actual' perceptions of which Strawson speaks. Here, however, we found ourselves left merely with metaphors, with just the tantalizing suggestion that what is crucial is the idea of an 'internal link' between actual and non-actual perceptions. Clarifying the idea of an internal link will be one of the tasks of the next chapter, in discussing Wittgenstein's philosophy.

Review and preview

1. Kant's central idea in the *Critique of Pure Reason* is that knowledge requires both understanding and sensibility, the sources of concepts and intuitions (sensory impressions), respectively. The imagination is appealed to in mediating between understanding and sensibility. The fullest account of this occurs in the first edition version of the Transcendental Deduction. The intuitions we receive through the senses are first combined in a complex intuition, previous intuitions are reproduced in imagination, and the synthesized intuitions are then conceptualized by the understanding.

2. In the second edition version of the Transcendental Deduction, however, the reproductive imagination is dismissed as merely empirical, and the emphasis shifts on to the productive, transcendental imagination, although we have to look elsewhere for an elucidation of this conception. Its role in our spatial-temporal experience, and in particular in drawing lines and transforming figures, was illustrated in problem-solving in Euclidean geometry.

3. The imagination also plays a crucial role in schematism, on Kant's view. In the case of sensible concepts, schemata are rules for generating images appropriate to the concepts, the schemata as well as the images being seen

as products of the imagination. It is in recognizing the centrality accorded to our imaginative activities, in mediating between images and concepts in the use of such rules, that a synthesis of rationalism and empiricism can be achieved.

4   Kant's talk of 'transcendental imagination' reflects a recognition that more than the (empirical) image-forming faculty is involved in human experience. The question is whether there might be some other characterization of the preconditions of human experience that does not appeal to anything as apparently mysterious as 'transcendental imagination'. One answer is provided by Wittgenstein, who, while sharing Kant's concern with the presuppositions of human experience, took a more naturalistic approach.

Further reading

There are now a number of English translations of Kant's *Critique of Pure Reason*. Until recently, the standard translation was Kemp Smith's (first published in 1929). Kemp Smith split up many of Kant's longer sentences into shorter ones, and the story goes that German-speaking students would learn English in order to read the Kemp Smith translation. But the authoritative translation – although it does not simplify Kant's sentences – is now Guyer and Wood's in the Cambridge edition (first published in 1997), which comes with a full introduction and helpful notes. I have used this translation here.

The best introduction to Kant's *Critique of Pure Reason* is Gardner (1999). For help with Kant's terminology, Caygill (1995) is excellent. Brief accounts of Kant's conception of imagination can be found in the general books mentioned in earlier chapters: Brann (1991, part I, chapter 3, section D), Kearney (1988, chapter 4) and Warnock (1976, part I). Although written more for Kant scholars, the fullest and best treatment of Kant's conception of imagination is Gibbons (1994). Chapter 1 discusses the Transcendental Deduction and chapter 2 schematism. Chapter 2 of Makkreel (1990), which can be recommended too, is also on Kant's conception of imagination in the first *Critique*.

Heidegger's book on Kant ([1929] 1991) is even more difficult than Kant's *Critique*. But there is an account of schematism (sections 19–23), and part III (sections 26–35) contains many insights into Kant's conception of the transcendental imagination and its anticipation of later developments. One book that develops Kantian ideas, and in particular his account of schematism, in emphasizing the role of the body in our mental activities is Johnson (1987). Chapter 6 is entitled 'Toward a theory of imagination', and outlines Kant's views.

Three classic papers on Kant and the imagination are Bell (1987), Crawford (1982) and Strawson ([1971] 1974). Bell discusses the schematism chapter and its relation to some of Wittgenstein's ideas. Crawford shows how Kant's conception of the creative imagination emerges from his reflections on mathematical methodology. As noted above, Strawson compares Hume's and Kant's views on the way that imagination informs perception, and he also brings in Wittgenstein's remarks on seeing-as (which we consider in the next chapter).

CHAPTER 5

Imagination and aspect perception

> One ought to ask, not what images are or what happens when one imagines anything, but how the word "imagination" is used.
>
> (Wittgenstein, *Philosophical Investigations*, § 370)

The main theme of the last four chapters has been the interrelationships between imagination, perception and thought, and the way in which appeals to imagination are made in describing or explaining certain kinds of cognitive experience. In this chapter we will explore these interrelationships further by looking at the work of Ludwig Wittgenstein (1879–1951), and in particular at his discussion of seeing-as, in which he too was concerned to clarify the way in which perception and thought seem to be fused together in certain kinds of visual experience. The kind of experience he had in mind was when we see something *as* something, such as seeing a figure as a picture of a duck. Seeing something *as* something is also described as perceiving an *aspect* of something. In looking at something, I may come to perceive an aspect of it that I had not noticed earlier: I come to see it in a different way, or *as* something else. 'Seeing-as' and 'aspect perception' are often used more or less synonymously – although strictly speaking, aspect perception might be taken as the genus of which seeing-as is a species. We can also *hear* something *as* something, such as the sound of a flute as a bird song or the roll of drums as thunder, or hear an aspect of something, such as a Bachian theme in a piece of modern music. In what follows we will focus on cases of seeing-as, but it is worth bearing in mind that analogous things can be said about other forms of aspect perception. Seeing-as – or aspect perception generally – is like 'normal' perception in some respects, and yet like thinking or interpreting in other respects. So the phenomenon of seeing-as raises just those questions about the relation between perception and thought that have been the theme of the previous chapters. Wittgenstein's discussion of seeing-as forms the topic of the second (and central) main section of the present chapter. I will begin, however, with some general comments Wittgenstein makes about imagination and mental images, outlining his method and the basic thrust of his philosophical thinking. In the third and final main section, the two discussions will be drawn together in considering the relationship between imagination and seeing-as, and the light that is shed on some of the issues explored in previous chapters.

Wittgenstein's *Philosophical Investigations* (*PI*), which was published posthumously in 1953, is arguably the most important philosophical work of the twentieth century. But it is also one of the most difficult to understand, not because it is written in the dense style of Kant, but because the structure of his arguments, the positive points he makes, and the targets of his criticism are far from obvious. Wittgenstein remarks in the preface that the nature of his investigation 'compels us to travel over a wide field of thought criss-cross in every direction' (*PI*, vii). Any one problem ramifies into all areas of philosophy, and can be investigated in many different ways, drawing on analogies and arguments from elsewhere. But there is more structure to the book than appears at first sight. Wittgenstein repudiates theory-building and thesis-stating in philosophy, seeking conceptual clarification rather than scientific explanation, which is why it is difficult to articulate the positive points he makes. But there is much of value that comes out of his wide-ranging conceptual clarifications. Although commentators have used his writings in attacking both traditional and current doctrines and positions, one of Wittgenstein's own main targets was his earlier work, the *Tractatus Logico-Philosophicus*, which was the only book he published in his lifetime, as a young man in 1921. In this work, he had offered an account of language and thought as gaining their meaning from picturing the world, and it was this picture theory that he criticized later, particularly in the first half of the *Investigations*. But he also discusses a wide range of other topics, including perception, mental imagery and imagination.

Wittgenstein's method of philosophizing was to write down remarks on the topics that were occupying him in notebooks, and then to select and refine those remarks, dictating them into typescripts that were often further cut up, reordered and revised. (The word processor would have been ideal for Wittgenstein, but unfortunately came too late.) Part I of the *Investigations* comprises remarks that were as polished and organized as Wittgenstein felt able to achieve, and we will consider the remarks on imagination and images from this part first. His remarks on seeing-as come from part II and are more provisional (although by no means first-draft material), being added by the editors; but we will come to these later in this chapter.

Let me make one general comment on the style of Wittgenstein's remarks before we begin. Those remarks take various forms – assertions, questions, suppositions, sketches of arguments, descriptions of everyday human practices, notes on our uses of language, parenthetical asides, thought experiments, analogies, aphorisms, and so on. But taken together they form a kind of dialogue with an imagined interlocutor. That interlocutor gives expression to views which Wittgenstein wants to examine, and asks questions about Wittgenstein's own views. The views that the interlocutor expresses are views that many people have held (though Wittgenstein rarely mentions particular names), or might be inclined to come out with in both everyday and philosophical contexts. Wittgenstein's remarks can be bewildering at first, but one gradually learns to enter into the imagined dialogue and to recognize when Wittgenstein is speaking in his own right and when his imagined interlocutor is speaking – which is often indicated by the use of double inverted commas in the text. Reading Wittgenstein can be frustrating at times, and making sense of his remarks can be slow and painful. But the effort soon reveals the depth and extraordinary richness of his philosophical thinking, even if one does not always agree with or understand everything he says. There are many ways into the heart of Wittgenstein's philosophy, and no single best way. What Wittgenstein says about imagination and aspect perception provides, I think, as good a route as any.

Wittgenstein on imagination and images

Wittgenstein's main concern in the part of the *Investigations* that deals primarily with the imagination (sections 363–402) is with the nature and role of mental images. But he also comments on his method, which we will consider first.

Wittgenstein's method

The key to Wittgenstein's method is the remark that forms the motto of the present chapter. Here is the whole of the relevant section:

> One ought to ask, not what images are or what happens when one imagines anything, but how the word "imagination" is used. But that does not mean that I want to talk only about words. For the question as to the nature of the imagination

is as much about the word "imagination" as my question is. And I am only saying that this question is not to be decided – neither for the person who does the imagining, nor for anyone else – by pointing; nor yet by a description of any process. The first question also asks for a word to be explained; but it makes us expect a wrong kind of answer.

(*PI*, § 370)

ACTIVITY

1 What is Wittgenstein's main methodological claim?
2 What alternative to his approach does he repudiate?

DISCUSSION

1 Wittgenstein's main methodological claim is that, in seeking a philosophical understanding of imagination, one should look at how the word 'imagination' is used.
2 The alternative approach he repudiates is to pursue some kind of introspective or empirical investigation – attempting to look inwards at one's private mental images or to describe some psychological process.

To explain the significance of Wittgenstein's main claim here, and the contrast he draws, let me return to the 'Wittgensteinian' account of imagining I suggested in chapter 1. 'Imagining', on this account, is to be understood not as denoting a specific kind of mental process, but as indicating an evaluation of a mental act on the part of the person using the word. It might indeed refer, in general terms, to 'thinking of something that is not present to the senses', but the key point is that, in calling such an act of thinking 'imagining', the person calling it such is showing a lack of commitment to the truth or existence of what is thought of. If anything like this is right, then it illustrates the importance of looking at the way that the word 'imagining' is used. The approach that Wittgenstein opposes simply assumes that 'imagining' denotes a specific kind of mental process, which it then proceeds to investigate by either introspection or empirical description.

There is an obvious objection to his method, however, which Wittgenstein implicitly recognizes and responds to in this passage. If we are being asked to look at how the word 'imagination' is used, then does this not reduce philosophy to mere lexicography? Wittgenstein's reply is that even if we say instead that our concern, as philosophers, is with the nature of imagination, we will still have to look at the use of the word 'imagination'. Wittgenstein does not deny that he is interested in the nature of imagination. He just suggests that expressing it like this is potentially misleading: it makes us expect the wrong kind of answer. It makes us expect some sort of specification of what is essential to imagination – an 'essence', understood as a distinctive kind of psychological process. But this is precisely what Wittgenstein repudiates. There may be any number of different psychological processes or social activities involved in experiences where we legitimately (i.e. meaningfully) talk of 'imagination', and we need to know what we mean by 'imagination' before any scientific investigation makes sense. But Wittgenstein does not repudiate talk of 'essence' altogether. In the very next section, he writes: '*Essence* is expressed by grammar' (*PI*, § 371). What imagination *is* is determined by the use that we make of the word 'imagination' – by its 'grammar', as he puts it. 'Grammar tells what kind of object anything is' (*PI*, § 373).

By 'grammar', Wittgenstein simply means the set of rules governing our use of language. But he understands by 'rules' more than just syntactic rules (the rules governing the way that words are put together in well-formed sentences); he also means the rules that govern the meaningfulness and appropriateness of using an expression in a certain way. Take the name 'Ludwig'. As a proper name, it can occupy the subject position in a sentence, as in 'Ludwig likes beetles'. But it is also part of its 'grammar' that it standardly refers (or purports to refer) to a particular person. It is in this sense that 'Grammar tells what kind of object anything is'. Or consider again the 'Wittgensteinian' account of imagining I suggested in chapter 1. If this account is right, then in calling an act of thinking 'imagining', I am evaluating that thinking in some way – and this too would count as part of the grammar of our use of 'imagining'. So even if I say that what I have been doing in the previous chapters is investigating the nature of imagination, that investigation might also be described as elucidating the grammar of our use of 'imagination' and its cognates. According to Wittgenstein, elucidating grammar is the main task of the philosopher, in seeking clarification of our most basic concepts.

Mental images

Although 'imagine' does not simply mean 'have an image', there is a close connection between the two in one of the core senses of 'imagine' (as we saw in chapter 1, pp.27–32), and it is this sense that is the main focus of Wittgenstein's attention. Now in ordinary contexts it may be perfectly harmless and legitimate to talk of 'having an image' when imagining something. But there is a great temptation (in certain philosophical contexts) to misconstrue this – to regard the image as the essential thing, as a kind of private, inner mental picture which somehow encapsulates the act of imagining. It is this misconstrual that is the main target of Wittgenstein's critique in sections 363–402.

It is important to stress at the outset that Wittgenstein is not denying the existence of mental images. (Nor can he be taken to be affirming it either, without clarification of what is meant by 'mental images'.) He is only repudiating a certain conception of mental images – as private mental entities that are in principle inaccessible to anyone other than the person 'having' them:

> The great difficulty here is not to represent the matter as if there were something one *couldn't* do. As if there really were an object, from which I derive its description, but I were unable to shew it to anyone.
>
> (*PI*, § 374)

On Wittgenstein's view, what counts as the object or image depends on the description. 'The mental picture is the picture which is described when someone describes what he imagines' (*PI*, § 367). For Wittgenstein, in other words, it is the description that determines the object rather than the object that determines the description.

The idea of the private mental object is one of the main targets of Wittgenstein's *Investigations*, and he attacks it in a variety of contexts. It was the central target in his so-called 'private language argument' in sections 243–315. His essential objection is that it makes no sense to appeal to such an object. It is not just that, since I cannot show any 'private' object I have to anyone else, there would be no way for others to verify that I have it, or what I say it is. I cannot even know what I mean by referring to it myself. For how do I know that the object is not always changing? To judge whether it has changed or not, I must already know how to describe or refer to it. But if I can do this in 'public' language, then the supposed object is accessible to others. And if I do this in a 'private' language, the terms of which have their meaning by referring to private mental entities, then we are back to square one.

Similar points are made in the remarks on imagination. The key question concerns the criteria of identity for images:

> What is the criterion for the sameness of two images? – What is the criterion for the redness of an image? For me, when it is someone else's image: what he says and does. For myself, when it is my image: nothing. And what goes for "red" also goes for "same".
>
> (*PI*, § 377)
>
> "Before I judge that two images which I have are the same, I must recognize them as the same." And when that has happened, how am I to know that the word "same" describes what I recognize? Only if I can express my recognition in some other way, and if it is possible for someone else to teach me that "same" is the correct word here.
> For if I need a justification for using a word, it must also be one for someone else.
>
> (*PI*, § 378)

According to Wittgenstein, it is what I say and do that determines what my image is, and whether it is the same as an image I described on a previous occasion. If this is so, then someone else is also in a position to make judgements about the images I have.

The problem of the inverted spectrum

Wittgenstein's view can be illustrated by considering the so-called 'problem of the inverted spectrum', which Wittgenstein himself alludes to in an earlier section of the *Investigations*, in explaining the idea of 'private experience' that is his central target.

> The essential thing about private experience is really not that each person possesses his own exemplar, but that nobody knows whether other people also have *this* or something else. The assumption would thus be possible – though unverifiable – that one section of mankind had one sensation of red and another section another.
>
> (*PI*, § 272)

ACTIVITY

Suppose that two of us are looking at the same patch of colour, which we both call 'red', and suppose too that we have also agreed, and would agree, on what to call every other colour that we have come across or might come across. Is it possible that when I look at this patch I have a 'red' sensation, while you have, say, a 'green' sensation? In other words, while we both *call* it 'red', is it possible that you are experiencing – 'inside', as it were – greenness, while I am experiencing redness? The suggestion is sometimes made that perhaps the colour spectrum as someone else experiences it is systematically 'inverted', so that the difference never comes out. What do you think that Wittgenstein's response to this problem would be?

DISCUSSION

We might admit that, in some sense, what goes on 'inside' you may be different from what goes on 'inside' me: perhaps there are indeed different neurophysiological processes. But *ex hypothesi*, we both call what is in front of us 'red', and have agreed, and would agree, on every other case. So we seem to have the same concept of 'red' in the sense that we apply it to the same objects. According to Wittgenstein, if there is, and could be, no outward manifestation of the supposed difference, then we should be taken to have the same visual sensation. If what we say and do, and would say or do, is exactly the same, then there are no grounds for claiming that we have different sensations.

According to Wittgenstein, the colour term 'red' does not *mean* the supposed 'private' sensation each of us has when we see something red, which would open up the possibility that we might all mean something different. If we all agree in our use of the term 'red', then what we mean by 'red' on each occasion is the same. This is not to say that there may be nothing 'private' involved. It is just that, even if there is, it is not the presence or absence of this that determines what I mean by 'red'. This is made clear in Wittgenstein's famous 'beetle-in-a-box' example. Wittgenstein is discussing pain sensation, but the point is intended to apply generally:

> If I say of myself that it is only from my own case that I know what the word "pain" means – must I not say the same of other people too? And how can I generalize the *one* case so irresponsibly?
> Now someone tells me that *he* knows what pain is only from his own case! – Suppose everyone had a box with something in it: we call it a "beetle". No one can look into anyone else's box, and everyone says he knows what a beetle is only by looking at *his* beetle. – Here it would be quite possible for everyone to have something different in his box. One might even imagine such a thing constantly changing. – But suppose the word "beetle" had a use in these people's language? – If so it would not be used as the name of a thing. The thing in the box has no place in the language-game at all; not even as a *something*: for the box might even be empty. – No, one can 'divide through' by the thing in the box; it cancels out, whatever it is.

That is to say: if we construe the grammar of the expression of sensation on the model of 'object and designation' the object drops out of consideration as irrelevant.

(*PI*, § 293)

We are tempted to think that sensation terms, such as 'pain' or 'red', get their meaning by designating private objects. But on Wittgenstein's view, whatever such objects may be, they are irrelevant in determining the meaning of the terms.

According to Wittgenstein, what holds in the case of sensations also holds in the case of images, which are often regarded too as private mental objects:

How do I know that this colour is red? – It would be an answer to say: "I have learnt English".

(*PI*, § 381)

At these words I form this image. How can I *justify* this?
Has anyone shewn me the image of the colour blue and told me that *this* is the image of blue?
What is the meaning of the words: "*This* image"? How does one point to an image? How does one point twice to the same image?

(*PI*, § 382)

We are not analysing a phenomenon (e.g. thought) but a concept (e.g. that of thinking), and therefore the use of a word. So it may look as if what we were doing were Nominalism. Nominalists make the mistake of interpreting all words as *names*, and so of not really describing their use, but only, so to speak, giving a paper draft on such a description.

(*PI*, § 383)

You learned the *concept* 'pain' when you learned language.

(*PI*, § 384)

"But when I imagine something, or even actually *see* objects, I have *got* something which my neighbour has not." – I understand you. You want to look about you and say: "At any rate only I have got THIS." – What are these words for? They serve no purpose. – Can one not add: "There is here no question of a 'seeing' – and therefore none of a 'having' – nor of a subject, not therefore of 'I' either'? Might I not ask: In what sense have you *got* what you are talking about and saying that only you have got it? Do you possess it? You do not even *see* it. Must you not really say that no one has got it? And this too is clear: if as a matter of logic you exclude other people's having something, it loses its sense to say that you have it."

(*PI*, § 398)

Whether we are talking about experiencing pain, having a sensation of redness, or having an image of something, it is tempting to think that the essential thing is the private object supposedly designated. But in each case, according to Wittgenstein, what determines what is meant by such talk is our use of the relevant language.

The problem of the missing shade of blue

A further illustration of Wittgenstein's governing idea can be provided by returning to Hume's problem of the missing shade of blue.

ACTIVITY

Look back at pages 65–9 above, where the problem of the missing shade of blue was discussed, and a distinction was drawn between 'pictorial' (or 'analogue') conceptions of imagination and 'descriptional' (or 'propositional') conceptions. Which did I suggest is Hume's official conception, and how might this be seen as responsible for the problem of the missing shade of blue? Which would you say better reflects Wittgenstein's conception, and what response to the problem does this conception suggest?

DISCUSSION

Hume's official conception, I suggested, is a pictorial rather than descriptional conception, and his conception also seems to be a paradigm example of the kind of view that Wittgenstein is criticizing. Arguably, it is just because Hume conceives ideas or images as private mental objects that the problem of the missing shade of blue is a genuine problem for him. For how can I have an idea or image of the missing shade of blue if no account can be offered of how the relevant object is generated (such as from a corresponding impression, on Hume's empiricist account)? Yet, as I suggested, there is a sense in which I do 'have an image' of the missing shade of blue. I recognize that there is a gap in the spectrum, and can describe it as, for example, 'the shade that is between this shade and that shade'. This suggests that a descriptional conception does better justice to the case; and this also seems to be the kind of conception that Wittgenstein has. On a descriptional conception, we might say, the supposed private object does indeed drop out of consideration as irrelevant, and the problem as to how I can have an idea or image of the missing shade of blue disappears. What determines whether I 'have an image' of the missing shade of blue, i.e. what determines what is meant by such talk, is what I say and do. If I show recognition that there is a gap, for example, and describe it in some appropriate way, then I can indeed be said to 'have an image' of it.

The underlying point here is not new. Thomas Reid, in his *Essays on the Intellectual Powers of Man* (1785), which essentially offers a critique of Humean empiricism, had argued that 'what is commonly called the image of a thing in the mind, is no more than the act or operation of the mind in conceiving it' (IV, i; 1983, 220). An 'image in the mind', he wrote, 'is only a periphrasis for imagination' (IV, ii; 1983, 231). What Wittgenstein adds to this is that the act or operation of the mind in conceiving or imagining something is manifested in how I describe it (in public language).

But how can a mere description, it might be objected, determine the image I have? Can any description not be interpreted or instantiated in many different ways? However, in this respect, we are no worse off than if we suppose that we have some private mental picture. For can any picture not be interpreted in many different ways? Any actual picture, diagram or illustration can be used to represent several different things. So what determines what the picture is a picture *of*? Here there is a temptation to treat the mental picture as a kind of super-picture, which is so perfect that there is no room for misinterpretation. Wittgenstein imagines someone succumbing to this temptation, and giving expression to such a view:

> "The image must be more like its object than any picture. For, however like I make the picture to what it is supposed to represent, it can always be the picture of something else as well. But it is essential to the image that it is the image of *this* and of nothing else." Thus one might come to regard the image as a super-likeness.
>
> (*PI*, § 389)

Images, we say, have intentionality: they are always images *of* something. But here, too, what they are images of is determined by what is said about and done with them. I may be the best authority on what my own images are images of, but since that is manifested in what I say and do, they are accessible to others. As we will now see, the importance of what I say and do in determining the experience that I can be said to have is also stressed in Wittgenstein's discussion of seeing-as, which offers one of the clearest illustrations of his general methodological approach.

Wittgenstein's discussion of seeing-as

Wittgenstein worked on the topic of seeing-as, together with other questions concerning psychological concepts, from 1946 until 1949. A selection of the remarks he wrote during this period, revised and reordered, eventually found their way into part II of the *Philosophical Investigations*. But preliminary selections were also made, forming two typescripts that were subsequently published as the two volumes of *Remarks on the Philosophy of Psychology* (*RPP*). In addition, the original manuscripts from the later part of this period (October 1948 to March 1949) have also been published as the first volume of *Last Writings on the Philosophy of Psychology* (*LW*). In what follows, we will focus on the discussion of seeing-as in the *Investigations*, but will also draw on some of the remarks from the other selections and manuscripts as appropriate.

The problem of seeing-as

Wittgenstein's discussion of seeing-as in part II of the *Philosophical Investigations* takes up the first 22 pages of section xi, which is by far the longest section of the part. The section opens as follows:

> Two uses of the word "see".
> The one: "What do you see there?" – "I see *this*" (and then a description, a drawing, a copy). The other: "I see a likeness between these two faces" – let the man I tell this to be seeing the faces as clearly as I do myself.
> The importance of this is the difference of category between the two 'objects' of sight.
>
> The one man might make an accurate drawing of the two faces, and the other notice in the drawing the likeness which the former did not see.
>
> I contemplate a face, and then suddenly notice its likeness to another. I *see* that it has not changed; and yet I see it differently. I call this experience "noticing an aspect".
>
> Its *causes* are of interest to psychologists.
>
> We are interested in the concept and its place among the concepts of experience.
>
> (*PI*, 193)

ACTIVITY

1. What are the two uses of the word 'see' that Wittgenstein distinguishes here?
2. Why is this distinction important, according to Wittgenstein?
3. What is characteristic of the experience that Wittgenstein calls 'noticing an aspect'?
4. What is Wittgenstein's interest in this experience?

DISCUSSION

1. Wittgenstein distinguishes between cases where, as we might put it, we 'simply' see (and report) what is before us and cases where we talk of seeing a relation between one thing and something else.
2. The importance, according to Wittgenstein, lies in the corresponding distinction between two 'objects' of sight. (Although Wittgenstein does not spell it out here, the 'object' of sight in the first case is (simply) the thing before us, whereas in the second case, it is something less tangible, something that is categorically different. We will see what Wittgenstein means in what follows.)
3. In 'noticing an aspect', I suddenly see a relation that something has to something else. Expressed in terms of the two senses of 'see', what I 'see' in the first sense seems not to have changed, while what I 'see' in the second sense is indeed now different.
4. Wittgenstein stresses throughout his work that his concern is with the concepts and not the causes of experience. (This will also become clearer in what follows.)

What is the problem that aspect perception raises? What is puzzling is that we do indeed talk, and feel justified in talking, about 'seeing' in such cases. And yet when we do, we are not using 'see' in the same way as in the standard, 'simple' cases. In aspect perception, what we 'see', in one sense of the word, is exactly the same, yet, in another sense of the word, it is utterly different. It is this puzzlement that forms the underlying motivation of Wittgenstein's concern with seeing-as, and which he articulates in various ways throughout his discussion:

> The expression of a change of aspect is the expression of a *new* perception and at the same time of the perception's being unchanged.

(*PI*, 196)

CHAPTER 5 IMAGINATION AND ASPECT PERCEPTION

"But this isn't *seeing*!" — "But this is seeing!" – It must be possible to give both remarks a conceptual justification.

But this is seeing! *In what sense* is it seeing?

"The phenomenon is at first surprising, but a physiological explanation of it will certainly be found." –
Our problem is not a causal but a conceptual one.

(*PI*, 203)

What is incomprehensible is that *nothing*, and yet *everything*, has changed, after all. That is the only way to put it. Surely *this* way is wrong: It has not changed in *one* respect, but has in another. There would be nothing strange about that. But "Nothing has changed" means: Although I have no right to change my report about what I saw, since I see the same things now as before – still, I am incomprehensibly compelled to report completely different things, one after the other.

(*RPP*, II, § 474)

Looking at a face and then seeing a likeness to another face – such as seeing the father's features in the son's – is just one example of aspect perception that Wittgenstein gives. He also takes the examples, among others, of a schematic cube, and, most famously of all, of the duck-rabbit to explore the problem. We will consider these two examples, and what Wittgenstein says about them, in turn.

The schematic cube

Wittgenstein introduces the example of the schematic cube immediately after his opening remarks:

You could imagine the illustration

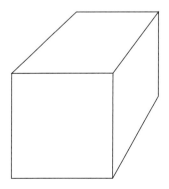

appearing in several places in a book, a text-book for instance. In the relevant text something different is in question every time: here a glass cube, there an inverted open box, there a wire frame of that shape, there three boards forming a solid angle. Each time the text supplies the interpretation of the illustration.

But we can also *see* the illustration now as one thing now as another. – So we interpret it, and *see* it as we *interpret* it.

Here perhaps we should like to reply: The description of what is got immediately, i.e. of the visual experience, by means of an interpretation – is an indirect description. "I see the figure as a box" means: I have a particular visual experience which I have found that I always have when I interpret the figure as a box or when I look at a box. But if it meant this I ought to know it. I ought to be able to refer to the experience directly, and not only indirectly. (As I can speak of red without calling it the colour of blood.)

(*PI*, 193–4)

ACTIVITY

1 What is Wittgenstein saying in the first two paragraphs?

2 What solution to the problem of seeing-as does talk of 'interpretation' suggest?

3 In the third paragraph Wittgenstein formulates a reply that someone (his imagined interlocutor) might make to the suggestion. What is this reply?

DISCUSSION

1 A figure such as a schematic cube may indeed be taken in different ways when it appears in a book, for example, but the context will determine its interpretation. However, even if the context determines which way the figure is to be taken, we can still see it in different ways (abstracting from the context). Nevertheless, in each case, we might insist, there is still 'interpretation' involved: we '*see* it as we *interpret* it'.

2 What Wittgenstein says in the first two paragraphs suggests that in aspect perception we 'interpret' the given object. In changes of aspect, then, what we 'see' may be the same in the first sense of 'see' but different in the second sense, since a different 'interpretation' is involved.

3 What Wittgenstein's imagined interlocutor is in effect saying is that talk of 'interpretation' does not do justice to the actual visual experience involved in aspect perception. We may indeed describe what we see in an 'interpretation', but this only refers to the experience 'indirectly'. Yet, as the interlocutor puts it, 'I ought to be able to refer to the experience directly'. Analogously, it might be suggested, I may describe red 'indirectly' as the colour of blood, but unless I can refer to an actual

> experience or sensation of red 'directly', then I cannot be said to really know what 'red' means.

It is not easy to work out exactly what Wittgenstein is arguing in this passage in introducing the example of the schematic cube. He wants to make the point that aspect perception involves interpretation of some kind, but recognizes that talk of interpretation is in danger of playing down the sensory character of the visual experience. This is what Wittgenstein's imagined interlocutor attempts to point out, but what underlies the interlocutor's objection is the conception of some kind of 'inner picture', which properly – or 'directly' – encapsulates the visual experience. As we have seen, Wittgenstein rejects this conception, but nothing is said here about what is wrong with it. Nor is it clear what implications this rejection has for the question as to how 'interpretation' *is* involved. The solution to the problem of seeing-as that talk of interpretation might be taken to suggest, then, is not a solution at all, but merely another way of putting the problem. Formulations of the puzzle in terms of the role of 'interpretation' can also be found frequently in Wittgenstein's remarks. Here is one example:

> The question now is: If one can see a figure according to an interpretation, does one see it according to an interpretation *every* time? And is there a well-defined difference between seeing which is not connected to any interpretation, and that which is?
>
> (*RPP*, II, § 359)

In asking the question again later in the *Investigations*, however, he also suggests, enigmatically, what may be needed to answer it:

> But how is it possible to *see* an object according to an *interpretation*? – The question represents it as a queer fact; as if something were being forced into a form it did not really fit. But no squeezing, no forcing took place here.
>
> When it looks as if there were no room for such a form between other ones you have to look for it in another dimension. If there is no room here, there *is* room in another dimension.
>
> (*PI*, 200)

Seeing-as seems to fall somewhere between 'simple' seeing and 'interpreting', and we find it difficult to fit it into either category. The problem is thus to find space between the two. But, as Wittgenstein remarks, it may be that we have to open up a further dimension to do so. What this dimension is we will see later in this chapter ('Wittgenstein's solution').

The duck-rabbit

Wittgenstein's most famous example is that of the duck-rabbit, which he introduces immediately after the passage discussed in the last activity.

> I shall call the following figure, derived from Jastrow [*Fact and Fable in Psychology*], the duck-rabbit. It can be seen as a rabbit's head or as a duck's.

> And I must distinguish between the 'continuous seeing' of an aspect and the 'dawning' of an aspect.
> The picture might have been shewn me, and I never have seen anything but a rabbit in it.
>
> Here it is useful to introduce the idea of a picture-object. For instance

> would be a 'picture-face'.
> In some respects I stand towards it as I do towards a human face. I can study its expression, can react to it as to the expression of the human face. A child can talk to picture-men or picture-animals, can treat them as it treats dolls.
>
> I may, then, have seen the duck-rabbit simply as a picture-rabbit from the first. That is to say, if asked "What's that?" or "What do you see here?" I should have

replied: "A picture-rabbit". If I had further been asked what that was, I should have explained by pointing to all sorts of pictures of rabbits, should perhaps have pointed to real rabbits, talked about their habits, or given an imitation of them.

I should not have answered the question "What do you see here?" by saying: "Now I am seeing it as a picture-rabbit". I should simply have described my perception: just as if I had said "I see a red circle over there." – Nevertheless someone else could have said of me: "He is seeing the figure as a picture-rabbit."

It would have made as little sense for me to say "Now I am seeing it as ..." as to say at the sight of a knife and fork "Now I am seeing this as a knife and fork". This expression would not be understood. – Any more than: "Now it's a fork" or "It can be a fork too".

One doesn't '*take*' what one knows as the cutlery at a meal *for* cutlery; any more than one ordinarily tries to move one's mouth as one eats, or aims at moving it.

If you say "Now it's a face for me", we can ask: "What change are you alluding to?"

I see two pictures, with the duck-rabbit surrounded by rabbits in one, by ducks in the other. I do not notice that they are the same. Does it *follow* from this that I *see* something different in the two cases? – It gives us a reason for using this expression here. ...

I am shewn a picture-rabbit and asked what it is; I say "It's a rabbit". Not "Now it's a rabbit". I am reporting my perception. – I am shewn the duck-rabbit and asked what it is; I *may* say "It's a duck-rabbit". But I may also react to the question quite differently. – The answer that it is a duck-rabbit is again the report of a perception; the answer "Now it's a rabbit" is not. Had I replied "It's a rabbit", the ambiguity would have escaped me, and I should have been reporting my perception.

(*PI*, 194–5)

ACTIVITY

1 Consider the case where I have only ever seen a rabbit in the duck-rabbit picture. What does Wittgenstein say I would reply to the question, 'What do you see here?' Which sense of 'see' would I be using in this reply?

2 Is Wittgenstein right about the reply I would give?

3 What is the point of Wittgenstein's cutlery example?

4 What conclusions can be drawn from Wittgenstein's discussion up to and including the cutlery example?

5 What is Wittgenstein saying in the penultimate paragraph of this passage?

6   Imagine now that I do recognize the ambiguity of the duck-rabbit picture. As Wittgenstein suggests, when asked what the picture is, I may say, 'It's a duck-rabbit' – or, we might add, 'I see a duck-rabbit'. In which sense would I now be using 'see'?

7   Can I see the duck-rabbit picture *as* a duck-rabbit picture?

DISCUSSION

1   Wittgenstein suggests that I would simply reply, 'A picture-rabbit'. (If I had not been introduced to the term 'picture-rabbit', then presumably I would say, 'A picture of a rabbit', or even just 'A rabbit' – understood as meaning a picture of a rabbit. I will use the last, simpler term in what follows, taking for granted that it refers to a picture-rabbit.) I would describe my experience, in other words, as 'I see a (picture-)rabbit' and not 'I see it *as* a (picture-)rabbit'. I would use 'see' in the first and not the second of the two senses that Wittgenstein had earlier distinguished.

2   Wittgenstein is surely right here. For to say 'I see it as a rabbit' implies that there are other ways of seeing it. But these are what I am assumed not to recognize. If I didn't know that there were other ways of seeing the picture, then I would simply report what I saw: 'I see a rabbit'. Of course, as Wittgenstein notes, someone else, who does appreciate the ambiguity of the duck-rabbit figure, can say of me, 'He sees it as a rabbit', but that only highlights the use of 'seeing-as' constructions to mark a contrast – to indicate that there are alternative possibilities.

3   The cutlery example reinforces the point just made. If it is obvious that something is a fork, then it makes no sense to say 'I see this as a fork' or 'I shall use this as a fork'. There are no other possibilities on the table, as it were. (Of course, cutlery sometimes comes in fancy designs, or is produced to serve several functions, where there may be genuine doubt as to what an item of cutlery is. In the case of a so-called 'spork', for example, which combines the functions of a spoon and a fork, I may well say, as I sit down to eat, 'I take this for a fork'.)

4   In the case we have so far considered, where I can only recognize a rabbit in the duck-rabbit picture, it makes sense both for me to say, 'I see a rabbit', and for you to say of me, 'He sees it as a rabbit'. Yet we are both referring to the same visual experience that I have. So this suggests that talk of 'seeing' or 'seeing-as' is not simply a matter of referring to a visual experience: there are other things involved. In such cases, talk of 'seeing-as' implies, while talk of simply 'seeing' does not imply, that there are alternative possibilities.

5   Wittgenstein asks us to consider the case in which I see two identical duck-rabbit pictures but in different contexts. Do I *see* something different? Wittgenstein does not answer this question directly; he merely says that we have a reason for using 'see' in this way. (There may also be reasons for not using it in this way. Wittgenstein often answers one question by giving an answer to a slightly different question. The strategy reminds us that we should not assume automatically that a question either makes sense or has a single answer. The issue is not so much whether we do see something different or not, as if there were a single determinate answer, as what is *meant* in using 'see' in the various possible ways.)

6   In saying 'I see a duck-rabbit', I would be using 'see' in the first sense. As Wittgenstein puts it, this would simply be the report of a perception – a recognition that what is before me is the ambiguous figure. There is a sense in which I can 'see' the duck-rabbit without 'seeing' it either *as* a duck or *as* a rabbit.

7   I can imagine a *use* for the sentence 'I see it as a duck-rabbit' – to indicate a contrast with the possibility of seeing the figure, say, as a map of a peninsula with a dot marking the location of buried treasure. The aspect switching that might be involved here may not have the visual interest of the switching from duck to rabbit aspects, but we can make some sense of talk of 'seeing' the figure *as* a duck-rabbit picture.

What is the general moral of this passage, regarding our use of the word 'see'? Even in the few cases considered here, our use of the word 'see' is far more complex than we might have thought at first. 'I see a rabbit', 'He sees a rabbit', 'I see it as a rabbit', 'He sees it as a rabbit', 'I see a duck-rabbit', 'I see it as a duck-rabbit' – all have different uses. We may distinguish two broad senses of 'see' – the simple sense and the sense involved in talk of 'seeing-as' – but this is only the start of conceptual clarification. There is much more to say about the two uses, and similarities and differences to be appreciated between and within the two categories.

Organization and inner picture

What I have just suggested is that the difference between 'seeing' (in the first, simple sense) and 'seeing-as' has to do not so much with the visual experience involved, which can be the same, as with the implications of our use of the relevant terms. 'Seeing-as' implies, while 'seeing' does not imply, that there are alternative ways of seeing. But is this right? Is there not a difference in my visual experience when I suddenly notice a new aspect, or when I switch from one aspect to another such as in the duck-rabbit case? Wittgenstein has his imagined interlocutor asking just this question:

> The change of aspect. "But surely you would say that the picture is altogether different now!"
> But what is different: my impression? my point of view? – Can I say? I *describe* the alteration like a perception; quite as if the object had altered before my eyes.
>
> (*PI*, 195)

How can the object I am looking at appear to have changed? One possibility is that, while the visual data I receive are the same, their 'organization' changes. It is this possibility that Wittgenstein goes on to discuss in taking the case of a puzzle picture – a picture in which there is a figure or figures hidden in what initially seems to be a simple image or scene. Before reading what Wittgenstein says, look at the example of a puzzle picture in Figure 4.

ACTIVITY

What hidden figures can you find in 'Old Swiss Mill'? Consider what happens when you suddenly see a figure and how it then affects your perception of the picture or the relevant part of the picture. (Spend no more than five or ten minutes looking for the figures: more appear – or seem to appear – the longer you look, and the point is not to find them all but to reflect on the process of seeing them. You can always return to the picture later as a break from trying to see what Wittgenstein is saying.)

DISCUSSION

What is wonderful about this puzzle picture, I think, is the sheer variety of the hidden figures. There are faces in the rocks and elsewhere, and lots of animals, particularly in the bottom part of the picture. Many of the figures form part of other figures, and aspect switching is sometimes required much as in the case of the duck-rabbit. There is also variety in the way that the figures are found, and the effect that seeing them then has – or so it seems to me. In some cases, such as in seeing the donkey's head on the right of the picture, the figure became clear to me very soon, and I find it difficult now to look at the picture without seeing the donkey. But at least the donkey might be taken to be a natural part of the scene. In other cases, such as in seeing the large cat in the trees on the top left, the figure that is seen seems to upset the balance and integrity of the picture: no such animal could 'really' be in the picture. Some

Figure 4 'Old Swiss Mill', published by Currier & Ives, New York, *c.*1872, lithograph, 22 × 32 cm. Photo: Library of Congress, Prints and Photographs Division (LC-USZ62-30528). 'Old Swiss Mill' is a particularly fine example of a puzzle picture. There is an extraordinary range of human and other animal figures hidden in the scenery. Indeed, every time you look at it, it seems, you notice a new one – or realize that one that you saw earlier can also be seen as something else. Some figures are such that once you see them, it is hard not to see them thereafter; other figures require an effort each time. Some figures seem substantial, others are mere outlines. Some are best seen close up, others from a distance. Some are well disguised, but clearly intended to be there; while other figures can be seen about which you are in some doubt as to whether they are 'really' there.

people have seen things that I have had much more difficulty seeing, and to see them each time myself, I have to go through a more deliberate process of 'construction', such as in the case of the (supposed) hare in the bottom right-hand corner of the picture, formed from the dog that is more obviously there and the two 'ears' between the roots of the tree above it.

While there are many differences in detail, in all the cases of finding a hidden figure it does seem natural to describe what is going on as a change in the 'organization' of the visual data one receives. Consider, for example, the donkey's head whose outline is formed by the branches of the tree in front of the house on the right of the picture. When you suddenly see it as a donkey's head, what initially seemed merely branches and the wall of a house become 'organized' or 'synthesized' into a donkey's head. Yet how are we to understand this 'organization'? It is not like organizing the books on your shelves, where some books are physically moved into different positions and the end result is different from how things were initially. Each element of the puzzle picture remains exactly where it is. Nor does change in 'organization' seem to be like change in colour. When I suddenly see the donkey's head, the shape of the donkey's head does not become coloured differently, though I might 'imagine' it a different colour or shade it in to indicate to someone else where the donkey is. The picture does not itself change when I see a hidden figure. But if 'organization' is not a property like colour, possessed by the object that is seen, then what is it? It is tempting to treat 'organization' instead as a property of some private mental image. Perhaps the relevant difference – between what is seen before and after finding the hidden figure – is located in some kind of difference of 'inner object'. But it is this suggestion that Wittgenstein is particularly concerned to reject. Here is what he says in taking the example of a puzzle picture:

> I suddenly see the solution of a puzzle-picture. Before, there were branches there; now there is a human shape. My visual impression has changed and now I recognize that it has not only shape and colour but also a quite particular 'organization'. – My visual impression has changed; – what was it like before and what is it like now? – If I represent it by means of an exact copy – and isn't that a good representation of it? – no change is shewn.
>
> And above all do *not* say "After all my visual impression isn't the *drawing*; it is *this* – which I can't shew to anyone." – Of course it is not the drawing, but neither is it anything of the same category, which I carry within myself.

The concept of the 'inner picture' is misleading, for this concept uses the '*outer* picture' as a model; and yet the uses of the words for these concepts are no more like one another than the uses of "numeral" and "number". (And if one chose to call numbers 'ideal numerals', one might produce a similar confusion.)

If you put the 'organization' of a visual impression on a level with colours and shapes, you are proceeding from the idea of the visual impression as an inner object. Of course this makes this object into a chimera; a queerly shifting construction. For the similarity to a picture is now impaired.

(*PI*, 196)

ACTIVITY

1. What does Wittgenstein suggest is wrong with appealing to an exact copy of my visual impression in trying to account for the change in 'organization' when I find a hidden figure in a puzzle picture?

2. Bearing in mind the attempt to explain 'organization', why is there a temptation to point 'inwards' in specifying the visual impression?

3. Why is the concept of an 'inner picture' misleading, according to Wittgenstein?

4. Why does putting the 'organization' of a visual impression on a level with colours and shapes assume that the impression is an inner object? And why does this make this object a 'queerly shifting construction'?

DISCUSSION

1. If I make an exact copy of my visual impression before and after finding a hidden figure, then no difference will be shown, since the picture does not itself change. So appeal to an exact copy cannot explain what happens in finding a hidden figure in a puzzle picture and, in particular, cannot explain the supposed change in 'organization'.

2. 'Organization', we want to say, is a property of my visual impression: change in organization is what accounts for the change in visual impression when I find a hidden figure. But if I try to draw what I see – to represent my visual impression in an exact copy – then no difference will be shown. No 'external' exact copy will capture the change. So there is a temptation to appeal to something 'internal'. Perhaps I have an exact copy 'internally', which does show the difference in organization.

3. The concept of an 'inner picture' is modelled on that of an 'outer picture', but this can easily make us think that an inner picture has all the properties of an outer picture except that it is somehow 'inside us'. Yet the very fact that an inner picture is 'internal' may make it very different (categorically

different) from an outer picture – just as numerals and numbers are very different. Perhaps someone chooses to call numbers 'ideal numerals', just as we might be tempted to call inner pictures 'ideal pictures' (pictures that are so perfect that they even embody 'organization', one might suggest). But such moves only obscure the differences, according to Wittgenstein.

4 If 'organization' is a property of an object just like colour or shape but cannot be exhibited in outer objects, then it can only be a property of inner objects. But if this is so, then we already have an essential difference between inner and outer objects: inner objects but not outer objects can possess the property of 'organization'. But now it looks as if there is an inherent contradiction in our appeal to inner pictures to account for seeing figures in puzzle pictures. On the one hand, we want inner pictures to be just like outer pictures, to embody the properties of visual impressions, yet, on the other hand, we attribute properties to them that outer pictures cannot have. Our idea of the inner object shifts about, depending on the role we want it to play.

Wittgenstein is not denying that it makes sense to talk of a change in 'organization' of my visual impression when I find a hidden figure in a puzzle picture. What he is denying is that 'organization' is to be understood as a perceptual property like colour or shape – and, in particular, as a property that is characteristic of an 'inner picture'. But how then are we to explain 'organization'? What we have to recognize here is the role that more complex cognitive activities and processes play in seeing a hidden figure or an aspect of something. Aspect perception is not simply a matter of passively receiving visual data or having some kind of image of something, but crucially involves actively interpreting what is seen in a certain way.

Returning to the case of the duck-rabbit, Wittgenstein goes on:

> If I saw the duck-rabbit as a rabbit, then I saw: these shapes and colours (I give them in detail) – and I saw besides something like this: and here I point to a number of different pictures of rabbits. – This shews the difference between the concepts.
> 'Seeing as ...' is not part of perception. And for that reason it is like seeing and again not like.
>
> (*PI*, 196–7)

In explaining what I see, I may indicate the relevant shapes and colours; but in explaining the aspect that I see, I will do something else, such as point to other pictures. Wittgenstein is not suggesting that pointing to other pictures is the only thing that shows the difference between seeing and seeing-as. There may be all sorts of things involved. But it is these additional things that determine the applicability of the concept of 'seeing-as'.

Returning to the question with which I began this section, then, we may indeed talk of a difference in visual experience when I suddenly notice a new aspect. But this difference is not to be located in any change of 'inner picture'. Appeal to an 'inner object' does not help us. We need to look at more complex activities and processes that are involved here, activities and processes that determine the difference between 'mere' seeing and seeing-as.

Seeing-as and interpreting

Wittgenstein rejects the appeal to 'inner pictures' in attempting to explain what goes on in aspect perception, but allows talk of 'organization', as long as 'organization' is not understood as a perceptual property like colour or shape. One way to understand 'organization' instead is as a function of how we *interpret* the visual data we receive in sense perception. This has the advantage of indicating the role that thought processes play in aspect perception. So how might thinking be involved?

ACTIVITY

Compare seeing the duck-rabbit as a duck with seeing it as a rabbit. How would you describe your own experience of seeing the two aspects? What differences are there? What goes on when you switch from one aspect to the other? Is there a change of 'organization'? Would talk of an 'inner picture' do justice to your experience? How would you say thinking is involved here?

DISCUSSION

What I would say, in my own case, is that I focus on different parts of the picture depending on which aspect I am seeing. When I see the duck-rabbit as a duck, I see it looking to the left, and imagine, for example, the two long protuberances opening up as a beak to receive food. When I see it as a rabbit, I see it looking to the right, and now see the two protuberances as ears. When I see it as a duck, I ignore the little dimple in the curve at the right, but when I see it as a rabbit, this dimple becomes the rabbit's mouth and even gives the rabbit a slightly watchful expression. (The duck just looks greedy.) Once I recognize these differences, I can switch from one to the other at will, simply fixing on either the left or the right side of the figure. There is a sense in which I do 'organize' what I see differently: I bring different parts together in different ways, and privilege some parts over others. As to whether or not I have some 'inner picture', this seems irrelevant to what I experience. Perhaps I can conjure up a mental image of the duck-rabbit which I can then also 'see' as either a duck or a rabbit, but what is important is not the mere having of the image, but the way I scan or focus on different parts of it. It is what I *do* with the picture or image that is relevant. It is here that we can say thinking comes in. For in 'organizing' or focusing on different parts of it, I conceptualize those parts differently. When I see the duck-rabbit as a duck, I conceive of the protuberances as a beak and think of this beak as opening and shutting. When I see the duck-rabbit as a rabbit, I conceive of the protuberances as ears and think of the rabbit as alert and listening. Thought processes inform the seeing of the figure under each aspect, different processes for different aspects.

Wittgenstein might disapprove of the way I have approached this issue. As he remarks at one point, 'Do not ask yourself "How does it work with *me*?" – Ask "What do I know about someone else?"' (*PI*, 206). Given that one of his main targets in the *Investigations* was the myth of the 'inner picture', it is understandable that he should say this. But there need be no real conflict between the descriptions that we give of our own experience and considerations of the criteria that we use for determining what other people see and think, since the descriptions we give are precisely what other people use in determining what we experience. Perhaps you would describe your own experience slightly differently from how I described mine, but I would be surprised if you were unable to take my description not just as a clue to what I experience, but as an expression of the kind of thing that others may well experience. (I certainly assumed this in the account I gave.)

The key point, though, is the role that thinking plays in aspect perception, and this is a continual theme in Wittgenstein's own discussion. As we saw earlier, however, Wittgenstein often talks of 'interpreting' rather than 'thinking'. But he clearly takes interpreting to be a form of thinking, as the following remark shows, made in reflecting on the duck-rabbit example:

> "Is it thinking? Is it seeing?" – Doesn't this really amount to "Is it *interpreting*? Is it seeing?" And interpreting is a kind of thinking; and often it brings about a sudden change of aspect.
> Can I say that seeing aspects is *related* to interpreting? – My inclination was indeed to say "It is as if I *saw* an *interpretation*". Well, the expression of this seeing *is* related to the expression of interpreting.
>
> (*LW*, I, § 179)

Elsewhere, however, Wittgenstein seems to play down the role of 'interpreting':

> Do I really see something different each time, or do I only interpret what I see in a different way? I am inclined to say the former. But why? – To interpret is to think, to do something; seeing is a state.
>
> (*PI*, 212)

But there is no conflict between these two passages, I think. In the first passage, Wittgenstein is remarking on the connection between seeing-as and interpreting, while still recognizing our impulse to talk of 'seeing' in aspect perception. In the second passage, our impulse to talk of 'seeing' is what is emphasized, making the point that seeing-as cannot be regarded as 'merely' interpreting. What these two passages highlight, though, is the way in which seeing-as seems to fall between seeing and interpreting (or thinking). It was suggested earlier that Wittgenstein's aim was to find space between seeing and thinking by opening up a further dimension. What might this further dimension be?

Wittgenstein's solution

In his discussion of seeing-as in the *Remarks*, Wittgenstein writes:

> It is seeing, *insofar as* ...
> It is seeing, only insofar *as* ...
> (That seems to me to be the solution.)
>
> (*RPP*, II, § 390)

Of course, at best, this can only be the schema of a solution. There are many similarities and differences between seeing and seeing-as, and the 'solution' suggested requires filling in the blanks. Malcolm Budd has taken this remark as providing a conclusion to Wittgenstein's discussion (1989, 97), although it was not a remark that found its way into the *Investigations*. But even with the blanks filled in, there remain important things to be said, as both Marie McGinn (1997, 195–204) and Stephen Mulhall (2001, 247–55) have argued. Wittgenstein's aim is not just to attack the myth of the 'inner picture', as if this alone would solve the puzzle about seeing-as, nor just to point out the similarities and differences between seeing and seeing-as, which hardly opens up that new dimension at which Wittgenstein hinted. Although Wittgenstein himself often plays down the revisionary thrust of his philosophy, his aim is to effect a reorientation in the way we understand psychological concepts. There is a crucial relation between seeing-as and *thinking*, which shows the categorical difference between seeing and seeing-as with which Wittgenstein himself chose to open his discussion.

Recall the paragraph quoted on page 148:

> If I saw the duck-rabbit as a rabbit, then I saw: these shapes and colours (I give them in detail) – and I saw besides something like this: and here I point to a number of different pictures of rabbits. – This shews the difference between the concepts.

(*PI*, 196–7)

Compare this paragraph with a remark that Wittgenstein makes later in the *Investigations*:

> The colour of the visual impression corresponds to the colour of the object (this blotting paper looks pink to me, and is pink) – the shape of the visual impression to the shape of the object (it looks rectangular to me, and is rectangular) – but what I perceive in the dawning of an aspect is not a property of the object, but an internal relation between it and other objects.

(*PI*, 212)

ACTIVITY What is the key difference between the concept of seeing and the concept of seeing-as that Wittgenstein is indicating in these two remarks?

DISCUSSION In the case of seeing, I perceive properties of the object seen; in the case of seeing-as, I perceive not (only) properties of the object seen, but (also) relations between the object and other things. In the first remark, Wittgenstein implies that seeing-as involves both types of perception. In the second remark, he seems to be restricting it to the second type. Clearly, seeing-as *presupposes* seeing: I must see something to see something *as* something. But what is *characteristic* of seeing-as is the perception of relations.

(This was the message, too, of Wittgenstein's opening remarks, the implications of which we will now explore.)

Wittgenstein calls the relations perceived in seeing-as 'internal relations'. The distinction between internal and external relations had been drawn in Wittgenstein's early work, the *Tractatus Logico-Philosophicus*. Here is the key proposition (4.123):

> A property is internal if it is unthinkable that its object should not possess it. (This shade of blue and that one stand, eo ipso, in the internal relation of lighter to darker. It is unthinkable that *these* two objects should not stand in this relation.) (Here the shifting use of the word 'object' corresponds to the shifting use of the words 'property' and 'relation'.)

The idea might be illustrated, developing Wittgenstein's own example, by distinguishing the following two statements:

(1) Cambridge blue is lighter than Oxford blue.

(2) Cambridge's blue is lighter than Oxford's blue.

Insofar as 'Cambridge blue' and 'Oxford blue' refer to particular shades of blue, it is inconceivable that these particular shades do not stand in the relation of lighter to darker: the first statement is necessarily true. Anyone who said that Oxford blue was lighter than Cambridge blue would not understand the meanings of the terms. The relation between the two shades of colour is an internal relation. But it is only a contingent fact that Cambridge University chose a lighter shade of blue for its colour than Oxford University. It is conceivable that the blue that Cambridge chose might have been darker than the blue that Oxford chose. The relation between the two choices of colour is an external relation (i.e. it depends on *external* conditions such as the predilections of each university). (1) expresses an internal relation, while (2) expresses an external relation.

How does seeing-as involve the perception of internal relations? In seeing the duck-rabbit as a rabbit, what I see is not just a property of the object seen but a relation between the duck-rabbit and other pictures of rabbits and/or actual rabbits. If there were no such relation, then there would be no seeing the duck-rabbit as a rabbit. It is inconceivable, in other words, that I could see the duck-rabbit as a rabbit without seeing some relation to either a picture of a rabbit or an actual rabbit. The relation is therefore 'internal', in Wittgenstein's sense.

What are the implications of this? First of all, we can see why Wittgenstein talks of a categorical difference between seeing and seeing-as. In seeing, we perceive the properties of objects themselves; in seeing-as, we perceive internal relations between objects. The 'objects of sight' in seeing-as – the internal relations – are categorically different from the 'objects of sight' in seeing. Second, in perceiving the properties of objects, we are relatively passive. When we open our eyes, we have no choice in the shapes and colours we see. In perceiving internal relations, on the other hand, we are much more active, since it is we who think of the other objects to which our primary object of sight is internally related. We will return to this in the next section. Third, seeing-as involves crucial presuppositions. To see the duck-rabbit as a rabbit, for example, I must already be familiar with rabbits or pictures of rabbits. I must have the concept of a rabbit, and be able to recognize rabbits or pictures of rabbits when I see them. As far as this latter point is concerned, Wittgenstein writes:

> "Now he's seeing it like *this*", "now like *that*" would only be said of someone *capable* of making certain applications of the figure freely.
> The substratum of this experience is the mastery of a technique.
>
> But how queer for this to be the logical condition of someone's having such-and-such an *experience*! After all, you don't say that one only 'has toothache' if one is capable of doing such-and-such. – From this it follows that we cannot be dealing with the same concept of experience here. It is a different though related concept.
>
> It is only if someone *can do*, has learnt, is master of, such-and-such, that it makes sense to say he has had *this* experience.
> And if this sounds crazy, you need to reflect that the *concept* of seeing is modified here.
>
> (*PI*, 208–9)

ACTIVITY

1 What is Wittgenstein's main point in this passage?

2 What is supposed to be queer? Is it queer?

DISCUSSION

1 Wittgenstein's main point is that the experience of seeing-as presupposes certain abilities: 'The substratum of this experience is the mastery of a technique.'

2 That experience should depend on the mastery of a technique might be supposed to be queer. And this might indeed seem queer if we take as our paradigm of 'experience' the sensation of having pain. Isn't experience

simply what happens to us – a result of what we passively receive from the outside world? Wittgenstein argues, however, that it should not seem queer once we recognize that we are not dealing with a single concept of experience. Both the concept of experience, as it applies in the case of sensation, and the concept of seeing, as it applies in 'simple' cases, are modified in the case of seeing-as.

The point that Wittgenstein is making here is fundamental to his philosophy. We all too readily assume that psychological terms refer to particular states or processes 'in the mind'. Yet our use of psychological language is enormously complex, and reflects not just mental processes, but also features of the wider context. When we talk of someone seeing something *as* something, we are not just reporting on their visual processes. We are also implying that they have grasped the concepts and mastered the techniques necessary to have that experience, concepts and techniques which themselves presuppose a certain language and culture – a whole 'form of life', as Wittgenstein puts it (*PI*, 226). This may be obvious in a case such as someone's seeing a particular painting as a parody of Post-Impressionism. But it is also true in simpler cases such as that of the duck-rabbit. This is the further dimension that Wittgenstein opens up in finding the space he wants between seeing and thinking.

Seeing-as and imagination

Wittgenstein's remarks on seeing-as have been highly influential in contemporary discussions of imagination. Yet in the account just given, the imagination has not been mentioned once. So how can his remarks have been influential? In the *Investigations*, Wittgenstein himself only refers to the imagination in two passages in these remarks. The first passage is concerned with seeing aspects of a triangular figure (*PI*, 207). In the second passage, towards the end of his remarks, he notes: 'The concept of an aspect is akin to the concept of an image'; and he points out the similarity between seeing an aspect and imagining in that both are subject to the will (*PI*, 213). There are more remarks on the relationship between seeing-as and imagining, however, in the manuscripts and typescripts from which the material for the *Investigations* was drawn. Perhaps the most significant are the following:

> I see something *in different connexions*. (Isn't this more closely related to imagining than to seeing?)
>
> It is as if one had brought a concept to what one sees, and one now sees the concept along with the thing. It is itself hardly visible, and yet it spreads an ordering veil over the objects.
>
> (*RPP*, I, §§ 960–1)

The first remark reflects the second of the three implications of Wittgenstein's account of seeing-as that I noted towards the end of the last section. Seeing-as involves the thinking of objects to which our primary object of sight (that which we see *as* something) is internally related. Is it not the imagination to which this ability to think of objects is attributed? In seeing a duck-rabbit as a rabbit, I do not need to relate the picture to any other picture or actual rabbit in front of me. It is enough for me, presumably, to *imagine* such a picture or rabbit. But if this is right, then the imagination would seem to be involved at the very heart of seeing-as. The second remark is yet a further example of the idea that Wittgenstein expresses, metaphorically, on a number of occasions. In noticing an aspect, a concept or thought somehow 'infuses' the perception. As he writes in the *Investigations*:

> It is almost as if 'seeing the sign in this context' were an echo of a thought. "The echo of a thought in sight" – one would like to say.
>
> (*PI*, 212)

If there are echoes of thought in sight, then is it not the imagination that is responsible? We will address this question directly shortly. First, however, to bring out the relevance of Wittgenstein's remarks on seeing-as for understanding imagination, let us return to some of the issues explored in earlier chapters and see what further light might now be shed on them.

Rationalism and empiricism

As noted at the beginning of chapter 2, the dispute between rationalists and empiricists is often characterized as one between those who privilege the role of reason in the acquisition of knowledge and those who regard knowledge as derived from sense experience. Aspect perception seems to bring together sense perception and thought in the most intimate way, and might be regarded as particularly problematic for both. So what implications does seeing-as have for the dispute between rationalists and empiricists?

Consider our experience of seeing the duck-rabbit as a duck and as a rabbit. Does the empiricist or the rationalist have the better resources to account for this experience? The empiricist would be right that there could be no such experience without sense perception. Seeing-as presupposes seeing: to see something *as* something, I must see it in the first place. If what has just been suggested is right, then I also have to 'imagine' some other object in seeing the relation; but this too the empiricist would be happy to explain – in terms of conjuring up the relevant image. The rationalist, on the other hand, would be right in stressing the contribution of something other than sense perception. But they would have to accept that sense perception is required too, and if their point were simply that there could be no experience of seeing the duck-rabbit as a duck without the *concept* of a duck, then this alone does not provide support for rationalism. For the concept of a duck is an empirical concept, which the empiricist (such as Locke or Hume) would take as some kind of idea or image.

It is not clear, however, what either the empiricist or the rationalist would make of the idea of an *internal* relation, which is central to Wittgenstein's account of seeing-as. One might initially think that the empiricist would have the easier time in explaining this. For if both our perception of the duck-rabbit and our image, say, of a rabbit are involved in seeing the picture as a rabbit, then it would seem a relatively straightforward mental operation to compare them – to see the relation between them. Seeing-as would just be the seeing of relations between ideas or images. Since all this goes on 'in the mind', does that not exhaust the conception of 'internal' relations? But this is not at all Wittgenstein's conception.

ACTIVITY

In cases in which an actual object is before me, I can be mistaken in saying, even in good faith, 'I see a rabbit'. Can I similarly be mistaken in saying of a picture, 'I see this picture as a (picture of a) rabbit'?

DISCUSSION

It is not clear in what sense I can be mistaken in aspect perception. In the case of seeing, I can be corrected and, in principle, be brought to see that I am wrong if I claim that I am seeing something that I am not. But there is nothing analogous in the case of seeing-as. If I claim, in all good faith, that I see a picture as a picture of a rabbit, then how could someone tell me I was wrong? If they challenge me, then I would be expected to explain what the relation is I see: 'These are the ears, this is the eye, this is the mouth ...', for example. Obviously, if I could offer no explanation at all, then there would be doubts as to what I was claiming. But we are supposing that I am acting in good faith, which is to say that some such explanation could be given. Of course, even with my explanation, someone else may be unable to see the aspect that I see. But that is just what we would say: they cannot see what I see. Any attempt to 'correct' me would seem out of place. In practice, though, what is most likely to happen is that they will just say: 'I can see what you mean, although it looks to me more like ...', or 'I suppose it does look a bit like a rabbit, but I see it as ...'.

In cases of seeing-as, the relation that is seen between the primary object of sight and something else is *constitutive* of the experience. It is not an accidental or external feature of the experience that this relation is seen, but an essential or internal feature. It is in this sense that Wittgenstein talks of 'internal' relations. And if this is right, then seeing-as is not quite the empirical process that the empiricist would have us believe. In seeing an aspect, I do not acquire knowledge about the world – at least in the way that I do in simply seeing something. What I learn, or exhibit mastery of, is a way of making connections between things – a technique of comparison rather than an item of information.

Does this mean that the rationalist can offer a better account of seeing-as? The rationalist may place greater emphasis on conceptual powers rather than sensory data, but in an important sense neither the rationalist nor the empiricist does justice to aspect perception. As traditionally characterized, the dispute between rationalists and empiricists concerns what is required for knowledge. But 'knowledge' is understood here as knowledge of the world or knowledge of facts. But if we can speak of knowledge in aspect perception, then it is knowledge *how* rather than knowledge *that*. In seeing something *as* something, what I know is how to make a certain comparison. I appreciate a connection rather than apprehend a fact. All this is part of what is involved in the distinction that Wittgenstein draws between seeing and seeing-as: between seeing properties and seeing internal relations. In the end, it is not clear that either rationalism or empiricism, as traditionally conceived, makes room for this distinction.

Seeing Wittgenstein as a Kantian

In her account of Wittgenstein's remarks on seeing-as, Marie McGinn emphasizes the link that exists in aspect perception between what is seen and the response that someone makes. In this way, she writes, 'the case of seeing-as works against our inclination to think of perception in terms of the influence of objects on a receptive faculty, and draws our attention to the role of an active, responding subject in determining the nature of visual experience, or in fixing what is seen' (1997, 195). This too suggests the inadequacy of empiricism to do justice to the phenomenon of aspect perception. But while it might be thought to support a more rationalist approach, what it really suggests is a Kantian conception. For, as we saw in the last chapter, 'the role of an active, responding subject in determining the nature of visual experience' was just what Kant stressed in his own critique of the 'way of ideas'.

Recall the comparison of Hume's and Kant's accounts of abstract ideas and the discussion of Strawson's conception of 'non-actual' perceptions (pp.116–21 above). To what extent might Wittgenstein be seen as a Kantian? Take my example of seeing a cat. According to Kant, to recognize it as a cat, I must know how to apply the concept of a cat, which requires being able to generate images of cats, such as arise from recalling past perceptions of cats. Such images or past perceptions inform my present perception. What is wrong with traditional empiricism is the assumption that perceptions are discrete mental images. On Kant's view, even a supposedly simple perception is actually complex – even the most momentary of perceptions is 'infused' with other perceptions. Wittgenstein, too, criticizes empiricism and recognizes the role that other perceptions and thoughts play in any current perception or image, and the abilities that are presupposed in having visual experiences. Kant emphasizes that I must have the ability to schematize; Wittgenstein emphasizes that I must have mastery of a technique.

Strawson, it will be recalled, in explaining Kant's claim that 'imagination is a necessary ingredient of perception itself' (see p.96 above), was concerned with the way that 'non-actual' (i.e. past or possible) perceptions are 'alive' in a present perception. The relation between them, he suggested, was an internal relation, an idea he took from Wittgenstein, but whose clarification I left dangling at the time. We can now return to Strawson and see how his account is completed. For according to Wittgenstein, what happens in seeing-as is that I see an internal relation between my primary object of sight and some other object or objects, a relation that is constitutive of my experience, in the sense that it would not be that experience without that relation. But these other objects may well be 'non-actual', in Strawson's sense. In seeing the duck-rabbit as a (picture of a) duck, I need not be seeing any actual ducks or other pictures of ducks. But there is some sense in which I must actively supply these 'non-actual' objects to have the experience I do. So what Wittgenstein says about seeing-as appears to fit the model that Strawson finds in Kant's conception of the role of imagination in perception. What had impressed Strawson was the striking similarity between these two conceptions, and it was on the basis of this that he built his account in 'Imagination and perception'.

But as Strawson admits, there seems to be one crucial difference between Kant and Wittgenstein. For, as we have seen, Wittgenstein emphasizes the link between perceptual experience and what I say and do, which is largely absent in Kant. However, what Wittgenstein emphasizes might be seen as a development or generalization of Kant's point. There is an internal relation not just between actual and non-actual perceptions and thoughts, but also between my experiences and what I say and do. (This, in fact, is the point that McGinn makes.) This is a strengthening and not a rejection of Kant's underlying insight – that any experience I have cannot be taken as an isolated 'given', independent of either the world of external objects or my own abilities, capacities, past perceptions and thoughts. What Wittgenstein adds is that neither can it be isolated from what I say or do. In this important sense, Wittgenstein might indeed be seen as a Kantian.

The relation between imagination and seeing-as

As noted above, Wittgenstein only refers to the imagination in two passages in his remarks on seeing-as. So can we really say that imagination is involved in seeing-as, on Wittgenstein's account? If not, then does the connection with Kant not break down? One of the contexts in which Wittgenstein mentions the imagination is in discussing the aspects of a triangle. Here is the paragraph in which the example is first given:

> Take as an example the aspects of a triangle. This triangle

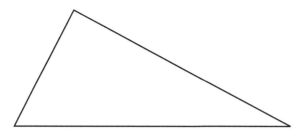

can be seen as a triangular hole, as a solid, as a geometrical drawing; as standing on its base, as hanging from its apex; as a mountain, as a wedge, as an arrow or pointer, as an overturned object which is meant to stand on the shorter side of the right angle, as a half-parallelogram, and as various other things.

(*PI*, 200)

A few pages later, he makes the following two remarks about this example:

> The aspects of the triangle: it is as if an *image* came into contact, and for a time remained in contact, with the visual impression.
>
> ... It is possible to take the duck-rabbit simply for the picture of a rabbit ... but not to take the bare triangular figure for the picture of an object that has fallen over. To see this aspect of the triangle demands *imagination*.
>
> (*PI*, 207)

ACTIVITY

Putting these two last remarks together, what is the main point that Wittgenstein is making here?

DISCUSSION

Wittgenstein is suggesting that imagination is only involved in some cases of aspect perception. In these cases something extra must indeed be added – an 'image' – which is appropriately attributed to the work of the imagination.

Does this contradict Strawson's claim about the connection between imagination and seeing-as? Strawson recognizes the question himself, but makes two points in response (1974, § 6, 59–63). First, in making sense of the *contrast* that Wittgenstein seems to be drawing here between cases of aspect perception that involve, and cases that do not involve, imagination, he remarks that we do often talk of 'imagining' in 'situations in which there is some sort of departure from the immediately obvious or familiar or mundane or established or superficial or literal way of taking things; situations in which there is some sort of innovation or extravagance or figure or trope or stretch of the mind or new illumination or invention' (ibid., 60–1). But, he goes on to add, such talk of 'imagining' is relative to the context and need not indicate any essential difference in perceptual process. This enables him to make his second point: namely, that there remains a kinship between seeing-as and imagining, which Wittgenstein himself notes in other places. Here are the remarks to which I referred earlier:

> The concept of an aspect is akin to the concept of an image. In other words: the concept 'I am now seeing it as ....' is akin to 'I am now having *this* image'.
> Doesn't it take imagination to hear something as a variation on a particular theme? And yet one is perceiving something in so hearing it.
>
> "Imagine this changed like this, and you have this other thing." One can use imagining in the course of proving something.
>
> Seeing an aspect and imagining are subject to the will. There is such an order as "Imagine *this*", and also: "Now see the figure like *this*"; but not "Now see this leaf green".
>
> (*PI*, 213)

Even in the standard cases of seeing-as, such as seeing the aspects of the duck-rabbit picture, then, there are similarities with standard cases of imagining, such as simply conjuring up an 'image' of something. In particular, both are subject to the will. But to return to Strawson's main point, the crucial connection lies in the internal relation that is involved in aspect perception. In seeing the duck-rabbit picture as a (picture of a) duck, what I see is an internal relation between the picture and real ducks or other pictures of ducks, none of which, however, may be present at the time. This is where it seems legitimate to talk of 'imagination' – in conjuring these other things up, whether as some kind of image or simply in thought. Wittgenstein himself writes: 'By noticing the aspect one perceives an internal relation, and yet noticing the aspect is related to *forming an image*' (*LW*, I, § 733). He may speak here only of aspect perception being *related* to image-formation; nevertheless, insofar as imagination covers more than just image-formation, but – in its most general sense – thinking of something in its absence, it seems reasonable to describe aspect perception too as involving imagination. To adapt Strawson's words in discussing Kant (see p.119 above), should we not register our sense of the kinship between aspect perception and image-formation by extending the title of 'imagination' to cover both capacities?

The clarification of mental concepts

As we have seen, Strawson's concern was to explain Kant's claim that 'imagination is a necessary ingredient of perception itself'. If Strawson is right about the connection between Kant and Wittgenstein, then Wittgenstein might be interpreted as holding that imagination is a necessary ingredient of aspect perception. At the same time, however, Strawson admitted that it was hard to make sense of all this without using metaphors. This is the first sentence of the key paragraph of Strawson's paper that was cited above (p.119): 'It seems, then, not too much to say that the actual occurrent perception of an enduring object as an object of a certain kind, or as a particular object of that kind, is, as it were, soaked with or animated by, or infused with – the metaphors are *à choix* – the thought of other past or possible perceptions of the same object'. Wittgenstein makes use of similar metaphors in trying to understand what is involved in aspect perception. He talks, for example, of a concept spreading 'an ordering veil over the objects' (*RPP*, I, § 961), of an 'echo of a thought in sight' (*PI*, 212), of an aspect as 'an inarticulate reverberation of a thought' (*RPP*, I, § 1036), and of an image coming into 'contact' with the visual impression (*PI*, 207). So if one did interpret Wittgenstein as holding that imagination is a necessary ingredient of aspect perception, should this not also be understood metaphorically?

As explained in the last chapter, Kant treated the imagination as a *faculty*, as a power to engage in certain kinds of cognitive activity. Indeed, according to Kant, we could not have experience at all without what he called 'transcendental imagination'; and it was this conception that was seized upon in Romanticism in glorifying the imagination. But as I suggested in the first chapter, and as we have now seen illustrated, the thrust of Wittgenstein's philosophy seems to be in the opposite direction. On Wittgenstein's view, instead of treating imagination as a mysterious power and 'imagining' as denoting a specific kind of mental process, we should look at the uses of the word 'imagination' and its cognates in attempting to understand the varieties of our imaginative experiences and the puzzling and often conflicting ways in which we describe them. This suggests, despite the connections already identified, that Wittgenstein's project is very different from Kant's. If Kant mystifies the imagination, then Wittgenstein's concern is to demystify it.

Wittgenstein's remarks on seeing-as provide an excellent illustration of his project of conceptual clarification. What is so puzzling about seeing-as is the tension we feel between describing it as 'seeing' and describing it as 'thinking' or 'interpreting'. Recall the remarks quoted on page 137:

> "But this isn't *seeing*!" – "But this is seeing!" – It must be possible to give both remarks a conceptual justification.
>
> But this is seeing! *In what sense* is it seeing?
>
> "The phenomenon is at first surprising, but a physiological explanation of it will certainly be found." –
> Our problem is not a causal but a conceptual one.
>
> (*PI*, 203)

Just a page later, Wittgenstein goes on:

> "Is it a *genuine* visual experience?" The question is: in what sense is it one?
>
> Here it is *difficult* to see that what is at issue is the fixing of concepts.
>
> A *concept* forces itself on one. (This is what you must not forget.)
>
> (*PI*, 204)

What Wittgenstein is concerned to clarify are the concepts we use, and indeed often feel compelled to use, in describing the phenomena of aspect perception. When we do describe them using a certain concept, it is because we see connections between its use here and its use in other contexts. In describing seeing-as as a form of 'thinking', for example, we might have in mind that both are subject to the will and involve the deliberate application of a concept. (Making sense of aspect perception is itself a form of aspect perception. In seeing seeing-as as a type of seeing, we are recognizing one set of relations; in seeing seeing-as as a type of thinking, we are recognizing another set of relations.)

Why does Wittgenstein think that a 'physiological explanation' cannot help in the project of conceptual clarification? The answer is provided in a later paragraph of the *Investigations*:

> Imagine a physiological explanation of the experience. Let it be this: When we look at the figure, our eyes scan it repeatedly, always following a particular path. The path corresponds to a particular pattern of oscillation of the eyeballs in the act of looking. It is possible to jump from one such pattern to another and for the two to alternate ... Certain patterns of movement are physiologically impossible; hence, for example, I cannot see the schematic cube as two interpenetrating prisms. And so on. Let this be the explanation. – "Yes, that shews it is a kind of *seeing*." – You have now introduced a new, a physiological, criterion for seeing.

And this can screen the old problem from view, but not solve it. – The purpose of this paragraph however, was to bring before our view what happens when a physiological explanation is offered. The psychological concept hangs out of reach of this explanation. And this makes the nature of the problem clearer.

(*PI*, 212)

At best, all that a physiological – or any scientific – explanation can provide is a new criterion for one of our psychological concepts. Even if we assume, let us say, that such an explanation shows a closer connection between seeing-as and 'simple' seeing than we initially thought, the task would remain to explain why we were tempted – and perhaps still are tempted – to describe seeing-as as a form of thinking. The philosophical puzzle would be left unresolved, in other words. And the problem may even be exacerbated, if the scientific explanation itself modifies our concepts so that further clarification is required, to explain the connections between the modified concepts and our original concepts.

Something similar might be said about Kant's appeal to the 'transcendental imagination' in 'explaining' our cognitive activities. As his talk of the imagination as a 'hidden art in the depths of the human soul' suggests (see p.112 above), this only screens rather than solves the relevant problems. Kant's appeal to the imagination is itself something that requires conceptual clarification – a clarification that I have sought to provide. Equally, we might describe aspect perception as requiring 'imagination', but this too may be more an expression of the problem than a solution. There may indeed be connections between our concepts of 'noticing an aspect' and 'forming an image' that make it natural to extend our use of the term 'imagination' to cover both. But the key task is to make clear these conceptual connections.

'Imagining' and 'seeing-as'

Let me conclude this chapter, and Part One as a whole, by returning to the question of the definition of 'imagining' explored in chapter 1.

ACTIVITY

On page 23 a definition of 'imagining' was suggested that was described as 'Wittgensteinian'. What was this definition, and in the light of the present chapter, to what extent do you think it is rightly called 'Wittgensteinian'?

DISCUSSION

'Imagining' was defined as 'thinking of something that is not present to the senses and that may or may not be true or existent, thinking which, in being called "imagining", indicates a lack of commitment to the truth or existence of what is thought of by the person calling it such'. The key point was that, in calling something 'imagining', we are not just referring to some mental activity but also evaluating that activity in some way – or, more specifically, refraining from committing ourselves to the truth or existence of what is being thought of. The definition was described as 'Wittgensteinian' because of the implicit rejection of the assumption that 'imagining' simply denotes some particular mental process. Given the contrast that Wittgenstein draws – at least in some places, such as in discussing the aspects of a triangle – between aspect perception that involves, and aspect perception that does not involve, 'imagination', it might be argued that this is not a definition that Wittgenstein would have provided. There is no suggestion in his writings that talk of 'imagining' reflects a lack of commitment *on the part of the person using the term* to the truth or existence of what is being thought of. And even if we took just the first part of the suggested definition – i.e. 'thinking of something that is not present to the senses' (adopting the general definition suggested by Stephenson's twelve conceptions of imagination; see p.11 above), then the contrast Wittgenstein draws would seem to rule out attributing this to him too. Furthermore, it might be pointed out that Wittgenstein seems to have image-forming particularly in mind in talking of 'imagining', and this suggests a more restricted conception of imagination than is reflected in the suggested definition.

To see how the suggested definition of 'imagining' might nevertheless be regarded as Wittgensteinian in spirit, recall what was said above (in 'The duck-rabbit', pp.140–3) about the implications of talk of 'seeing-as'. Take the case where I can only recognize a rabbit in the duck-rabbit picture. In this case, I noted, it makes sense both for me to say, 'I see a rabbit', and for you to say of me, 'He sees it as a rabbit'. Yet we are both referring to the same visual experience that I am having. So it cannot be the case that 'seeing' and 'seeing-as' simply denote two different mental processes. Talk of 'seeing-as' implies, while talk of 'seeing' does not imply, that there are alternative possibilities – as recognized *on the part of the person using the term*. But this is analogous to talk of 'imagining', which also implies commitments *on the part of the person using the term*. Of course, these commitments are only one feature of the use of the relevant terms, and there may be other commitments in other contexts. But it does show that there is more to our use of such terms than simply the denoting of a mental process, which, as I have argued, is one of Wittgenstein's fundamental points. The suggested definition of 'imagining' might indeed be seen as Wittgensteinian in spirit, then, although the purpose in suggesting it was not to lay down an authoritative definition but just to highlight the point that has just been made.

Review and preview

1. In seeking a philosophical understanding of imagination, Wittgenstein advocates looking at how the word 'imagination' is used, a strategy deliberately employed to undermine the temptation to appeal to inner mental processes or private objects in explaining our imaginative activities and experiences.

2. Our main focus has been on Wittgenstein's discussion of seeing-as. In noticing an aspect of something, what we see in one sense remains the same, and yet in another sense seems entirely different; and this was the puzzle that motivated Wittgenstein's concern. Seeing-as both presupposes seeing but at the same time involves something more – some concept, thought or image that 'infuses' the perception. What is central to his account is the idea of an internal relation. In aspect perception, what I see is an internal relation between my primary object of sight and something else, a relation that is constitutive of my experience and that is manifested in what I say and do.

3. While Wittgenstein only twice talks about the imagination in his remarks on seeing-as in the *Investigations*, there is a kinship between aspect perception and image-formation and there are grounds for claiming that the imagination is involved in aspect perception. These grounds were seen in exploring the connection between Wittgenstein and Kant, centring on the idea of an internal relation. Despite this connection, however, Wittgenstein's project of conceptual clarification can also be taken as a critique of Kant's philosophy and of the Romantic glorification of the imagination that it inspired. For arguably, while Kant mystifies the imagination, Wittgenstein's concern is to demystify it.

4. Like the concept of imagining generally, the concept of seeing-as is related to both the concept of seeing and the concept of thinking. These interrelationships have been the main theme of Part One. But like imagining, too, seeing-as can also exhibit creativity, since it is we who

supply the 'non-actual' things to which our primary object of sight is seen to be internally related. We will turn to the issue of creativity in Part Two.

Further reading

Wittgenstein's two main works are the *Tractatus Logico-Philosophicus*, which is available in two English translations (each of which has its advocates; I have used the one by Pears and McGuinness here), and the *Philosophical Investigations* (*PI*), which was first published posthumously in 1953 (in an English translation by G.E.M. Anscombe). In focusing on the *Investigations* here, I have used the second edition of 1958. Sections 363–402 of part I are the main sections on imagination, and section xi of part II contains his remarks on seeing-as. Other works which include material that later found its way into the *Investigations*, and to which I have referred here, are the two volumes of *Remarks on the Philosophy of Psychology* (*RPP*), and the two volumes of *Last Writings on the Philosophy of Psychology* (*LW*).

McGinn (1997) can be recommended as an introduction to the central themes of the *Investigations*, and Budd (1989) to Wittgenstein's philosophy of psychology. McGinn discusses the private language argument in chapter 4, the attack on the idea of the private mental object in chapter 5, and seeing and seeing-as in chapter 6. Budd discusses seeing aspects in chapter 4 and images in chapter 5. Glock (1996) contains helpful entries on the main concepts and topics in Wittgenstein's philosophy. Hacker (1986) offers an account of both Wittgenstein's early and later philosophy, with chapter 9 on the private language argument. Chapter 5 of Hanfling (1989) is also on the private language argument. The most comprehensive commentary on part I of the *Investigations* is the four volumes by Baker and Hacker (1980, 1985, 1990, 1996 – the last two by Hacker alone), volume 3 of which contains a chapter on the private language argument and a chapter on imagination. Bennett and Hacker (2003, section 6.3) offer a Wittgensteinian critique of work on the imagination by cognitive scientists.

The following works mentioned in previous chapters contain accounts of Wittgenstein: Bell (1987), Brann (1991, part I, chapter 3, section D), Strawson ([1971] 1974), Warnock (1976, part II) and White (1990, chapter 10). Mulhall (2001) is devoted to the topic of seeing aspects.

Part Two
Creativity

CHAPTER 6

Creativity and originality

> The very essence of the creative is its novelty, and hence we have no standard by which to judge it.
>
> (Carl R. Rogers, *On Becoming a Person*, 1961)

In Part One we explored a number of different conceptions of imagination. The imagination is often seen as the source of creative activity, and this came out at various points, most notably in considering Kant's conception of the transcendental imagination. But what *is* creativity, and how – if at all – can it be explained? What is the relationship between imagination and creativity? These are the questions that we address in Part Two. We will focus on the issues of the definition and explanation of creativity in this chapter, and turn to the role of the imagination in creativity in the next chapter.

This chapter has three main sections. In the first we will consider how creativity might be defined, and in the second and third we will explore the question of the explanation of creativity. As Carl Rogers's remark (quoted above) suggests, it is tempting to think that creativity not only involves originality but also, precisely because of this, cannot be judged or explained. On this view, creativity is not a mystery whose solution has yet to be found, but a mystery whose solution is impossible. We will look at a recent attempt by Margaret Boden to explain creativity, drawing on computational psychology, and David Novitz's critique of her account. Novitz offers his own 'recombination theory', and we will consider this theory and some of the problems that it raises too.

The definition of creativity

What is creativity? Clearly, whether creativity can be explained depends on what is meant by 'creativity'. At the same time, however, as we will see, the definitions of creativity that have been given are often motivated by views of what can be explained.

Creativity as novel combination

If asked to give a dictionary definition of 'creativity', what would you say?

ACTIVITY

'Creativity' means the ability to create, where 'create', according to the *Concise Oxford Dictionary* (6th edn), means 'bring into existence, give rise to; originate'. 'Creation' is sometimes understood as producing something out of nothing, as when theologians speak of God's creation. But in its ordinary use, it just means the production of something new or original out of existing material.

DISCUSSION

If 'creation' just means the production of something new out of what already exists, then there is an obvious model of how this occurs – the model provided by empiricist associationism. On this view, as we saw in chapter 3, new ideas are simply the result of combining or rearranging existing ideas. Take the case of imagining a winged horse. Here I simply combine the idea of a horse with the idea of wings. Creativity would seem to be both easy to define and simple to explain.

The assumption has been made here that imagining a winged horse *is* creative. But is this right? If not, then what (if anything) might make it creative?

ACTIVITY

The idea of a winged horse, understood as combining the idea of a horse with the idea of wings, is something that can be accidentally or mechanically generated. But you might feel that the mere accidental or mechanical generation of something would not be regarded as a creative act. Of course, winged horses do not exist in nature, and so there is a sense in which an idea or image of such a being is our own creation. But the key issue, I think, concerns the role that such an idea or image plays. If a combination of two or more things is to count as creative, then – so it might be argued – it must have some kind of value or meaning. What might give the idea of a winged horse value? If we call the winged horse we imagine 'Pegasus', say, and tell a story about him in which his winged nature is an intrinsic part, then our imagining takes on a more creative character. In the story of Pegasus in Greek mythology, for example, the combination of horse and wings is neither arbitrary nor accidental, and to this extent the invention of Pegasus might be regarded as creative.

DISCUSSION

Arguably, then, the mere combining of two or more things is not in itself creative. A distinction needs to be drawn between valuable or meaningful combinations and arbitrary or meaningless combinations. Merely adding the idea of wings to the idea of a horse is not creative unless it has significance in some wider context. So creativity seems to require not just novelty or originality, but also value or meaning. But is this generally true, or is there something else required too? We will look further at this question in the next section. I have also taken the simplest kind of example in introducing the issue – combining the idea of a horse with the idea of wings to generate the idea of a winged horse. But do all cases of creativity involve combination? We will turn to this question in the next but one section, and it will form a main theme in the rest of the chapter.

Creativity as exemplary originality

In chapter 1 we considered the question of the definition of 'imagining', and examined Berys Gaut's account in section 2 of his paper, 'Creativity and imagination' (the main argument of which will be discussed in the next chapter). In section 1 he offers a definition of creativity, which we will look at here.

ACTIVITY

Read section 1 of 'Creativity and imagination' (Reading 6), and answer the following questions:

1 What is the widest sense of 'creative', according to Gaut, and what does he suggest is its core sense?

2 What is Gaut's main point in the second and third paragraphs?

3 Do you agree that the two examples Gaut gives in the fourth paragraph do not show creativity?

4 What is the third condition that Gaut thinks is needed for genuine creativity? Is he right?

5 How, then, does Gaut define 'creativity'? How convincing do you find his account?

DISCUSSION

1 In its widest sense, according to Gaut, 'creativity' involves the bringing into being of something new, understood as including 'creative

destruction'. But in its core sense, he suggests, it means the production of something 'original', which he glosses as 'saliently new'.

2   Gaut's main point in the second and third paragraphs is that creativity involves making something that is not just original but also valuable. Originality may have value in itself, but this is not the only source of value. When we talk of the creativity exhibited by Picasso and Braque in their Cubist paintings, for example, we have in mind not just the originality but also the artistic merit of the paintings. The production of an art work that is merely original but has little artistic merit, Gaut argues, is not regarded as genuinely creative.

3   In the first case, insofar as I had no intention to produce a work of art, Gaut is surely right that I did not act creatively. In the second case, I certainly intend to produce something original and valuable, so to this extent we might be more inclined to describe my successful act as creative. But the mere mechanical generation of the result is not itself creative; if there is creativity involved here, then it is located more in the recognition or development of this result. We will consider an example of such a mechanical search procedure – Goodyear's discovery of vulcanization (which Gaut mentions in a footnote to this paragraph) – later in this chapter.

4   Gaut specifies the third condition as 'flair'. If 'flair' just means whatever it is that turns the production of something original and valuable into creation, then the claim that flair is needed may be true but trivial. But what the specification does do is indicate the importance of *how* something is produced. As his two examples suggest, the making of something does not count as creative if it is done unintentionally or mechanically. When we talk of making something by 'flair', we mean more than just producing something intentionally and non-mechanically; the term gives expression to the kind of thing that we might feel is also required for an act to be creative.

5   According to Gaut, 'creativity' (in its core sense) means the making of something original and valuable by flair. If creativity involves bringing something new into being, then originality would seem to be of its essence, although there is more to say about what exactly 'originality' means. But as we saw in the last section, originality on its own is insufficient: the product of a creative act must also have value. Furthermore, if we take the two examples Gaut gives in the fourth paragraph seriously, then the process too must meet a certain condition. According to Gaut, the process must

exhibit 'flair'. There is more to say about both value and flair as well, but we might be inclined to agree with Gaut that something like originality, value and flair are the three 'vital ingredients' of creativity.

In the second paragraph, Gaut refers to Kant. We looked at Kant's first *Critique*, the *Critique of Pure Reason*, in chapter 4. But Kant also wrote two other *Critiques*, the *Critique of Practical Reason*, on ethics, and the *Critique of Judgement*, the first half of which concerns aesthetics. In sections 46–50 of the latter, Kant offers an account of genius, the genius being someone who exhibits exceptional creativity. Essentially, Kant defines genius in terms of 'exemplary originality', and what he means by 'exemplary' is something that sets an example or provides a model for others to follow. Gaut appeals to Kant in arguing that creativity requires value as well as originality. But what Kant means by 'exemplary originality' is not quite the same as the 'originality plus value' of which Gaut speaks. If something is exemplary, then in serving as a model for others, it possesses value. But there may be other ways for a product to possess value, so 'originality plus value' covers more than 'exemplary originality'. If this is right, then Gaut's specification of 'flair' can be seen as a recognition of the need to restrict the definition of creativity further to bring it more into line with Kant's conception of genius. For, it might be suggested, appreciating the 'exemplariness' of a work of art may well involve appreciating the 'flair' with which it was produced. Take the first case Gaut describes in the fourth paragraph. Flailing around on a canvas in a dark room is not a good example to follow to produce a stunningly good abstract painting: at least 99.9 per cent of the time it will not work. So too, in the second case, mechanically producing something would not count as 'exemplary' in Kant's sense. To this extent, then, Kant's characterization of genius as requiring exemplary originality already captures what Gaut wants.

Most people would agree, I think, that creativity involves the production of something that is both original and valuable (in some sense of those terms). Yet, as we have seen, something else seems to be required too. Kant talks of 'exemplary originality' and Gaut talks of 'flair', and both accounts might be viewed as attempts to fill out or go beyond the condition of 'value'. But there are also attempts to fill out or go beyond the condition of 'originality'. One such attempt is made by Margaret Boden, to whose work we now turn.

Psychological and historical creativity

In 1990 Margaret Boden published *The Creative Mind* (with a second edition in 2004), in which she offers answers to the questions of what creativity is and how it can be explained – and, in particular, explained by psychology. In 1994 she published a paper entitled 'What is creativity?', which summarizes her account. We will focus on the latter here and, in particular, on the first three sections, which are included as Reading 3.

ACTIVITY

Read the first thirteen paragraphs of the first section of Boden's paper, 'The definition of creativity', and then answer the following questions:

1. After introducing her paper in the first three paragraphs, Boden goes on to criticize what she calls the 'combination theory'. What is this theory, and what are the two objections she raises to it in the fifth and sixth paragraphs?
2. Neither of these first two objections constitutes her main objection to the combination theory. How does she state her main objection?
3. What is Boden's distinction between psychological (P-) and historical (H-) creativity?
4. Which of the two types of creativity is Boden interested in, and why?
5. What is Boden's position on the issue of value?

DISCUSSION

1. According to what Boden calls the 'combination theory', creativity is defined in terms of the 'novel combination of old ideas'. What she has in mind is the empiricist model discussed above, and just as I did, she objects to such an account for ignoring value. She also objects that such an account typically fails to explain how the novel combinations come about.
2. Boden's main objection to the combination theory is that it can only explain, at best, novel ideas that *did not* happen before, not novel ideas that *could not* have happened before.
3. Psychological (P-) creativity occurs when someone has a valuable idea that could not have arisen before in their mind. Historical (H-) creativity occurs when someone has a valuable idea that not only could not have arisen before in their mind but also did not arise before in anyone else's mind. H-creativity is thus a species of P-creativity.
4. Boden is interested in P-creativity. H-creativity is a matter for historians and cannot be systematically explained – except insofar as all H-creative ideas are P-creative ideas, the explanation of which is Boden's concern.

5   Boden certainly holds that creative ideas must be valuable, but their value is not something that she thinks it is the task of psychology to explain – although she does admit that 'criteria of valuation sometimes enter into the originating process itself'.

ACTIVITY

Read the rest of the first section of Boden's paper, 'The definition of creativity', and then answer the following questions:

1   What is it to say that an idea 'could not' have arisen before, according to Boden?
2   What is Boden's objection to Chomsky's conception of linguistic creativity?
3   What, then, is Boden's distinction between what she calls mere 'first-time novelty' and 'radical originality'?
4   How does Boden's account of creativity compare with Gaut's?

DISCUSSION

1   An idea 'could not' have arisen before, according to Boden, if there was no 'generative system' within which the idea could have been generated in accordance with the rules of that system.
2   Boden's objection is to Chomsky's use of the word 'creativity'. While an infinite number of new sentences can be generated by the rules of language, Boden does not regard this as genuine creativity.
3   'First-time novelty' refers to what, as a matter of fact, occurs for the first time, but is generated by the same set of rules as are other things. 'Radical originality' refers to what *could not* have arisen before, in the sense that there was no generative system before, by the rules of which it could have been generated.
4   Both Gaut and Boden are concerned with what is needed over and above originality (i.e. mere novelty) and value for the production of something to be genuinely creative. According to Gaut, this is 'flair'. According to Boden, it is 'radical originality'. It would be tempting to put the two accounts together, and to suggest that what 'flair' involves is the establishment of a new generative system. But this is hardly what Gaut means, although it might be taken to include it.

If we bring in Kant's conception of genius, too, then we have three accounts of creativity, all of which define creativity in terms of originality, value and something else – 'exemplariness', 'flair' or 'radical originality'. Let us keep these possibilities in mind in turning now to the issue of how creativity is to be explained.

Boden's theory of creativity and Novitz's critique

Gaut did not expand on what he meant by 'flair', which almost seems a term for that mysterious *je ne sais quoi* that turns mere valuable originality into creativity. And if Boden and Kant are right that genuine (or exceptional) creativity requires the establishment of new rules or models, then the prospects for explaining creativity appear bleak. Indeed, if something can only be explained by showing how it was generated by the rules of a system, then it looks as if the establishment of a new set of rules or generative system is impossible to explain. We will look here at Boden's response to this problem, before considering some objections to her account that have been raised by David Novitz.

Boden's theory

The second section of Boden's paper is entitled 'Exploring and transforming conceptual spaces'. A 'conceptual space' is essentially what she had called a 'generative system' in the previous section, and the idea of a conceptual space is offered as the key to the explanation of creativity.

Read the second section of Boden's paper, and answer the following questions:

ACTIVITY

1. How does Boden define a 'conceptual space', and how is the idea meant to be the key to the explanation of creativity?
2. What is Boden's point in taking the example of the Mad Tea-Party from Lewis Carroll's *Alice's Adventures in Wonderland*?
3. Boden goes on to discuss the case of the development of post-Renaissance western music, and mentions two composers here, J.S. Bach and Schoenberg. On the basis of this discussion (paragraphs 7 to 10), and her earlier account of the distinction between first-time novelty and radical

originality, which of them would she regard as the more creative? Do you agree?

4   What is the example of Mendeleyev's periodic table meant to show?

5   Boden identifies two ways of transforming a conceptual space. What are these two ways, and what examples does she give to illustrate each?

DISCUSSION

1   Boden defines a 'conceptual space' as 'the generative system that underlies [a given domain of thinking] and defines a certain range of possibilities: chess moves, or molecular structures, or jazz melodies'. A conceptual space, in other words, is a rule-governed system whose rules and principles determine what can and cannot be done within it. Boden's key idea is, then, that creativity involves the exploration and transformation of conceptual spaces.

2   The Mad Tea-Party is offered as a simple example of a conceptual space – governed by the rule of moving round the table when things get dirty or used up. But, as Alice realized, it has its limitations. An exploration of that space soon establishes what is wrong, requiring a revision or addition to the rule – i.e. a transformation of the space – which the creatures, of course, seem not to recognize.

3   The implication is that Schoenberg is the genuinely creative composer, since it was he who transformed the 'generative system' of tonal harmony. ('Generative system' is the better term to use than 'conceptual space' in the case of music. Boden just uses 'space', as well as 'generative system', in the relevant passage. But the underlying idea is the same.) Yet many people would regard Bach as the more creative – as the real genius here.

4   Mendeleyev's periodic table is offered as another example of a conceptual space whose initial articulation led to an exploration of that space and, through that, to new discoveries. Exploration of a conceptual space is itself a form of creativity, according to Boden, but the creativity involved here is not as radical as it is in transforming a conceptual space.

5   A conceptual space can be transformed either by dropping or by negating one of its governing rules or constraints. Boden gives two examples of the former: Schoenberg's dropping the home-key constraint in developing atonal music, and the dropping of Euclid's fifth axiom, the notorious parallels postulate, in creating non-Euclidean geometry. Kekulé's discovery of the benzene ring is given as an example of negating a constraint, in this case the assumption that all organic molecules are based

on strings of carbon atoms, understood topologically as an open curve. Kekulé's famous dream of a snake biting its own tail led him to conceive of the benzene molecule as a closed curve.

To bring out Boden's central – and perhaps most controversial – idea, let us focus here on the case of music. Does Boden really want to claim that Schoenberg was more creative than Bach? She does not deny that Bach was creative. She admits that exploration of a conceptual space or generative system is one form of creativity and can lead to novel ideas, such as new forms of harmonic modulation. But, as she put it, 'exploring a conceptual space is one thing: transforming it is another'. The implication is clear: Bach may exhibit creativity, but it is of an inferior kind to that exhibited by Schoenberg in moving to the atonal system. What Schoenberg did was to transform the system of tonal music by dropping one of its governing principles: the home-key constraint.

Boden's account of the case of music suggests, however, that there is more to radical creativity than simply changing one or more of the rules of a system. That system needs to be thoroughly explored first before a transformation can be effective. The potential of the system needs in some sense to have been exhausted, first, to realize what its limitations are and, second, to understand its rules sufficiently for making appropriate changes. If this is right, then we can see how Boden thinks that radical creativity is superior to mere first-time novelty for it presupposes the production of first-time novelty, and then goes further – effecting what amounts to a conceptual (or generative) revolution. Schoenberg is a good case in point, for he went through a rich tonal period, as exemplified in the high romanticism of *Verklärte Nacht* and the *Gurrelieder*, before his atonal music emerged. This is not to endorse the claim, though, that Schoenberg exhibited greater creativity than Bach.

Creativity and computational psychology

What implications does Boden's conception have for the question of the explanation of creativity? At the end of her second section, Boden writes that 'in calling an idea creative one should specify the particular set of generative principles with respect to which it is impossible'. The specification of these principles, she goes on to argue in the third section of her paper, entitled 'The relevance of computational psychology', is something that computers can help us with. For what we can do with a computer is simulate the relevant generative system and see just what it can and cannot do.

ACTIVITY

Read the third section of Boden's paper. What are the four 'Lovelace questions' that Boden distinguishes, and what is her answer to each one? Which is the key question for Boden, and do you agree with her answer?

DISCUSSION

As Boden reports it, Lady Lovelace was notoriously dismissive of the claim that computers could have anything to do with creativity. But Boden suggests that we distinguish four questions, which she calls 'Lovelace questions' in honour of Lady Lovelace. The first question is whether computers and computational psychology can help us understand human creativity, and to this question Boden's answer is a resounding 'Yes'. The second and third questions concern whether computers could ever *appear to be* creative or *appear to recognize* creativity; and to these questions Boden's answer is a more qualified 'Yes'. The fourth question (which is the one that Lady Lovelace had primarily in mind) is whether computers could ever *be* creative, and this question Boden leaves aside on the ground that it is a philosophical and not a scientific question. Boden's main interest is in the first question, and given her conception of creativity as involving the exploration and transformation of a conceptual space, we might agree with her answer – to the extent that computers can simulate the relevant conceptual space.

ACTIVITY

Bearing in mind what was said earlier in discussing the definition of creativity, do you think that computers could ever *be* creative?

DISCUSSION

If Gaut is right and creativity requires originality, value and flair, then we might feel that computers could never *be* creative. For even if a computer could generate something that is both original and valuable, could it ever produce it by 'flair'? Perhaps flair is too strong a requirement, but if we agree with Gaut that a creative act must be both intentional and non-mechanical, then this would seem to rule out computer creativity. Of course, it might be objected that this begs the question *against* computer creativity, but most people would presumably agree with Gaut that the two cases he describes in the fourth paragraph of section 1 of his paper do not exhibit creativity. On Kant's conception of creativity, too, computers could not *be* creative, since what they generate could never be 'exemplary' in the sense he had in mind. According to Boden, creativity requires originality and value, too, but the additional requirement that she specifies – radical originality – would seem to leave open the question of whether computers could *be* creative. If a computer could produce something original and valuable, then why could it not also produce something radically original and valuable?

Clearly, what answer we give to the philosophical question of whether computers could *be* creative depends on our conception of creativity. However, even if we take creativity to require 'flair', we might still agree with Boden that computers can help us understand creativity to the extent that there are conceptual spaces involved, which can be simulated by a computer program. Take an idea that is both original and valuable. What determines whether it is also radically creative? According to Boden, if that idea cannot be generated by any existing conceptual space, then it counts as radically creative. Furthermore, if we can specify a transformation of one of those conceptual spaces, by means of which the idea *can* be generated, then we have an explanation of why it counts as radically creative. Simulating conceptual spaces by a computer program thus provides a way of identifying and explaining creativity. In the rest of her paper and in her book (1990, 2004), Boden discusses a range of computer simulations to support her theory. The details need not concern us here. We can agree that her conception of creativity is ideally suited to provide a role for computational psychology. The philosophical question is whether that conception is adequate.

Novitz's critique of Boden

In 1999 David Novitz published a paper entitled 'Creativity and constraint', criticizing Boden's conception of creativity and offering his own theory. We will consider his own theory below, after looking first at his critique of Boden's account. He outlines that account in the first three sections of his paper and then, in section IV, raises three objections, which he articulates by presenting what he claims are counter-examples.

Read the first five paragraphs (up to 'exploration of such spaces') of section IV of Novitz's paper, 'Computers and human beings', which, together with the first half of section V, is included as Reading 4. What is the objection that

ACTIVITY

Novitz raises here to Boden's theory? (Novitz talks, in the first paragraph, of 'Boden's constraint', by which he means her claim that the ascription of creativity always involves reference to some specific conceptual space.)

DISCUSSION   Novitz's first objection concerns Boden's thesis that radical creativity involves the transformation of a conceptual space after prior exploration of it. Novitz argues, on the contrary, that too close an involvement with a given conceptual space may actually – for social reasons such as position in a community – inhibit its transformation. And as a matter of fact, there are many people, normally regarded as creative, who seem not to have explored the relevant conceptual space before their creative activities. He gives the example of Henri Matisse, whose new approach to the use of colour in painting seems to have been aimed – at least, if his own account of it is right – solely at producing what he himself found satisfying. So too, Novitz suggests, it was Pablo Picasso's fascination with African tribal carvings that played a greater role in the development of Cubism than any intention to transform the existing artistic tradition through prior exploration of it.

ACTIVITY   How convincing is this first objection to Boden's account? How might one reply on Boden's behalf?

DISCUSSION   The objection may be convincing on one reading of Boden's thesis. As I stated it, Boden's thesis is that radical creativity involves the transformation of a conceptual space after prior exploration of it. This way of formulating it leaves it open whether a radically creative person has to have explored that space for themselves. Is it not enough that that space *has been* explored – whether by them or by others? We might require that the radically creative person is at least aware that that space has been explored, but do they have to have actively explored every detail of it for themselves? Perhaps the tradition that they end up transforming has become so tired and stale that it is obvious that its limits have been reached and its potential exhausted.

Recall the distinction that Boden drew, towards the end of section 1 of her paper, between whether an idea is creative or not and how an idea actually arose. Boden's main concern is with the first question. All that is required for an idea to be creative is that there *is* an appropriate conceptual space that has been explored and then transformed. Whether the person in whose mind the idea actually arose explored the space thoroughly themselves is only relevant to the second question. Perhaps this constitutes a qualification to what Boden herself meant, rather than a straightforward defence, but it does seem the more reasonable position and still in keeping with her central aim.

Novitz's second objection, however, goes deeper, raising a question about the very idea of a conceptual space.

ACTIVITY

Read paragraphs 6 to 9 of section IV of Novitz's paper, and answer the following questions:

1 To what thesis is the case of Jenner's development of the smallpox vaccine intended as a counter-example?
2 Is it a genuine counter-example?
3 In paragraph 7 Novitz formulates a dilemma for Boden's account. What is this dilemma?
4 Can Boden give a different response to the one that Novitz suggests in paragraph 8?
5 What is the example of Edison's invention of the phonograph meant to show?

DISCUSSION

1 The case is intended as a counter-example to Boden's thesis that radical creativity requires the existence of an appropriate conceptual space.
2 The case does not seem to be a knock-down counter-example. Although there may have been no previous conceptual space involving the idea of vaccination, there were various conceptual spaces without which the new conceptual space could not have been developed – concerning, for example, infection and the fact that one could only get some diseases once. Certainly, Novitz's claim that Jenner developed a new conceptual space *ab initio* (i.e. from scratch) seems too strong. But this brings us on to the issues raised by paragraph 7.
3 The dilemma concerns the specification of a conceptual space. Either a conceptual space is specified so loosely that computational psychology cannot be employed in explaining creativity. Or a conceptual space is specified so tightly that there will be many counter-examples to Boden's account.

4   Novitz suggests that Boden would respond, in effect, by tackling the dilemma by its second horn, simply excluding the cases that Novitz thinks are counter-examples. But she could also tackle the dilemma by its first horn. Even if a conceptual space is a loose cluster of ideas, there may still be value in employing computational psychology. It is just that a number of simulations may then have to be run – offering alternative systematizations of the conceptual spaces – to help us understand what creativity there is.

5   Edison's invention of the phonograph is offered as a second counter-example, but it does not, I think, raise any further issues.

Novitz is right to probe at just what is meant by 'conceptual space', and there is a danger that the term is made so vague as no longer to be helpful, but some flexibility is a good thing and a way can then be found to respond to Novitz's criticism.

Novitz's final objection concerns the case of Goodyear's discovery of vulcanization (which was mentioned above), and he concludes with a summary of his three objections.

ACTIVITY

Read the rest of section IV of Novitz's paper (paragraphs 10 to 15), and answer the following questions:

1   To what thesis is Goodyear's discovery of vulcanization intended as a counter-example?
2   Is it a genuine counter-example?
3   How might Boden respond?
4   How can Boden's theory be both too exclusive and too inclusive?

DISCUSSION

1   The case is intended as a counter-example to the thesis that radical creativity occurs whenever there is a transformation of a conceptual space.

2   Here the description of the case is crucial, and there is a lot of slippage in what it is that Novitz is calling 'creative'. Distinctions need to be drawn – between different senses of 'idea' as well as between the creativity of an idea, of the development of an idea, of a person, of a particular action of a person, of a discovery or invention, and so on. Boden talks mainly of *ideas* being creative, though she understands 'idea' in a very broad sense (see paragraph 7 of the first section of her paper). Novitz talks indiscriminately

of the idea of vulcanization, Goodyear's development of that idea, the discovery of vulcanization, and Goodyear's invention, all as candidates for the ascription of 'creative' (whether truly or falsely). The intuition underlying Novitz's account is surely right. The mere accidental or mechanical generation of the result is not creative (as noted in discussing Gaut's definition above). It is what we do with that result that is important. So if by 'idea' here we mean the mere stumbling on an occurrence of vulcanization, then this is not creative. But if by 'idea' we mean the development of the whole conception of vulcanization, then this *is* creative. Goodyear may not have been as creative a person as, say, Picasso or Einstein; but it may reasonably be claimed that his development of the conception of vulcanization was creative, precisely because it transformed our understanding of rubber.

3 Boden might stress the point I have just made – that on her understanding of 'idea', it covers the development of the whole conception of vulcanization. There is nothing in her work to suggest that she would regard the mere stumbling on an occurrence of vulcanization as creative; indeed, the very centrality of her notion of a conceptual space rules this out. What makes an 'idea' creative is not the mere possibility of its leading to a transformation of a conceptual space, but its actual role in that transformation.

4 According to Novitz, Boden's theory both excludes some things that ought to count as radically creative and includes some things that ought not so to count. There is nothing inconsistent in Novitz's allegation, then, although we might disagree with it.

Being fair to flair

Boden's main thesis – at least insofar as it is the target of Novitz's second and third objections – might be summarized thus: radical creativity occurs if and only if there is transformation of a conceptual space (which we can take to presuppose prior exploration of it, whether or not this is done thoroughly by the person exhibiting the creativity). Such transformation is thus seen as both a necessary and a sufficient condition for radical creativity. Novitz's objections can then be summed up as the claim that such transformation is neither a necessary nor a sufficient condition for radical creativity. It is not a necessary condition, as the Jenner example is intended to show; and it is not a sufficient condition, as the Goodyear example is intended to show. (This is another way of saying that Boden's theory is both too exclusive and too inclusive, respectively.) The Goodyear example does not, I think, show that transformation of a conceptual space is not a sufficient condition for radical creativity, once care is taken in specifying what it is that is radically creative, and assuming that the result has value. The Jenner example is harder to deal with, for Novitz is right that there is a vagueness in the notion of a conceptual space. It seems reasonable to claim that transformation is not a necessary condition – that there are other ways in which radical creativity can be exhibited – for example, in explorations of a conceptual space that reveal its unexpected depths or rich resources.

As far as this latter claim is concerned, Boden does concede something to the objection. In the last section of her paper (not included in Reading 3), where she considers the question of how creativity might be measured, she writes:

> It is significant, here, that some musicians regard Mozart as a greater composer than Haydn *even though* they allow that Haydn was more adventurous, more ready to transform contemporary musical styles. Mozart's superiority, on this view, lay in his fuller exploration (and tweaking) of musical space, his ability to amaze us by showing us what unsuspected glories lie within this familiar space. Whether this musical judgment is faithful to Haydn's and Mozart's work is irrelevant. The point is that it is one which can intelligibly be made. It follows that no creativity metric could be adequate that ignored structural exploration, focusing only on structural transformation.
>
> (1994a, 114)

Boden does not endorse the view that Mozart was more creative than Haydn, but she does allow that it is 'intelligible'.

Boden seems to be suggesting here that musical judgement is essentially a matter of assessing how well a musical space is explored and/or transformed. This suggestion reflects a purist view that might well be questioned. Musical composition does not simply involve exploring and transforming musical spaces, but is typically undertaken with other aims in mind too. Consider Haydn's *The Seven Last Words of our Saviour on the Cross* (which exists in orchestral, choral, string quartet and piano versions), a series of penitential meditations, or the music that Mozart wrote for *Don Giovanni*, with its sophisticated characterization and tragicomedy, and *The Magic Flute*, with its masonic symbolism. These are unquestionably works of genius, yet their genius lies in the matching of the music to the extra-musical themes. If we still want to speak of conceptual spaces, then it might be suggested that what both Haydn and Mozart do in these works is bring together a number of different conceptual and musical spaces. Their astonishing creativity lies more in the combination or synthesis of these spaces than in the exploration or transformation of just one of them.

If this is right, then it returns us to the point from which we began our consideration of Boden's theory. Creativity requires originality and value, but also something else. Boden suggests 'radical originality', but it may be more important to specify a condition concerning the *way* in which the creative result is achieved. Gaut talks of 'flair', which may not be the ideal word here, but it is significant that Novitz uses it too in summing up his three objections to Boden's account. What is important is not just the 'flair' involved in the production of the relevant work, but the inspiration it provides for others, as Kant emphasized in requiring the work to be 'exemplary'. Of course, flair or exemplariness may be less easy for a computer to simulate in 'explaining' creativity, but this is no doubt a conclusion that many would be happy to accept. In the end, perhaps, one might well wonder whether Boden's theory was driven too much by the concern to find a role for computational psychology.

Novitz's recombination theory

How might we do better justice to such cases as that of Mozart? Novitz offers his own theory in section V of his paper, which he calls the 'recombination theory'. He dispenses with the idea of a conceptual space on the grounds that, as he puts it, 'people may be radically creative even when they do not transform anything as well-defined as a conceptual space' (1999, 76). Instead, he returns to the combination theory that he suggests Boden was too swift to dismiss at the beginning of her account (p.175 above), and modifies it.

Creativity and recombination

Read the extract from section V of Novitz's paper that is included in Reading 4, and answer the following questions:

ACTIVITY

1. As we have seen, creativity tends to be defined in terms of originality, value plus something else. Does Novitz's definition fit this model? If there is a 'something else', what is it?

2. Does Novitz's definition succeed in including the Jenner case (which Novitz argued Boden's theory did not)?

3. Does it succeed in excluding the Goodyear case (as Novitz conceives it)?

4. If creativity requires recombination on Novitz's view, how can aspect perception be creative?

5. Is Novitz right to add the qualification 'or would have been' in the specification of his second – surprise – condition?

6. We talk of 'creating' a fuss, a disturbance, a mess, as Novitz admits. Why is this not real creativity, according to Novitz? Is he right?

7. Can you think of any counter-examples or objections to Novitz's own theory?

DISCUSSION

1. Novitz also specifies three conditions. His second condition captures the originality requirement and his third condition the value requirement. His first condition provides a fairly minimal 'something else'. Creativity requires a recombination of things (ideas, techniques or objects) which – however it actually arose – is then *deliberately used* to satisfy the second and third conditions.

2. According to Novitz, Boden's theory excluded the Jenner case because there was no conceptual space that Jenner transformed. But Jenner did deliberately bring together a number of things in developing the idea of vaccination, which was both surprising and valuable. So it satisfies Novitz's definition.

3. As Novitz conceives the Goodyear case, the discovery of vulcanization was accidental although it led to transformation of our understanding of rubber. On Boden's theory, it comes out as radically creative, but it is unclear that it would be excluded by Novitz's theory, since the first condition allows chance recombination and Goodyear does seem to have then deliberately capitalized on his discovery. (As we will see, Novitz recognizes the problem in a later paper.)

4. Although aspect perception does not involve a recombination of the physical parts of what is seen, Novitz does allow that it involves bringing

into play other (ideational) things such as beliefs and descriptions. So it can be creative.

5   I have suggested that Novitz's second condition captures the originality requirement. But he specifies it in terms of the result being 'surprising' rather than original. Something is 'surprising' *to* someone, so if there is no one (appropriate) around to be surprised, and a creative work had to *be* surprising, then it could not count as creative. But this seems counterintuitive: whether a work is creative depends on its character, and is creative whether or not there is anyone around to appreciate it. It is just that, *were there* to be appropriate people around, they would be surprised.

6   This is where the value condition comes in. Insofar as the fuss, disturbance or mess made has no value, it does not count as creative, according to Novitz. Although we do speak of 'creating' as a kind of making, the term is also used in opposition to 'destroying', and certainly in aesthetic contexts carries connotations of value. The problem is in specifying just what this value is – or how much of it is required.

7   Consider the attack on the World Trade Center and the Pentagon on 11 September 2001. Was this creative? The attack was meticulously planned and co-ordinated, and it was undoubtedly surprising to almost the entire population of the world. Although it caused several thousand deaths and widespread anguish and outrage, it was intended to be of real value to some people. It seems, therefore, to fulfil Novitz's definition; but his remarks suggest that he would not wish to count it as creative. He might argue that it will prove to have been thoroughly harmful in the long term; but might it not also prove to have had at least some beneficial consequences for some people?

In discussing the similar case of the development of nuclear weapons, Novitz comes to the conclusion that this *was* creative, since it was intended to save the free world (1999, 78–9). But equally, those who planned the attack of September 11th might argue that it was intended to save the Islamic world, and their *intention* is what is crucial in deciding whether the attack was creative on Novitz's definition. So it is not clear that his definition captures what he wants, and there remain difficulties with the value condition.

Creativity and value

In a paper published four years later entitled 'Explanations of creativity' (2003), Novitz returns to the topic and modifies his recombination theory. He recognizes that his earlier theory does not sufficiently exclude the Goodyear case, and that to do so he needs to say more about the act of recombination itself. As he puts it, 'It is the intrinsic cleverness, brilliance, delightfulness, or beauty – that is, the intrinsic value – of the act that is missing in such a case and that inclines us to think of the recombination as ordinary or banal, hence as less than creative' (2003, 186). According to his revised theory, then, an act is creative if and only if it involves:

1 the intentional or chance, yet intrinsically valuable, recombination of existing clusters of ideas, techniques, or objects – where this recombination is subsequently deliberately used or deployed

2 in ways that result in something that is (or would have been) surprising to – hence, not predicted by – a given population; and, furthermore,

3 in ways that are intended to be, and are either actually or potentially, of instrumental value to some people.

(2003, 191, n.15)

ACTIVITY

1 What is the difference between this revised theory and Novitz's original theory?

2 Is it an improvement? Are there still problems, or any new ones?

DISCUSSION

1 The first condition now includes the specification that the recombination be 'intrinsically valuable', while the third condition qualifies the value involved here as 'instrumental value'.

2 The revised theory does now exclude the Goodyear case (as Novitz understands it) – depending on what is meant by 'intrinsic value'. All that Novitz says about 'intrinsic value' is what has just been quoted: he has in mind the 'intrinsic cleverness, brilliance, delightfulness, or beauty' of the act. This offers one way of expanding on what Gaut calls 'flair', but further specification might still be requested. More problematically, however, the revised theory still leaves itself open to the other objection I raised – that the attack of 11 September 2001 also comes out as creative, which is not

what Novitz would want. For the attack was undoubtedly cleverly conceived and planned, and so would count as having 'intrinsic value'.

Novitz recognizes the main objection that might be raised to his theory, even in its revised form – the difficulty, as he puts it, 'that a single, intrinsically valuable, recombination can be intended both to harm and to benefit different groups of people' (2003, 187). He is thinking of the development of nuclear weapons, which he still wants to argue was creative, on the grounds that it was *intended* to be beneficial. But so too was the attack of September 11th – for the Islamic world. Novitz writes that 'there are robust moral constraints on creativity, for an intentionally immoral act – one that is designed to hurt and to harm – cannot also be a creative act' (ibid.). This suggests that he would deny that the attack exhibited creativity. However, whether he would deny this or not, what is crucial is that his theory implies that judgements of creativity are dependent on moral evaluations. Yet this seems too strong a position to adopt, since two of us can surely agree on the creativity of an act while disagreeing on its moral implications. We might accept that creative acts must be 'intrinsically valuable', in some such sense as Novitz has in mind, and we might also require that they have 'instrumental value', in some such sense as Kant had in mind in talking of 'exemplariness'. But judgements of creativity are frequently made without moral evaluations, and there seems no reason to demand that they involve them.

Review and preview

1 As the comparison of Gaut's, Kant's and Boden's accounts of creativity suggests, creativity is typically defined in terms of originality, value and something else – 'flair' (Gaut), 'exemplariness' (Kant) or 'radical originality' (Boden).

2 According to Boden, genuine creativity involves the exploration and transformation of a generative system or conceptual space, and hence creativity can only be explained by reference to such systems. In his critique of Boden's theory, Novitz offers a number of counter-examples aimed to show that transformation of a conceptual space is neither a necessary nor a sufficient condition for creativity. Boden might arguably

be defended in the Goodyear case, but both the Jenner and Mozart cases suggest that transformation is not a necessary condition.

3   Novitz offers his own alternative theory of creativity, the recombination theory. However, while it rightly places greater emphasis on combination and value, it might be thought to go too far in requiring judgements of creativity to involve moral evaluation.

4   In previous chapters a number of different conceptions of imagination were explored, revealing some of the ways in which the imagination has been seen as involved in creative activities of the human mind. Having now considered what 'creativity' might mean, and some of the issues that arise in attempting to explain it, we are now in a position to look in more detail at the relationship between imagination and creativity. We turn to this in the next and final chapter.

Further reading

Boden's paper (1994a) is a good place to start in exploring the topic of creativity. As mentioned, it summarizes the account offered in her book (Boden 1990, 2004). The paper is part of a collection edited by Boden (1994b), which contains further essays on creativity, mainly by psychologists.

Although focusing on art, the best collection of philosophical papers on creativity is Gaut and Livingston (2003). This includes both Gaut (2003), which is included as Reading 6, and Novitz (2003).

Creativity is a huge topic of interest among psychologists and cognitive scientists. Sternberg (1999) can be recommended as the most comprehensive survey to date of research in this area.

CHAPTER 7

Creativity and imagination

'Only connect ...'

(E.M. Forster, *Howards End*, 1910)

In the first five chapters of this book we explored some of the interrelationships between imagination, perception and thought, and some of the ways in which the imagination has been appealed to in making sense of human experience. In the last chapter we turned to the issue of creativity, looking in particular at a recent debate over the definition and explanation of creativity. In this final chapter, the various threads will be brought together in considering the question of the relationship between imagination and creativity.

We will focus on Berys Gaut's paper, 'Creativity and imagination' (2003), which directly addresses the issue of the relationship between imagination and creativity, and which is included in full as Reading 6. In section 1 of his paper he offers a definition of creativity, which was considered (and broadly endorsed) in the last chapter, and in section 2 he provides an analysis of imagination, which was examined (more critically) in chapter 1. In sections 3 and 4 he discusses two models of how the imagination works in creative activities, which he calls the 'display' and the 'search' models. We will consider these in the first main section of this chapter, and I will introduce a third model, the 'connection' model. In the second main section these models will be illustrated by taking two examples of the creative imagination at work. We will look, first, at aspect perception – Wittgenstein's account of which was explored in chapter 5 – and, second, at the making of metaphor, which has often been regarded as a paradigm example of creative activity, and which Gaut discusses in section 5 of his paper.

The role of imagination in creativity

What role does the imagination play in creativity? Perhaps surprisingly, the question is rarely addressed explicitly in philosophical discussions.

Sometimes it is just assumed that the imagination *is* creative and that all creativity is due to the imagination. But one direct attempt at answering the question has been made by Berys Gaut in 'Creativity and imagination'. We will examine the account he provides in sections 3 and 4 of his paper here, and consider an alternative account that arguably does greater justice to the kinds of cases discussed both in this book and by Gaut himself.

Creative acts and imagining

In the first two sections of his paper, Gaut explains what he means by 'creativity' and 'imagination'. As we saw in the last chapter, he defines 'creativity' in terms of originality, value and flair. As we saw in chapter 1, he defines 'imagining' as 'thinking of something without alethic or existential commitment, i.e. without commitment to its truth or falsity, existence or non-existence', although I raised doubts about whether this captures all the standard cases in which we talk of 'imagining'.

The third section of his paper is entitled 'Models of creativity'. After a one-page introduction, he considers two models of how the imagination might work in relation to creativity, the 'display' model and the 'search' model. We will examine these two models in the next section. We will look first at his introduction.

ACTIVITY

Read the introduction to section 3 of Gaut's paper (the first four paragraphs), and answer the following questions:

1 Why does Gaut think that a creative act does not require an imagining? How convincing are the purported counter-examples he gives?

2 Why does Gaut think that not every imagining involves a creative act? Is he right?

3 What conclusion does Gaut draw from these considerations?

DISCUSSION

1 Creative acts do not *require* imagining, according to Gaut, because there are cases in which creativity occurs without imagining taking place. The two counter-examples he offers are both cases of creativity supposedly occurring through dreaming rather than imagining – Russell's solving of difficult logical problems and Kekulé's discovery of the benzene ring. (Boden discusses the case of Kekulé in section 2 of her paper, 'What is creativity?' – see Reading 3.) In response to this, however, one might argue

that it is the *rethinking* of what was dreamt that constitutes the creative act. Gaut himself suggests (in the fourth paragraph of section 1) that a creative act must be *intentional*, but merely dreaming something is arguably not intentional. What would definitely be intentional is the rethinking of what is dreamt in solving the relevant problem or making the relevant discovery, and this rethinking would surely count as 'imagining'. If this is right, then Gaut has not established that creative acts do not require imagining.

2   Gaut suggests one sense in which all imaginings are creative, insofar as they 'go beyond what is given to belief and to perception'. But in the sense of 'creativity' that he defined in section 1, not all imaginings are creative, since there are many cases of imagining which involve neither originality nor value (nor presumably 'flair'). Fantasizing, he suggests, is one form of imagining that, in general, cannot be counted as creative for just this reason. Perhaps we might want to stress that there are *degrees* of originality, value and flair, so that all imaginings are creative, at least to a minimal extent. However, in the interesting sense of 'creativity' with which we were concerned in the previous chapter, I am inclined to agree with Gaut that there are many cases of imagining that do not count as genuinely creative.

3   Gaut concludes from his considerations that there are no necessary relations between creativity and imagination, i.e. that creativity neither implies nor is implied by imagination.

We might agree with Gaut that not all imaginings are creative in the broad sense of 'creativity' endorsed in the previous chapter, but it is less clear that there are examples of creative acts that do not involve imagining (in the sense of 'imagining' that Gaut has in mind). Gaut has himself admitted that a creative act must be intentional, which presumably involves *thinking* of something. If, at the same time, that creative act *originates* something, then since that something did not exist prior to the creative act, the thinking that was involved must have been a thinking without commitment to its existence (at the time it was thought of). So, by Gaut's own definition, 'imagining' must have been involved. Even if imagination does not imply creativity, then, creativity may imply imagination.

The display and search models

In sections 3.1 and 3.2 of his paper, Gaut considers two models of how the imagination is involved in creativity and draws two further distinctions.

ACTIVITY

Read section 3.1 of Gaut's paper, and answer the following questions:

1. What is the 'display' model? How might the model be illustrated?
2. What is wrong with the display model, according to Gaut?
3. What is the distinction between passive and active creativity? How does the distinction help Gaut to say what is wrong with the display model?

DISCUSSION

1. According to the 'display' model, the imagination displays the results of creativity to the creative person, but does not itself generate the results, which arise from some other source such as the unconscious. Gaut gives the examples of Russell's and Kekulé's creativity to illustrate the model. In these two cases the creative idea is supposedly generated in dreaming, and if the imagination does then have a role (as indeed it arguably does, though perhaps in a different way), then it is merely to 'display' that idea to consciousness. In the case of Kekulé, for example, what the imagination presumably displays is the image of a snake eating its own tail, which inspired the idea of the ring structure of the benzene molecule.
2. According to Gaut, the display model accords the imagination a merely peripheral role in creativity, which does not do justice to the deeper connection between imagination and creativity that we feel must exist.
3. Passive creativity occurs when a new idea simply 'pops into one's head', such as supposedly occurred in the cases of Russell and Kekulé. Active creativity, on the other hand, involves a deliberate process of trying out different approaches, ideas or solutions until the right one is found. The display model, on Gaut's view, may do justice to passive creativity, but it does not capture the supposed role of imagination in active creativity.

ACTIVITY

Read section 3.2 of Gaut's paper, and answer the following questions:

1. What is the 'search' model? How might this be seen as doing greater justice to the role of the imagination in creative activities than the display model?

2   Why does Gaut think that the search model is misleading about an important aspect of active creativity?

3   What does Kasparov's creativity consist in, according to Gaut?

4   How is Gaut's discussion of Kasparov and Shallow Pink meant to show the need to distinguish between imagination as a *source* of creativity and imagination as a *vehicle* for creativity?

5   What is Gaut's diagnosis of what is wrong in the glorification of the imagination in Romanticism?

6   What is Gaut's final conclusion?

DISCUSSION

1   According to the 'search' model, the imagination is involved in grasping and searching through a range of different possibilities and then selecting the most appropriate one. Since trying out possibilities until the right one is found is just what active creativity involves, the search model is clearly suited to it. To the extent that active creativity is more important than passive creativity, then, the search model does greater justice to the role of the imagination in creative activities than the display model.

2   According to the search model, active creativity involves searching through a range of possibilities and then selecting the best one. But this is something that can be done mechanically, whether by Deep Blue or a 'Shallow Pink', which seems the very opposite of a creative process as Gaut understands it.

3   According to Gaut, Kasparov's creativity consists in *pre-selecting* a much smaller range of possibilities to consider.

4   In Gaut's view, both Kasparov and Shallow Pink use their imaginations in surveying possibilities. But while Kasparov uses his imagination creatively, Shallow Pink does not. This suggests that Kasparov's creativity cannot simply have its *source* in his imagination, since Shallow Pink also uses his imagination in surveying possibilities. Instead, Gaut suggests, Kasparov's imagination serves only as a *vehicle* for his creativity – as the medium in which the possibilities are surveyed.

5   Gaut criticizes the Romantics for failing to respect the distinction between imagination as the source and imagination as the vehicle of creativity. The Romantics saw the imagination as the source of all creativity (and indeed, inspired by Kant, as the source of all human experience), but according to Gaut they should have seen it only as a vehicle of creativity.

6   Gaut's final conclusion is that imagination is involved in the creative process as the vehicle of active creativity.

In section 3 of his paper, then, Gaut draws three key distinctions – between the display and search models, between passive and active creativity, and between the source and vehicle of creativity. The first two distinctions are closely related: the display model captures passive creativity, while the search model does greater justice – though not full justice – to active creativity. The third distinction is introduced to motivate Gaut's central claim that the role of the imagination in creativity is as the vehicle of active creativity. Let us look a little further at the first two distinctions, before turning in the next section to what Gaut says himself (in section 4 of his paper) in clarification of his central claim.

ACTIVITY

Look again at the example of problem-solving in Euclidean geometry in appendix 1. Do Gaut's two models have any application here?

DISCUSSION

Problem-solving in Euclidean geometry might be taken to illustrate very well Gaut's distinction between the display and search models, and the more important role of the latter. On the one hand, the imagination may be involved in simply and somewhat passively exhibiting representations of given geometrical figures. On the other hand, it may more actively be engaged in trying out different auxiliary constructions in the hope of hitting on a set that enables the problem to be solved. Insofar as creativity is exhibited in geometrical problem-solving, it lies in finding appropriate auxiliary constructions, and the search model would thus appear to do greater justice to what is going on here than the display model.

However, as Gaut argues, merely searching though possibilities can be a very mechanical process carried out just as well – or even better – by a computer. In the case of problem-solving in Euclidean geometry, it would be relatively easy to generate different possible auxiliary constructions by drawing further lines and circles (in accord with Euclid's first three postulates) in progressively more complex combinations. Eventually, it would seem, we would be bound to hit on a construction that makes a solution possible. So if there is creativity involved, then it cannot consist in merely searching through different possibilities. What is crucial is the *selection* of possibilities; and where there is an indefinite number, ingenuity may be required in narrowing them down and inspiration may be required in choosing the right one. So creativity is located less in the searching through than in the selecting of possibilities. If the search model is therefore the better model of the role of the imagination in (active) creativity, it looks as if the imagination cannot be taken as a *source* of creativity. If its role lies in searching, then the imagination might indeed seem able merely to serve as a *vehicle* of creativity. So is Gaut right that the imagination should be seen as a vehicle rather than a source of creativity? We will look further at just what Gaut means by this claim in the next section, before considering an alternative model.

Imagination as the vehicle of active creativity

In section 4 Gaut clarifies his central claim that the role of the imagination in creativity lies in serving as the vehicle of active creativity.

Read section 4 of Gaut's paper, and answer the following questions:

ACTIVITY

1. According to Gaut, how does imagination differ (in its commitments) from belief and intention? Why does he therefore think that imagination is suited 'of its nature' to serve as the vehicle of active creativity?

2. As we have seen, Gaut defines 'imagining' as 'thinking of something without alethic or existential commitment'. But in the fifth paragraph of this section, he admits that I can imagine what I also believe to be true. Why, on his account, does this not constitute a counter-example to his definition? Do you find what he says convincing?

3. How, then, does Gaut see the connection between imagination and creativity? Is he right?

DISCUSSION

1. According to Gaut, imagination involves neither a commitment to truth, unlike belief, nor a commitment to action, unlike intention. It is because it is free from such commitments that it is ideally suited to serve as a vehicle for active creativity, which involves trying out or playing with different possibilities.

2. On Gaut's account, while I may indeed believe that what I imagine is true, or 'aim' at truth in imagining something, such a belief or aim is merely 'extrinsic' to the act of imagining itself. In other words, my act of imagining is the act of imagining it is regardless of whether I believe that what I imagine is or will be true. Gaut is right, I think, that we can talk of

someone 'imagining' what they also believe is true (see Stevenson's first, third and eighth conceptions discussed in chapter 1). But why should such a belief be regarded as *extrinsic* to the act of imagining? Take the case of Macbeth 'imagining', as we would say, a dagger in front of him. Here the belief that there is such a dagger is *intrinsic* to the act of imagining – or so it seems reasonable to claim. I do not myself, then, find what Gaut says here convincing.

3   Although Gaut makes the point again that creativity does not *require* imagination (which we considered above), he nevertheless concludes that there is a 'constitutive connection' between imagination and creativity, in that imagination, as he puts it, is 'peculiarly suited' to be the vehicle of active creativity. Insofar as creativity involves thinking of possibilities, then we might agree that there is a constitutive connection with imagination, for thinking of possibilities is one of the kinds of things that we call 'imagining'. But it only follows from this that the imagination is just a vehicle and not a source of creativity if the imagination is involved *merely* in thinking of possibilities. Gaut considers its role in 'displaying' ideas, where it is presumably also seen as a vehicle and not a source of creativity, this time in passive rather than active creativity, but he does not consider other roles that the imagination might play.

If all we have are the display and search models of the role of imagination in creativity, then it is perhaps not surprising that the imagination can only be seen as a vehicle and not a source of creativity. But are these the only models, and if not, then is there some way of according the imagination a more substantial role, a role in which it might even be regarded as a *source* of creativity? We will consider a third model in the next section.

The connection model

As we have seen, Gaut draws three distinctions – between the display and search models, between passive and active creativity, and between imagination as a source and as a vehicle of creativity. From his discussion of these distinctions, Gaut concludes that the main role of the imagination in creativity is as the vehicle of active creativity. However, in reaching this conclusion, Gaut's initial distinction seems to have been lost, in the sense that the display model now seems to overshadow the search model. For if imagination is the vehicle rather than source of creativity, then this seems to fit the display rather than search model. Ideas may not be simply 'popping into one's head', but even in the more active process of searching, the role of the imagination would now seem only to be to display the results of that search (so that the selection can take place). Although, as we will see, Gaut goes on to discuss examples of creative uses of imagination, most notably in inventing metaphors, the imagination is not itself seen as creative.

The example of problem-solving in Euclidean geometry, however, suggests that there is a third model of the role of the imagination in creative activity, which might be called the 'connection' model, which does construe it as a more creative power. The imagination may be involved in searching for and displaying new ideas, but what is often crucial is the connecting of one idea to another. In the example given in appendix 1, it is the use made of previous results – from I, 47 and II, 5 of Euclid's *Elements* – that enables the solution to be found. For what the first result shows (which is Pythagoras' theorem) is that a square is equal in area to two other squares, if the latter lie on the two shorter sides of a right-angled triangle, on the longer side of which lies the former. So if we are trying to construct a square of a certain area, then this opens up the possibility of doing so by finding two other squares. What the second result shows is that a rectangle is equal in area to the difference between two squares, if a line is cut up in a certain way (see Figure 7 of appendix 1). So if we can construct two squares from the initial rectangle, then by Pythagoras' theorem we may be able to construct the square we want. If this reconstruction of the creative process is right (and there may, of course, be other possibilities), then the first two (connected) strokes of inspiration are the realization that these two previous results can be applied in solving the present problem. What remains is to link the two results together, i.e. (referring again to Figure 7 of appendix 1) to show how to get from GE and GF to GE and GH, which requires a third stroke of inspiration – conceiving of GF and GH as radii of the same circle. In all three strokes of inspiration, then, what is involved is connection. Searching and displaying play a role, but the real creativity would seem to lie in making fruitful connections.

On the connection model too, however, the imagination still functions as a vehicle for the creative process. Perhaps we recognize that both II, 5 and II, 14 of Euclid's *Elements*, say, start from a rectangle, and we are led to follow through the implications of this. But in making this connection, the imagination might also be regarded as a source of creativity. Bringing the two together – among other things – is what makes possible the solution, and it is to the imagination that we assign this bringing together. If this is right, then we might see the example as illustrating Kant's distinction between the reproductive and productive imagination. The imagination may have both a reproductive role, in recalling and displaying previous ideas or results, and a productive or creative role, in selecting and connecting some of those ideas or results.

ACTIVITY

How might the connection model be taken to apply to Gaut's example of Kasparov's chess-playing?

DISCUSSION

As Gaut argues, what is crucial is the *pre-selection* of possible moves, which is where bringing earlier results to bear is relevant. As Gaut himself puts it, Kasparov 'may also use his imagination in seeing a current position as a variation of one with which he was previously familiar' (section 3.2). In other words, it is precisely in connecting his current position with positions he recalls from other games that Kasparov is able to narrow down the range of possibilities.

Kasparov's current position need not be identical with positions from past games – if it were, mere memory might determine what is and what is not the best move. But there will be similarities in certain respects which suggest possible strategies. Creativity in chess lies in finding a good and unexpected move (so that we have both value and originality) which is inspired but not determined by previous experience. Since it is the imagination that enables previous experience to be used in this way, it might appropriately be regarded as a source and not just as a vehicle of creativity.

From the inadequacy of the search model, Gaut drew the conclusion that the imagination was merely a vehicle of creativity. Gaut may be right, in many cases, that creativity does not consist in running through the range of possibilities and then selecting, but involves pre-selecting. But pre-selecting requires connecting, which is where the imagination might be argued to have its creative role to play. So what the inadequacy of the search model might really be taken to show is the need for the connection model, which might allow us to retain the view that the imagination itself is creative.

Computation and combination

ACTIVITY

Recall the discussion of Boden's and Novitz's theories of creativity in the previous chapter. With which theory does the connection model of the role of imagination in creativity fit better?

DISCUSSION

Neither Boden nor Novitz says very much about the imagination in their accounts. But it seems clear that the connection model fits better with Novitz's than with Boden's theory. On Boden's theory, radical creativity involves the exploration and transformation of a conceptual space. But there is no obvious reference here to connection. As I argued, Boden's theory seems to do little justice to the creativity that Haydn and Mozart showed, for example, in bringing together different conceptual and musical spaces (see pp.186–7 above). On Novitz's 'recombination theory', on the other hand, as its name suggests, connection or recombination is central, and is made explicit in the first condition for creativity that he specifies (see p.188 above).

Although Boden does not do so in her 1994 paper, she does address the issue of creative connection in chapter 6 of her book, *The Creative Mind*. She here appeals to connectionist computer systems, in which Parallel Distributed Processing (PDP) networks are used to model the associative operations of the human mind. Such systems can engage in various forms of 'pattern-completion' or 'analogical pattern-matching', for example (see 1990, 118–33; 2004, 131–46). If this is so, then it only reinforces the point that connection may be a more important element of creativity than transformation.

The creative imagination

In considering the role of the imagination in creativity, we have taken the examples of chess-playing and geometrical problem-solving (with brief mention again of Haydn and Mozart). But how does the connection model I have suggested apply in other, more obvious cases of creativity? We will look here at two further examples: first, that of aspect perception, which we explored in chapter 5, and second, related to it, that of metaphor-making, which is often taken as a paradigm of creative activity.

Aspect perception

Creativity in chess-playing, I have just argued, has its source in seeing one's current position as similar (though not identical) to positions that one recalls (whether consciously or unconsciously) from previous games. In view of our exploration of seeing-as in chapter 5, this should come as no surprise. Seeing an aspect of something arguably does involve imagination, and in a form that may exhibit creativity.

ACTIVITY Look back in particular at the discussion of the relationship between imagination and seeing-as on pp.160–2. What form of connection is involved in aspect perception?

DISCUSSION As Wittgenstein characterizes it, in noticing an aspect of something, I see an internal relation between my primary object of sight and something else. In seeing the duck-rabbit picture as a (picture of a) duck, for example, I see an internal relation between the picture and real ducks or other pictures of ducks. As it might also be put, I must 'imagine' these ducks or other pictures of ducks in some way – as 'non-actual perceptions', in Strawson's terminology – in order to see the relevant aspect. What happens in aspect perception, then, is that I *connect* my 'non-actual perceptions' with my primary object of sight; and creativity is exhibited to the extent that the connections I make are original and fruitful.

As we saw in the last chapter in discussing Novitz's recombination theory of creativity, Novitz also uses aspect perception to illustrate his account. The fact that the recombination or connection here is what Novitz calls 'ideational' – involving ideas, beliefs, theories, or anything else 'non-actual' – is no objection to that account. Of course, these connections must be original ('surprising', in Novitz's terms) and valuable in some way to count as creative, and there may be argument over what 'valuable' means, but the essential point about the role played by connection remains.

Clearly, the richer the range of experiences I have to drawn upon, the more I might be creative (even within the constraints of a particular domain). This makes sense, I think, of one feature of exceptional creativity – or 'genius' – that comes out in biographical accounts. It is often thought that genius is an innate talent, but this downplays the huge role played by immersion and obsession –

immersion in the relevant domain of activity and obsession with pursuing the relevant projects. Mozart is perhaps the obvious example. Trained and pushed – 'hot-housed', as we might now say – by his father, he lived and breathed music to such an extent that he had an abundant source of musical ideas to connect and shape into new works, and a mastery of techniques (to bring in something Wittgenstein emphasizes) to realize those new works in feasible ways. Haydn's genius, too, was partly a function of the huge demands that were put on him to compose and conduct musical pieces for the Esterházy family, in whose service he was employed from 1761 until his death in 1809. And to return to Kasparov's chess-playing, here we find immersion and obsession to an unprecedented extent as well. Of course, such immersion and obsession is not sufficient for genius or exceptional creativity. But it might at least be taken as a necessary condition. As the Goodyear example shows, merely stumbling across what turns out to be a fruitful connection is not in itself a sign of creativity. Whether Goodyear can be regarded as creative or not depends on how he developed his 'accidental' discovery. Certainly, there seems to have been enough immersion and obsession here to make it reasonable to talk of 'creativity', even if not to the same degree as in the case of Mozart or Haydn.

Metaphor

At the end of his discussion of seeing-as, Wittgenstein remarks on the connection that exists between the concepts of 'seeing an aspect' and 'experiencing the meaning of a word' (*PI*, 214). This can be explained as follows. In grasping the meaning of a word that I see written down or hear spoken, I do not simply see or hear the word, or see or hear the word and have at the same time some corresponding thought. I *experience* the word *as having a particular meaning*. This connection extends to the role that the creative imagination plays in the relevant phenomena. Just as creativity may be exhibited in aspect perception, so too it may be involved in experience of meaning. This is perhaps illustrated most clearly in our use and understanding of metaphor, and indeed metaphor-making is often offered as a paradigm example of the work of the creative imagination.

In 'Creativity and imagination', Gaut devotes section 5 to metaphor-making. He begins with Kant's account of genius, which, as I mentioned in chapter 6, Kant essentially defines in terms of 'exemplary originality', where what he means by 'exemplary' is something that sets an example or provides a model for others to follow. What is characteristic of genius or exceptional creativity, according to Kant, is 'spirit', which he defines as 'the faculty for the presentation of **aesthetic ideas**' (*CPJ*, § 49). It is Kant's conception of an 'aesthetic idea' that Gaut first explains and then uses to motivate his own discussion of metaphor.

ACTIVITY

Read the first six paragraphs of section 5 of Gaut's paper, and answer the following questions:

1. As Gaut reports him, what does Kant mean by an 'aesthetic idea'?
2. Gaut gives two examples of his own to illustrate Kant's conception of an aesthetic idea, and notes four of Kant's examples. Can you suggest any further examples?
3. Why does Gaut claim that Kant has metaphors in mind in talking of aesthetic ideas? Do you think Gaut is right?

DISCUSSION

1. As Gaut quotes him (from section 49 of the *Critique of Judgement*), Kant defines an 'aesthetic idea' as 'a presentation of the imagination which prompts much thought, but to which no determinate thought whatsoever, i.e., no [determinate] concept, can be adequate'. In other words, an aesthetic idea is a sensory representation that gets us thinking but which cannot be summed up in any conceptual form.

2. Various examples may have occurred to you. Here are two of my own. Look back, first, at Figure 1 in chapter 1 (p.29). Blake's 'Divine image' – as expressed in either the poem or the illustration – is a good example of an aesthetic idea. Literally, the illustration shows someone hammering something on an anvil, and it might be interpreted broadly as depicting the brutal side of our nature suppressing our sensitive side. But any number of more specific things might be taken as suggested, and there is no single 'correct' interpretation. Its possible meanings resist summary. Gaut gives a sculptural and an architectural example, and sculpture, in particular, provides many examples of sensory representations that may prompt much thought without being definitively conceptualizable. A further example is provided in Figure 5.

3. According to Gaut, all four of Kant's examples can be understood as involving the metaphorical attribution of some property to something. An eagle cannot literally hold lightning in its claws, for instance, but in

Figure 5 Giovanni Anselmo, *Untitled*, 1968, granite, fresh lettuce and copper, 0.7 x 0.23 x 0.37 m, Centre Pompidou-MNAM-CCI, Paris. Photo: RMN. Courtesy of the artist and Marian Goodman Gallery, New York.

In 2001 there was a special exhibition at the Tate Modern in London on the work of the Italian 'Arte Povera' movement in the period 1962–72. One of the sculptures that was particularly thought-provoking was by Giovanni Anselmo, officially untitled but also known as 'Eating structure'. As the picture shows, it consisted in a lettuce squashed between two blocks of granite, the smaller block tied round the larger by a copper wire. But what does it represent? As one starts to think about it, all sorts of meanings and issues open up. What happens when the lettuce dries out? The smaller block will then fall. To maintain it in its state, then, the sculpture has to be 'fed' with a new lettuce every day. The idea may be simple, but it is an effective way to raise questions, and make one think, about the nature of the artistic object and our role in its upkeep, the relationship between art and nature, and the role of the imagination itself in the appreciation of art. What we have here, then, is an excellent illustration of what Kant meant by an 'aesthetic idea'.

portraying it as doing so we are symbolizing – and stimulating thought about – God's power. Furthermore, according to Gaut, metaphors satisfy Kant's definition of an 'aesthetic idea': they prompt much thought but cannot be paraphrased literally, and good metaphors are both original and valuable. Although Kant's examples may be interpreted as metaphors, however, his conception of an aesthetic idea seems to me to be wider than that of a metaphor. Aesthetic ideas include, as Gaut himself recognizes, non-linguistic sensory representations such as sculptural and architectural forms. Of course, as Gaut's talk of 'visual and other sensory metaphors' indicates, the notion of metaphor, which has its home in spoken and written language, can itself be used metaphorically – i.e. applied to what is non-linguistic – but there seems no reason to restrict Kant's conception of aesthetic ideas merely to metaphors. Describing the sculpture in Figure 5, for example, as a 'metaphor' does not seem to do justice to the richness of its semantic properties. Nevertheless, we might agree with Gaut that metaphors are good examples, even paradigm examples, of aesthetic ideas and can be used to illustrate the workings of the creative imagination.

ACTIVITY

Read the rest of section 5 of Gaut's paper, and his conclusion in section 6, and answer the following questions:

1 As we saw in the last chapter, Gaut defines creativity in terms of originality, value and flair. On Gaut's conception, then, how does the invention of a metaphor exhibit creativity?

2 How is the imagination involved in the making and understanding of a metaphor?

3 What is the objection that Gaut considers to his claim that metaphor-making is a paradigm of creative imagination? How does he reply to this objection, and what do you think of his reply?

4 In the penultimate paragraph of section 5, Gaut criticizes Kant's definition of an 'aesthetic idea'. What is his criticism, and what is the modification he suggests?

5 Although Gaut does not himself talk of the connection model of the role of the imagination in creativity, to what extent does this model apply in the case of metaphor?

1. A newly invented metaphor is clearly original and has value if it is 'apt', as Gaut puts it. Gaut is less explicit as to how 'flair' is manifested, since this is partly a function of originality and aptness. But his remarks about bringing together two otherwise disparate domains suggest that flair in metaphor-making is exhibited in the way that this is done.

2. In creating a metaphor, the imagination is involved in seeing the connection that lies at its heart – for example, in seeing certain similarities between men and wolves in saying 'Men are wolves'. In understanding a metaphor, the imagination is involved in thinking of the subject of the metaphor as having various of the properties suggested by the comparison. In both cases, the imagination is involved in seeing something from a new perspective.

3. The objection that Gaut considers is that metaphors could be mechanically generated by a Deep Blue or Shallow Pink, which would not count as creative. In reply, Gaut denies the analogy between chess-playing and metaphor-making that might suggest that a sophisticated computer or idiot savant could produce successful metaphors. There are no definite rules governing metaphor-making, unlike in the case of chess-playing, Gaut argues, nor are there clear criteria for a successful metaphor in the way that there are clear criteria for a successful chess move. This might seem a surprising reply, since Gaut has already dealt with the issue of mechanical generation in specifying, in section 1 of his paper, that creativity requires 'flair'. Since the merely mechanical generation of something does not involve flair, it cannot exhibit creativity. However, as Gaut goes on to admit, a good metaphor could still be mechanically generated (among a host of bad ones, perhaps), so we are still left with the problem that metaphor-making is not necessarily a creative act. At this point, though, Gaut concedes to the objection and qualifies his earlier claim. Even if not all metaphor-making is a paradigm of creative imagination, creative metaphor-making *is* a paradigm. This might seem trivially true, but Gaut remarks that his main claim is just the heuristic one – that metaphor-making illuminates the creative process in a particularly clear way. All we need for this are some paradigm cases of metaphor-making – creative ones, of course. As Gaut puts it, 'Paradigms are still paradigms, even when they are very uncommon.'

4. Kant defines an 'aesthetic idea' as 'a presentation of the imagination that prompts much thought, but to which no determinate thought ... can be adequate'. But bad metaphors as well as good metaphors can prompt

much thought, Gaut argues, so this definition will not do as it stands. (The production of aesthetic ideas characterizes genius, according to Kant, so this does constitute an objection, although Kant would presumably reply that an aesthetic idea must also be 'exemplary', which bad metaphors are not.) Instead, Gaut suggests, we should require that an aesthetic idea or good metaphor 'guide' our thought, 'guide' in the sense of directing us to see and explore the connection that lies at the heart of the idea or metaphor.

5   The connection model captures very well, I think, what goes on in metaphor-making, as Gaut's own account (implicitly) shows. In imagining men as wolves, for example, we do indeed connect our knowledge of wolves with our knowledge of human behaviour. Gaut himself talks of the imaginative act in good metaphor-making bringing together disparate domains and revealing apt connections.

Metaphors are a good example, then, both of what Kant means by 'aesthetic ideas' and of the role that the imagination plays in connecting ideas or conceptual domains in creative activity. The meaning of a metaphor is not exhausted by any literal paraphrase, but its value lies in the aptness and richness of the comparison it suggests. This comparison involves bringing together different concepts or domains of thought, which is where the imagination comes in. But does this mean, after all, that the imagination is a source and not just a vehicle of creativity? In metaphor-making, what lies at the heart of the creative process is the connecting of two or more things, and we have also seen this illustrated in the case of problem-solving in Euclidean geometry. Is connecting not a paradigm example of something that is attributed to the work of the imagination? If so, then we have found one sense in which we can talk of the imagination as a source of creativity, and given some content to our conception of the 'creative imagination'.

Metaphors in discussions of imagination

In section 5 of his paper, Gaut remarks that metaphors are 'surprisingly common in many domains of creative thought', not only in literature and other areas of art but also in science and philosophy. The question naturally arises as to what metaphors are used, and the role they play, in discussions of imagination and creativity. Indeed, have metaphors not been used in asking the very question of whether imagination is a 'source' or a 'vehicle' of creativity? How can imagination literally be a source or a vehicle of creativity? We have seen what sense might be given to such talk, but is this not just one attempt to unpack the metaphors?

ACTIVITY

Looking back over what has been covered in this book, what other examples are there of metaphors being used?

DISCUSSION

Metaphors, of one kind or another, are far more prevalent in philosophical debate than one might initially think, and we may all make use of them more often than we care to admit. The use of metaphors was perhaps most obvious in Strawson's explanation of Kant's claim that 'imagination is a necessary ingredient of perception itself' (see pp.118–21 above). Strawson talks of present perceptions being 'soaked with or animated by, or infused with' what he calls 'non-actual' perceptions, and of the latter being 'alive' in present perceptions, and makes the point himself about how difficult it is to give anything other than a metaphorical description of this. Indeed, is Kant's own claim not itself metaphorical? Can imagination be literally an 'ingredient' of perception? Wittgenstein too, we saw, makes use of metaphors in attempting to understand the phenomenon of aspect perception. He talks, for instance, of an 'echo of a thought in sight', and of an image coming into 'contact' with the visual impression (see p.163 above). And to note just one further example here, central to Margaret Boden's account of creativity is the idea of a 'conceptual space', which she too admits is a metaphor, although one that she thinks computational psychology can help fill out (see the last paragraph of the section entitled 'Exploring and transforming conceptual spaces' of Reading 3).

Other examples of the use of metaphors might have been given here, and many more can be found in philosophical discussion more generally. Of course, what is initially used as a metaphor gradually acquires more prosaic meanings. It is not simply that freshly baked metaphors soon become stale, but that if they work at all, as Gaut has stressed, then they *guide* our thought, directing us to explore and articulate the connections that lie at their heart. In articulating these connections, more literal meanings become established, and the metaphor no longer strikes us as a metaphor. But while some metaphors may be relatively easily paraphrased in clarifying what they mean, or the philosophical point that they are being used to make, other metaphors may be open to conflicting interpretations and may be philosophically confusing rather than enlightening. We have seen what sense might be given to the idea of imagination as a 'source' of creativity, for example, but there is a great temptation to construe the imagination as a mysterious power, as we find in Kant's philosophy and Romanticism. Discussions of imagination may be particularly prone to metaphorical descriptions, and there may be much work to be done in clarifying such descriptions. On the other hand, if we are more romantically minded, the pervasiveness of metaphor might be taken to show just how fundamental the work of the creative imagination is. In making sense of anything, we must apply the ideas and conceptual tools we already have, and this will inevitably mean extending their use from one domain to another, suggesting and establishing connections, enriching our understanding, and in turn provoking further questions. But perhaps expressed like this, nothing mystifying or controversial has been said. In the end, the issue is not whether there *is* such a thing as 'creative imagination', as what we *mean* in talking of imagination in the various ways we do. Discussions of imagination may themselves reveal the work of imagination, but if so, then imagination is also required in the interpretive task of understanding those discussions.

Review

1 We have considered three models of the role that the imagination plays in creative activities. We looked first at the two models that Gaut discusses – the display and search models – and I endorsed his criticisms of those models. But rather than concluding with him that the imagination is only a vehicle of creativity, I suggested a third model, the connection model, which might be taken to do greater justice to the role of the imagination in acting as a source of creativity.

2 The role that the imagination plays in connecting ideas or conceptual spaces was illustrated in the cases of aspect perception and metaphor. I concluded by commenting on the pervasive use of metaphors in philosophical discussion.

Further reading

Gaut's paper, 'Creativity and imagination' (2003), which is included as Reading 6, is contained in Gaut and Livingston (2003), which includes other papers on creativity, including Novitz (2003), which was referred to in the last chapter, and a useful general introduction. Boden (1990, 2004) was also cited in the previous chapter.

There are several English translations of Kant's *Critique of Judgement*. For a long time, the standard translation was Meredith's (1952; the translation of the 'Critique of Aesthetic Judgement', which is the first and most influential part, dates from 1911). A new translation (with good notes) by Pluhar appeared in 1987. But what will now become the standard translation is Guyer and Matthews's in the Cambridge edition of Kant's works (under the title *Critique of the Power of Judgment*, published in 2000), which comes with a helpful introduction, notes and glossary. I have used this one here (cited as *CPJ*), though Gaut relies on Pluhar's translation. For an introductory essay on the main topics of the 'Critique of Aesthetic Judgement', Schaper (1992) can be recommended. But the most thorough book on the subject, which includes a chapter on Kant's account of genius, is Allison (2001).

Appendix 1 Imagination and creativity in Euclidean geometry

Problem-solving in Euclidean geometry provides a good case study for exploring the role of imagination in thinking and the nature of creativity. Here is an example that is simple enough to be accessible but rich enough to be instructive.

An example of problem-solving in Euclidean geometry

Proposition 14 of Book II (hereafter II, 14) of Euclid's *Elements* sets the following problem: 'To construct a square equal to a given rectilineal figure'. A diagram is provided (Figure 6), the only addition here being that the square EHIJ has been constructed, whereas Euclid draws just the one side EH, and simply refers to EHIJ as the square on EH (which we can also designate as EH^2).

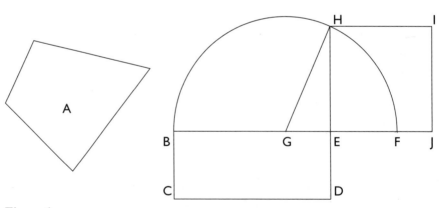

Figure 6

The aim, then, is to construct a square with the same area as A. Now Euclid has already shown how to construct a *rectangle* equal to a given rectilineal figure (I, 45), so assuming that the rectangle BCDE is equal to A, the problem here is to construct a square with the same area as BCDE. The solution can be set out as follows.

Solution to II, 14

Starting from rectangle BCDE, extend side BE to F, such that EF = ED. Then bisect BF at G, and draw a semi-circle with centre G from B to F (clockwise). Extend line DE to H where it intersects the semi-circle. EH is then the side of a square (EHIJ) of the same area as BCDE.

The important point about these constructions is that they can all be achieved by one or other of the three legitimate operations within Euclidean geometry (the ruler and compass principles): drawing a line between any two points, extending a line, and drawing a circle (or segment of a circle) with any given centre and radius (in accordance with Euclid's first three postulates). But while this does indeed result in a square equal in area to BCDE, we also need to demonstrate that this is so. Euclid's proof can be formulated as follows.

Proof of II, 14

Since BF has been cut into equal segments at G (BG and GF) and unequal segments at E (BE and EF), we know from a previous result (II, 5) that the rectangle formed with sides BE and EF (equivalent to BCDE) together with the square formed with side GE is equal in area to the square formed with side GF. We can write this as follows:

$GF^2 = BCDE + GE^2$

But, adding the line GH, we also know from Pythagoras' Theorem (I, 47) that the square on GH is equal in area to the sum of the squares on GE and EH (since GEH is a right-angled triangle), i.e.:

$GH^2 = EH^2 + GE^2$

But GF = GH (since this is the radius of the circle), so $GF^2 = GH^2$. Thus (making use of Euclid's first axiom or common notion that 'Things which are equal to the same thing are also equal to one another'):

$BCDE + GE^2 = EH^2 + GE^2$

Subtracting GE^2 from both sides (making use of Euclid's third axiom that 'If equals be subtracted from equals, the remainders are equal'), the desired result is reached:

$BCDE = EH^2$, i.e. BCDE = EHIJ

Pythagoras' Theorem is well known. The other theorem used here may be less familiar. It can be illustrated in Figure 7, extending the constructions of Figure 6.

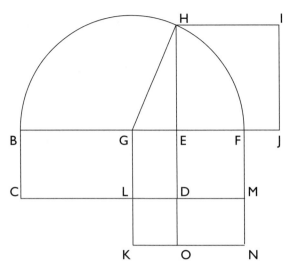

Figure 7

GKNF is the square on GF, DO results from extending ED, and DM results from extending CD. The theorem states that BE × EF (i.e. BCDE) + GE² = GF². The proof can be given as follows. (Euclid's own proof depends on other, previously established theorems; see *Elements*, I, 382–3. Allowing the figure to partly speak for itself, I have simplified here to avoid being drawn back further.)

Proof of II, 5

BCDE + GE² = BCDE + LKOD (since LKOD is equal to the square on GE)

= BCLG + GLDE + LKOD (since BCDE = BCLG + GLDE)

= GLMF + GLDE + LKOD (BCLG = GLMF, since BG = GF)

= GLMF + DONM + LKOD (GLDE = DONM, since if ED = EF, then GL = ON, and LKOD is a square)

= GKNF, i.e. GF²

The use of this theorem together with Pythagoras' Theorem is not the only way to prove that BCDE = EHIJ. Nor is it necessarily the simplest. The following alternative proof, referring to Figure 8, involves fewer additional constructions.

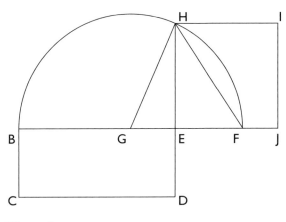

Figure 8

Alternative proof of II, 14

Add lines BH and HF. Since any angle inscribed in a semi-circle is a right angle, <BHF is a right angle; in which case triangle BHE is similar to triangle HEF. So the ratio of BE to EH is the same as the ratio of EH to EF, i.e. BE × EF = EH².

This proof might seem simpler, but we would need to have shown that any angle inscribed in a semi-circle *is* a right angle, and to have developed sufficiently the theory of proportions. This was not something that Euclid had done in the first two books of the *Elements*, so he would not have been able to rely upon it at this stage in his work. The proof just given can be found in Book VI (Proposition 13).

Imagination and creativity in Euclidean problem-solving

The solution to the problem posed in II, 14 of Euclid's *Elements* is ingenious, and aesthetic terms readily spring to mind in describing both the solution and the experience one has in thinking through it. The strategy is neat, the proof is elegant, and there is pleasure generated in appreciating how it works. Throughout history, mathematicians, scientists and philosophers have been inspired by Euclidean geometry, and given the success demonstrated here in squaring the rectangle, one can understand the enduring fascination with the attempt to square the circle. Geometrical problem-solving not only captures the imagination but also requires imagination in its operation. Faced with the task of constructing a square equal in area to a given rectangle, it is far from obvious how we are to proceed. Why should the square be constructed on the corner of the rectangle, for example? And even if we are presented with Figure 6 itself, and told to show that EHIJ is equal in area to BCDE, the solution cannot simply be read off, since further – auxiliary – constructions may be needed, as Figures 7 and 8 show. And as we have also seen, there is more than one possible solution; which solution is the most appropriate depends on what has already been established. Imagination and creativity are clearly called for. Indeed, if the solution were merely a matter of mechanically carrying out certain operations, then would it not have soon become obvious that squaring the circle was impossible? Squaring the circle has held the fascination it has just because the role of creativity in problem-solving has been recognized.

Of course, there are constraints on the process: construction must proceed in accord with Euclid's first three postulates, and if we make use of other theorems, then we must be in a position to prove these too. If we have worked our way through the first two books of Euclid's *Elements* up to II, 14, and are then set the task of solving this problem (which is the last one in Book II), then we have a source of previously established results to draw upon, which may greatly facilitate the task. But this still leaves us with choices, and ingenuity is required in making an appropriate choice. Euclid's own solution relies upon the theorems proved in I, 47 and II, 5, but there are other ways to solve the problem, as Euclid himself shows in Book VI. That there are constraints, then, does not remove the need for imagination and creativity. On the contrary, the constraints are necessary for creativity to flourish, and recognition of them arguably only enhances our appreciation of the ingenuity involved in the solutions that are offered.

But how exactly do imagination and creativity come in here? Problem-solving in Euclidean geometry clearly involves 'construction', but this takes a number of different forms. In any case of problem-solving, there is an initial 'given' (the rectangle BCDE, in this example), which must first be constructed in setting out the problem, and the task is then to construct a further figure (the square EHIJ) on the basis of what is given. But these are not the only constructions that are involved. As we have seen, auxiliary constructions are also needed in getting from what is given (the rectangle) to what is sought (the square). Although these constructions must also be in accord with Euclid's first three postulates, it is here that creativity is required. Appropriate auxiliary lines have to be added both to construct the desired figure and to prove that the desired figure has the relevant properties (that EHIJ is equal in area to BCDE).

This suggests that a distinction should be drawn between construction in the sense of simply exhibiting a given figure and construction in the sense of generating new lines which are neither part of what is given nor part of what is sought, but which are nevertheless required to solve the problem. The constructions need not be physically drawn. They can be *imagined*, and indeed, even if they are drawn, we should think of what goes on in the imagination as logically prior. What is physically drawn is only an external record of what is imagined. So this suggests that there is a distinction, too, between two roles that the imagination can play: exhibiting the relevant geometrical figures in a specific (visualizable) form and generating new geometrical objects. This corresponds to the distinction that Kant drew, in the *Critique of Pure Reason*, between the reproductive and the productive imagination. To represent a rectangle or square to ourselves, in first grasping the conditions of the problem, we need to reproduce an image in 'empirical intuition'; but we also have the power to engage in 'pure' imagination, producing lines that are not there in the initial specification of the problem. The real creativity thus lies in the use of the 'pure' imagination.

Appendix 2 The structure of Kant's *Critique of Pure Reason*

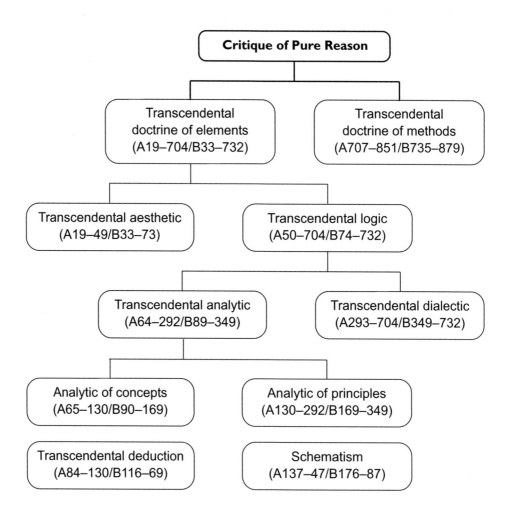

Figure 9 The structure of Kant's *Critique of Pure Reason*, insofar as it is relevant to Kant's conception of imagination

Glossary

abstract ideas (as understood in relation to British empiricism, in particular) ideas that embody our understanding of abstract or general terms – terms that apply to more than one object, such as 'cat' or 'person'; also known as **general ideas**.

aesthetic idea (as understood by Kant) a sensory image or representation that prompts much thought but which cannot be conceptualized in any definite form.

alethic commitment commitment to the truth (or falsity) of something; cf. **existential commitment**.

a posteriori (as understood by Kant) dependent on a particular experience; (more generally) something is said to be known a posteriori if it is known through some particular experience; often defined in opposition to **a priori**: what cannot be known a priori can only be known a posteriori.

a priori (as understood by Kant) what is necessarily prior to, or a precondition of, experience; (more generally) something is said to be knowable a priori if it can be known independently of any particular experience; contrasted with **a posteriori**.

associationism (as understood in relation to Hume's philosophy, in particular) the view that the operations of the human mind are to be explained in terms of the association of ideas, governed by the **principles of association**.

categories (as understood by Kant) the most fundamental concepts of human experience, which structure our thought and without which human experience would not be possible, such as the concepts of unity, reality, substance and causality; also known as **pure concepts**.

conceptual space (as understood by Boden) a domain of thinking or human activity governed by a certain set of rules or constraints, which define a range of possibilities; also known as a **generative system**.

corporeal imagination (as understood in relation to Descartes's philosophy) the physical (as opposed to mental) faculty of having or processing images in the brain; to be distinguished from both **sensory imagination** and **intellectual imagination**.

dramatic imagining (as understood by Gaut) imagining what it is like to be someone else or to be in someone else's position.

empirical imagination (as understood in relation to Hume's and Kant's philosophy) the faculty of imagination responsible for the empirical association and reproduction of ideas, in accordance with the **principles of association**; to be distinguished (in Kant's philosophy) from the **transcendental imagination**.

epistemological atomism (as understood in relation to Hume's philosophy) the view that knowledge and belief are based on simple sensory impressions and ideas, understood as discrete mental entities.

existential commitment commitment to the existence (or non-existence) of something; cf. **alethic commitment**.

experiential imagining (as understood by Gaut) a form of imagining with a rich and distinctive experiential aspect, which includes both **sensory imagining** and **phenomenal imagining**.

external relation (as understood in relation to Wittgenstein's philosophy) a non-constitutive or contingent relation; a relation in which one thing stands to another thing is an external relation if that (first) thing would still be what it essentially is even if that relation did not obtain; contrasted with **internal relation**.

general ideas (as understood in relation to British empiricism, in particular) see **abstract ideas**.

generative system (as understood by Boden) see **conceptual space**.

historical (or H-) creativity (as understood by Boden) the creativity that an individual person exhibits in coming up with a surprising and valuable idea that not only is new to them but also occurs for the first time in human history; it is thus a species of **psychological creativity**.

intellectual imagination (as understood in relation to Descartes's philosophy, in particular) the mental faculty responsible for *supposition*, such as forming hypotheses, conceiving of and engaging in thought experiments, and raising sceptical doubts; to be distinguished from both **corporeal imagination** and **sensory imagination**.

internal relation (as understood in relation to Wittgenstein's philosophy) a constitutive or necessary relation; a relation in which one thing stands to another thing is an internal relation if that (first) thing would not be what it essentially is if that relation did not obtain; contrasted with **external relation**.

intuition (as understood by Kant) a raw (i.e. unconceptualized) sensory impression or representation.

non-actual perception (as understood by Strawson) a perception that is somehow involved (e.g. presupposed or anticipated) in a given experience but which is not *actually* present.

objectual imagining (as understood by Gaut) imagining a particular object.

phantasia (from the ancient Greek) the faculty of apprehending or experiencing **phantasms**.

phantasm an image or appearance; from the Greek term *phantasma* (plural *phantasmata*), which originally meant something like an occurrence of something appearing to be such-and-such.

phenomenal imagining (as understood by Gaut) imagining what it is like to have a certain experience, such as imagining what it is like to feel wet; a type of **experiential imagining**.

principles of association (as understood in relation to Hume's philosophy, in particular) the principles governing the association of ideas, such as the principle of resemblance.

productive imagination (as understood by Kant) the faculty responsible for actively synthesizing our **intuitions** and for freely producing new ideas or representations, such as images exemplifying concepts (see **schematism**), or **aesthetic ideas**, and which lies at the basis of all our cognitive activities; also described as the **transcendental imagination** and distinguished from the **reproductive imagination** or **empirical imagination**.

propositional attitude an attitude adopted towards a proposition; believing that philosophers love beetles, for example, is described as adopting the attitude of belief towards the proposition expressed by the sentence 'Philosophers love beetles'.

propositional imagining (as understood by Gaut) imagining *that* something is the case – or 'entertaining' a proposition, as it is also put.

psychological (or P-) creativity (as understood by Boden) the creativity that an individual person exhibits in coming up with a surprising and valuable idea that is new to them; to be distinguished from **historical creativity** (a specific form of psychological creativity).

pure concepts (as understood by Kant) see **categories**.

reproductive imagination (as understood by Kant) the faculty responsible for reproducing ideas or representations; what Kant sees as merely the **empirical imagination**, to be distinguished from the **productive imagination** or **transcendental imagination**.

schema (plural schemata; as understood by Kant) a rule for generating images appropriate to a given empirical concept or for specifying how a **pure concept** (i.e. **category**) applies to the spatial-temporal world.

schematism (as understood by Kant) the art of operating with **schemata**.

sensibility (as understood by Kant) the faculty responsible for passively receiving **intuitions**; contrasted with **understanding**.

sensory imagination (as understood in relation to Descartes's philosophy) the mental (as opposed to physical) faculty that is responsible for perceiving ('in the mind's eye', so to speak) the images that occur in **corporeal imagination**; to be distinguished too from **intellectual imagination**.

sensory imagining (as understood by Gaut) imagining that takes a sensory form, such as visually imagining a wet cat; a type of **experiential imagining**.

transcendent (as understood by Kant) whatever lies beyond the limits of human experience; to be distinguished from **transcendental**.

transcendental (as understood by Kant) whatever functions as a necessary precondition of human experience; to be distinguished from **transcendent**.

transcendental imagination (as understood by Kant) the faculty of imagination that is the precondition of all human cognitive activity; see **productive imagination**.

transcendental unity of apperception (as understood by Kant) the unity of consciousness that is presupposed in all human experience.

understanding (as understood by Kant) the faculty responsible for actively supplying and using concepts; contrasted with **sensibility**.

way of ideas (as understood in relation to British empiricism) the approach that seeks to explain human cognitive activity in terms of ideas and their operations, as exemplified, in particular, by **associationism**.

Bibliography

Abbreviations in the text refer to the following sources in the Bibliography:

CPJ: Kant, *Critique of the Power of Judgment*.

CPR: Kant, *Critique of Pure Reason*.

Essay: Locke, *An Essay concerning Human Understanding*.

LW: Wittgenstein, *Last Writings on the Philosophy of Psychology*.

PI: Wittgenstein, *Philosophical Investigations*.

Principles: Berkeley, *A Treatise concerning the Principles of Human Knowledge*.

PW: Descartes, *The Philosophical Writings of Descartes*.

RPP: Wittgenstein, *Remarks on the Philosophy of Psychology*.

Treatise: Hume, *A Treatise of Human Nature*.

ALLISON, H.E. (2001) *Kant's Theory of Taste*, Cambridge, Cambridge University Press.

BAKER, G.P. and HACKER, P.M.S. (1980) *Wittgenstein: Understanding and Meaning*, Oxford, Blackwell.

BAKER, G.P. and HACKER, P.M.S. (1985) *Wittgenstein: Rules, Grammar and Necessity*, Oxford, Blackwell.

BELL, D. (1987) 'The art of judgement', *Mind*, 96, pp.221–44.

BENNETT, M.R. and HACKER, P.M.S. (2003) *Philosophical Foundations of Neuroscience*, Oxford, Blackwell.

BERKELEY, G. (1975) *A Treatise concerning the Principles of Human Knowledge*, in M.R. Ayers (ed.) *Philosophical Works*, London, Dent (first published 1710, 2nd edn 1734).

BLACKBURN, S. (1994) *The Oxford Dictionary of Philosophy*, Oxford, Oxford University Press.

BLAKE, W. (1970) *Songs of Innocence and of Experience*, ed. G. Keynes, Oxford, Oxford University Press (first published 1789, 1794).

BODEN, M.A. (1990) *The Creative Mind: Myths and Mechanisms*, London, Weidenfeld and Nicolson.

BODEN, M.A. (1994a) 'What is creativity?', in M.A. Boden (ed.) *Dimensions of Creativity*, Cambridge, Mass., MIT Press, pp.75–117.

BODEN, M.A. (ed.) (1994b) *Dimensions of Creativity*, Cambridge, Mass., MIT Press.

BODEN, M.A. (2004) *The Creative Mind: Myths and Mechanisms*, 2nd edn, London, Routledge.

BRANN, E.T.H. (1991) *The World of the Imagination*, Lanham, Maryland, Rowman and Littlefield.

BUDD, M. (1989) *Wittgenstein's Philosophy of Psychology*, London, Routledge.

CAYGILL, H. (1995) *A Kant Dictionary*, Oxford, Blackwell.

COLERIDGE, S.T. (1983) 'On the imagination', in J. Engell and W.J. Bate (eds) *Biographia Literaria*, Princeton, Princeton University Press, pp.295–306 (essay first published 1817).

COTTINGHAM, J. (1986) *Descartes*, Oxford, Blackwell.

COTTINGHAM, J. (1993) *A Descartes Dictionary*, Oxford, Blackwell.

CRAWFORD, D. (1982) 'Kant's theory of creative imagination', in T. Cohen and P. Guyer (eds) *Essays in Kant's Aesthetics*, Chicago, University of Chicago Press, pp.151–78.

CURRIE, G. and RAVENSCROFT, I. (2002) *Recreative Minds*, Oxford, Oxford University Press.

DESCARTES, R. (1984–91) *The Philosophical Writings of Descartes*, trans. J. Cottingham *et al.*, 3 vols, Cambridge, Cambridge University Press.

ENGELL, J. (1981) *The Creative Imagination: Enlightenment to Romanticism*, Cambridge, Mass., Harvard University Press.

EUCLID (1956) *The Thirteen Books of The Elements*, trans. T.H. Heath, 3 vols, New York, Dover.

GARDNER, S. (1999) *Kant and the Critique of Pure Reason*, London, Routledge.

GAUT, B. (2003) 'Creativity and imagination', in B. Gaut and P. Livingston (eds) *The Creation of Art*, Cambridge, Cambridge University Press, pp.148–73.

GAUT, B. and LIVINGSTON, P. (eds) (2003) *The Creation of Art*, Cambridge, Cambridge University Press.

GIBBONS, S. (1994) *Kant's Theory of Imagination*, Oxford, Oxford University Press.

GLOCK, H.-J. (1996) *A Wittgenstein Dictionary*, Oxford, Blackwell.

GLOCK, H.-J. (ed.) (2001) *Wittgenstein: A Critical Reader*, Oxford, Blackwell.

GUTTENPLAN, S. (ed.) (1994) *A Companion to the Philosophy of Mind*, Oxford, Blackwell.

HACKER, P.M.S. (1986) *Insight and Illusion*, rev. edn, Oxford, Oxford University Press.

HACKER, P.M.S. (1990) *Wittgenstein: Meaning and Mind*, Oxford, Blackwell.

HACKER, P.M.S. (1996) *Wittgenstein: Mind and Will*, Oxford, Blackwell.

HAMLYN, D. (1994) 'Imagination', in S. Guttenplan (ed.) *A Companion to the Philosophy of Mind*, Oxford, Blackwell, pp.361–6.

HANFLING, O. (1989) *Wittgenstein's Later Philosophy*, London, Macmillan.

HEIDEGGER, M. (1991) *Kant and the Problem of Metaphysics*, trans. R. Taft, 5th edn, Bloomington, Indiana University Press (first published 1929).

HOBBES, T. (1994) *Leviathan, with Selected Variants from the Latin Edition of 1668*, ed. E. Curley, Indianapolis and Cambridge, Hackett (first published 1651).

HUME, D. (1975) *An Enquiry concerning Human Understanding*, ed. L.A. Selby-Bigge, 3rd edn rev. P.H. Nidditch, Oxford, Oxford University Press (first published 1748, 1777).

HUME, D. (1978) *A Treatise of Human Nature*, ed. L.A. Selby-Bigge, 2nd edn, Oxford, Oxford University Press (first published 1739–40).

HUSSERL, E. (1990) *On the Phenomenology of the Consciousness of Internal Time*, trans. J.B. Brough, Dordrecht, Kluwer (first published 1966).

JOHNSON, M. (1987) *The Body in the Mind: The Bodily Basis of Meaning, Imagination, and Reason*, Chicago, University of Chicago Press.

KANT, I. (1929) *Critique of Pure Reason*, trans. N. Kemp Smith, London, Macmillan (first published 1781, 2nd edn 1787).

KANT, I. (1952) *Critique of Judgement*, trans. J.C. Meredith, Oxford, Oxford University Press (first published 1790, 2nd edn 1793).

KANT, I. (1987) *Critique of Judgement*, trans. W. Pluhar, Indianapolis, Hackett (first published 1790, 2nd edn 1793).

KANT, I. (1997) *Critique of Pure Reason*, trans. P. Guyer and A.W. Wood, Cambridge, Cambridge University Press (first published 1781, 2nd edn 1787).

KANT, I. (2000) *Critique of the Power of Judgment*, ed. P. Guyer, trans. P. Guyer and E. Matthews, Cambridge, Cambridge University Press (first published 1790, 2nd edn 1793).

KEARNEY, R. (1988) *The Wake of Imagination: Toward a Postmodern Culture*, London, Routledge.

KEYNES, G. (1970) 'Introduction' and 'Commentary', in W. Blake, *Songs of Innocence and of Experience*, ed. G. Keynes, Oxford, Oxford University Press.

LOCKE, J. (1975) *An Essay concerning Human Understanding*, ed. P.H. Nidditch, 4th edn, Oxford, Oxford University Press (first published 1690, 4th edn 1700).

MCGINN, M. (1997) *Wittgenstein and the Philosophical Investigations*, London, Routledge.

MAKKREEL, R.A. (1990) *Imagination and Interpretation in Kant: The Hermeneutical Import of the Critique of Judgement*, Chicago, University of Chicago Press.

MULHALL, S. (2001) 'Seeing aspects', in H.-J. Glock (ed.) *Wittgenstein: A Critical Reader*, Oxford, Blackwell, pp.246–67.

NOVITZ, D. (1999) 'Creativity and constraint', *Australian Journal of Philosophy*, 77, pp.67–82.

NOVITZ, D. (2003) 'Explanations of creativity', in B. Gaut and P. Livingston (eds) *The Creation of Art*, Cambridge, Cambridge University Press, pp.174–91.

PEARS, D. (1990) *Hume's System*, Oxford, Oxford University Press.

REID, T. (1983) *Essays on the Intellectual Powers of Man*, in *Inquiry and Essays*, ed. R.E. Beanblossom and K. Lehrer, Indianapolis, Hackett (first published 1785).

ROLLINS, M. (1989) *Mental Imagery*, New Haven, Yale University Press.

SCHAPER, E. (1992) 'Taste, sublimity, and genius: the aesthetics of nature and art', in P. Guyer (ed.) *The Cambridge Companion to Kant*, Cambridge, Cambridge University Press, pp.367–93.

SCHOULS, P.A. (2000) *Descartes and the Possibility of Science*, Ithaca, Cornell University Press.

SEPPER, D.L. (1996) *Descartes's Imagination: Proportion, Images, and the Activity of Thinking*, Berkeley, University of California Press.

SHEPARD, R. and METZLER, N. (1971) 'Mental rotation of three-dimensional figures', *Science*, 171, pp.701–3.

SORELL, T. (1983) *Descartes*, Milton Keynes, The Open University.

STERNBERG, R.J. (ed.) (1999) *Handbook of Creativity*, Cambridge, Cambridge University Press.

STEVENSON, L. (2003) 'Twelve conceptions of imagination', *British Journal of Aesthetics*, 43, pp.238–59.

STRAWSON, P.F. (1974) 'Imagination and perception', in *Freedom and Resentment*, London, Methuen (essay first published 1970).

STROUD, B. (1977) *Hume*, London, Routledge.

TYE, M. (1991) *The Imagery Debate*, Cambridge, Mass., MIT Press.

TYE, M. (1994) 'Imagery', in S. Guttenplan (ed.) *A Companion to the Philosophy of Mind*, Oxford, Blackwell, pp.355–61.

WARNOCK, M. (1976) *Imagination*, London, Faber.

WHITE, A.R. (1990) *The Language of Imagination*, Oxford, Blackwell.

WILKINSON, R. (1999) *Minds and Bodies*, Milton Keynes, The Open University.

WILKINSON, R. (2000) *Minds and Bodies*, London and New York, Routledge.

WITTGENSTEIN, L. (1958) *Philosophical Investigations*, trans. G.E.M. Anscombe, 2nd edn, Oxford, Blackwell (first published 1953).

WITTGENSTEIN, L. (1961) *Tractatus Logico-Philosophicus*, trans. D.F. Pears and B. McGuinness, London, Routledge, rev. pb edn 1974 (first published in English 1922, trans. C.K. Ogden).

WITTGENSTEIN, L. (1980) *Remarks on the Philosophy of Psychology*, 2 vols, vol.1 trans. G.E.M. Anscombe, vol.2 trans. C.G. Luckhardt and M.A.E. Aue, Oxford, Blackwell.

WITTGENSTEIN, L. (1982) *Last Writings on the Philosophy of Psychology*, vol.1, ed. G.H. von Wright and H. Nyman, trans. C.G. Luckhardt and M.A.E. Aue, Oxford, Blackwell.

WITTGENSTEIN, L. (1992) *Last Writings on the Philosophy of Psychology*, vol.2, ed. G.H. von Wright and H. Nyman, trans. C.G. Luckhardt and M.A.E. Aue, Oxford, Blackwell.

WU, D. (ed.) (1998) *Romanticism: An Anthology*, 2nd edn, Oxford, Blackwell.

YOLTON, J.W. (1984) *Perceptual Acquaintance*, Oxford, Blackwell.

Readings

Imagination and imagery
Alan R. White

Source: White, A.R. (1990) *The Language of Imagination*, ch.12, Oxford, Blackwell, pp.88–92.

Imagination does not imply imagery since much imagination is of what is non-sensory, just as much memory consists in recalling dates, times, arguments, rather than faces and places, and cannot, therefore, contain any imagery. That is, what is described in describing what one here imagines could not be a picture. This is the case, whatever form of imagination we consider. For instance we can imagine, or be unable to imagine, what the neighbours will think or why someone should try to kill us, just as we can imagine that the neighbours envy us or that someone is trying to kill us. Yet none of these imagined situations is something picturable in visual, auditory or tangible terms and, therefore, none is something pertaining to imagery. If what we imagine is either doing something or ourselves or another doing it, what we imagine may be some picturable activity, such as putting out to sea or walking in a procession, or it may be some non-picturable activity, as when I imagine being unjustly accused, or imagine myself or you allowing so-and-so or agreeing to such-and-such. Furthermore, whereas imagining oneself or another doing something observable, for instance lying in the sun or mowing the lawn, could involve picturing oneself or him engaged in such action, imagining doing something observable, for example lying in the sun or mowing the lawn, does not involve imagining – nor, *a fortiori*, picturing – oneself or another doing it. It makes sense to say 'I can picture myself or him mowing the lawn', but not 'I can picture mowing the lawn'. Equally, if what I can or cannot imagine is anything more unlikely than this or more silly than that, these are not things which are easily or at all reduced to imagery. I can also as easily imagine a difficulty or an objection as I can imagine an elephant or a bus. But only for the latter would the presence of imagery be at all plausible. Even when what we imagine is whether we perceive (see, hear, etc.) something, it is not *what* we think we perceive that we imagine, but *whether* we perceive it. Philosophers often misinterpret our common question 'Did I see, hear, smell so-and-so or did I only imagine it?' as if the 'it' referred to 'so-and-so', whereas it really refers to 'that I saw, heard, smelt so-and-so'.

[...]

If imagery implies the existence of images ... it is relevant that what we can have an image of can only be that which something else, namely the image, can resemble in some copyable way. It is because something can look like, sound like, feel like, smell or taste like, something else, that the former can be an image, as it can be a copy, of the latter. This is equally true when we include physical images, such as idols of wood or stone, phenomenal images, such as reflections in mirrors or pools, psychological images, such as after-images and hallucinations, or the mental images of dreams, memory and imagination. So something can look like a dagger, sound like a cat, or smell like gas, but however much something may seem, appear, or look, to be a difficulty, a solution, an insult or a hint, it cannot literally look like, sound like or smell like one, however metaphorically it may do so. This is why one cannot have copies or images of any of these. Even in the sensory, there are features which are imaginable, but not capable of being put in imagery. One can imagine, for example, that some man, no men or all men have red hair, that the black horse is here now or not there then, but there is no imagery for 'some', 'all' or 'none', or for 'here', 'now' or 'there'. Imagining that so-and-so is not such-and-such is as easy as imagining that it is, but there is no image of so-and-so as not being such-and-such. Furthermore, though visual and auditory imagery is plausible on the analogy of pictures and echoes, the existence of olfactory and taste imagery is as debatable as that of paintings of smells and tastes.[1] Yet imaginary tastes and smells are as common as imaginary sights and sounds and we can 'smell' or 'taste' something in our imagination. It is easy to imagine that someone is in great pain, but what would imagery of a pain be like? Imagery is confined to the copyable and the picturable, but imagination is not. Because one can paint or draw how one imagined something looked or sounded like, it does not follow that one can paint how one imagined a problem could be solved. Similarly, my ability to imagine how a clock looked or sounded or would look or sound, but not my ability to imagine how a problem was or would be solved, might manifest itself in imagery as it might in drawings or recordings. Even the element of likeness or copying etymologically expressed in 'image' has its limitations in 'mental', as contrasted with sensation or physical, images. For what makes my image of my uncle an image of him is not so much its pictorial likeness to him but that it is how I picture him, even if this is other than he is.

[...]

The possibility, and the common occurrence, of instances of imagining in various forms which do not or could not contain any imagery shows that imagination does not imply imagery. It is even clearer, as would now be generally admitted in contrast to the claims of Descartes and Hume, that the presence of imagery does not imply imagination. Imagery may occur in dreams, by night or by day, in memory and recollection, in expectation, wishing, and in various forms of thought. Various occurrences, such as the uttering or hearing of words, may arouse imagery in us without making us imagine anything. Even more vivid imagery, though perhaps imagery of a different kind, is an ingredient of after-images, hallucinations and, perhaps, some illusions. Imagery is also arguably a component of seeing one thing as another, as when one sees a particular figure as, for example, either a set of steps or an overhanging cornice or sees the duck-rabbit as a duck.[2]

A more relevant and more debatable problem is whether the presence of imagery in imagination, when it is present, in any way contributes to making it an instance of imagination. In other words, does any imagery present play an essential role in the imagination? The short answer is that imagery has characteristics which imagination has not and lacks characteristics which imagination has.

Though one can produce imagery to order, as when one indulges in day-dreams, or recalls what one has perceived in the past, in a way that one cannot produce sights or sounds to order, imagery often has an objectivity and independence of the imager. One can contemplate, inspect and scrutinize one's imagery. Like a picture or drawing, an image, especially an eidetic or an after-image, often lies passive before one. One's imagery often presents one with unexpected features. It can come and go independently of one. Having imagery, but not imagining, is an experience. Imagination, on the other hand, is very much under one's voluntary control, even though often one can't help imagining that, for instance, one is being persecuted or that one has heard a noise. What one imagines is what one conjectures, not what is present to one. One can't be surprised by the features of what one imagines, since one put them there. One reads off from one's imagery, but puts in what one imagines. One's inability to imagine when, where or why something is or to imagine X as a Y is not an ability to produce imagery, but to think of a possibility. To explain someone's inability to produce imagery by citing the poverty of his imagination is not to explain something by itself. Imagination is active and, as many philosophers ancient and modern have emphasized,[3] very much subject to our will.

Imagery lacks the essential features of imagination. It is particular and determinate, whereas imagination can be general and indeterminate.[4] One is imagining exactly the same thing when one imagines that, for example, a sailor is scrambling ashore on a desert island, however varied one's imagery may be. We can imagine being chased by a striped tiger without imagining how many stripes it has, but the striped tiger of our imagery must have a definite number of stripes.[5] On the other hand, though one can easily imagine that one is being chased by ninety-nine tigers and one's friend kills thirty-three of them, it is difficult to believe that any imagery one has would distinguish this case from that in which one imagined that one was chased by ninety-seven tigers of whom thirty-one were shot by one's friend.[6]

Even more importantly, imagery does not express anything, whereas imagination does. Merely to ask someone to have or produce imagery of a sailor scrambling ashore is no more to ask him to imagine anything than if one were to ask him to draw a picture of such a scene. A sign of a stag crossing a road does not say that the stag is crossing. To have an image of red grass is not necessarily to imagine grass being red or that grass is red. The imagery of a sailor scrambling ashore could be exactly the same as that of his twin brother crawling backwards into the sea, yet to imagine one of these is quite different from imagining the other. The imagery of such different things as memory, expectation, day-dreaming and imagining could be identical. Our imagery, like a sound film, of someone saying something does not differ from that of someone criticizing, explaining, commending, repeating, or replying to something, but there is a world of difference between imagining each of these. The difference between having imagery and imagining explains why we don't, despite what philosophers say, usually talk simply of 'imagining X', but of 'imagining that X is Y', 'imagining what or when or where X is', 'imagining X Ving', 'imagining X as Y', 'imagining X in certain circumstances'.[7] To have an image of X is not necessarily to imagine anything.

Notes

[1] E.g. Ryle 1949, and Vendler 1984; contrast Hume *Treatise*, and Matthews 1971, 160-2.

[2] Wittgenstein, *Philosophical Investigations* p. 213; Ishiguro 1967; Dilman 1968.

[3] Aristotle, *De Anima* 427b; Locke, *Essay* II.xxx; Sartre 1940; Wittgenstein, *Zettel* 621, 627; Berkeley, *Principles* 28, 29, 36; *Three Dialogues* 215, 235.

[4] Cp. Berkeley, *Principles* s.10; Kant, *Critique of Pure Reason* A141 = B180; Aristotle, *De Memoria* 450a 1-5; contrast Sartre 1940, ch. 1.5.

[5] This is currently highly debatable. Dennett 1969 says yes; contrast, e.g., Bennett 1971 s.7, Mackie 1976, 123, Fodor 1975, 177-95, Block 1983, who argues (a) a picture need not be photographic – e.g. a line of print could be shown as a squiggle – and (b) there need be no determinate answer to the number of stripes in a (mental or physical) picture of a tiger. He suggests that mental pictures may be more like drawn than looked-at pictures. The debate at least suggests that mental images are in many ways unlike physical images such as pictures.

[6] Descartes, *Meditation* VI, because he assimilates imagining and imagery thinks that this indistinguishability would hold for both.

[7] Wittgenstein, *Zettel* s.69, says that to imagine X in situation Y is to imagine that X is in situation Y; cp. Ryle 1949, 256.

Bibliography

Bennett, J. 1971. *Locke, Berkeley, Hume*, Oxford.

Block, N. 1983. The photographic fallacy in the debate about mental imagery. *Nous*, 17, 651–61.

Dennett, D.C. 1969. *Content and Consciousness*. London.

Dilman, I. 1968. Imagination. *Analysis*, 28, 90–7.

Fodor, J.A. 1975. *The Language of Thought*. New York.

Ishiguro, H. 1967. Imagination. *Proceedings of the Aristotelian Society*, Suppl. 41, 37–56.

Mackie, J.L. 1976. *Problems from Locke*. Oxford.

Matthews, G.B. 1969. Mental copies. *Philosophical Review*, 78, 53–73. Reprinted in *Ryle*, eds O.P. Wood and G. Pitcher 1971, 157–80. London.

Ryle, G. 1949. *The Concept of Mind*. London.

Sartre, J.-P. 1940. *L'Imaginaire*. Trans. Philosophical Library Inc. New York, 1972.

Vendler, Z. 1984. *The Matter of Minds*. Oxford.

Wittgenstein, L. 1953. *Philosophical Investigations*, eds E. Anscombe and R. Rhees. Oxford.

— 1967. *Zettel*, eds E. Anscombe and G.H. von Wright. Oxford.

Imagining and supposing
Alan R. White

Source: White, A.R. (1990) *The Language of Imagination*, ch.16, Oxford, Blackwell, pp.137–8, 141–2.

Though one can be as mistaken in imagining that p as one can in supposing that p, supposing, unlike imagining, is something one can also be justified or unjustified in. Wrongly imagining is not quite like wrongly supposing, since though both are wrong because things are other than one imagined or supposed them to be, in supposing that p, though not in imagining that p, one has committed oneself to p, whether or not one thinks that p. Supposing that p, unlike imagining that p, is something it may be fair or unfair, reasonable or unreasonable, to do, something one may have good, bad or no reason for doing. To say that one cannot suppose that p, for example that the audience would be interested in the topic, is to suggest a limit on what one is justified in doing, whereas to say that one cannot imagine that p is to suggest a restriction on what one is capable of doing.

[...]

We have seen that though one can admit, either that one cannot imagine or that one cannot suppose that, for example, many people will be interested in this topic, the reason for the 'cannot' is of a different kind in the two cases, the former referring to one's inability to conjure up such a possibility, the latter to one's lack of justification for committing oneself to such a hypothesis. For the same reason, though one can either imagine or suppose, for example, that A killed B in Rome during the summer in order to rob him of his wallet, one can be sensibly asked 'Can you imagine when or where or why A killed B', but not 'Can you suppose ...'. The reason is that one is being asked whether one can come up with or hit upon a possibly correct or plausible answer to the question. On the other hand, one can be asked 'When or where or why, do you suppose, A killed B?' but rather dubiously 'When or where or why, do you imagine, A killed B?' because one is being asked what is the answer, correct or not, which one does put forward either as a possibility or as a hypothesis. To suppose is here to hypothesize, that is, put forward as a hypothesis, not to think of a hypothesis; whereas to imagine is to think of a possibility. Imagining an answer may call for a feat or a flight of imagination, but there are no feats or flights of supposition. One can say either 'Imagine that a bomb has gone off in a crowded shop' or 'Suppose that ...', but while one can add 'Can you imagine what would happen?', one cannot add 'Can you suppose what would happen?' Equally, there may be limits or bounds to one's imagination, but not to one's supposition. We say 'I can't imagine anything more dangerous (more beautiful, significant, evil)', but not 'I can't suppose ...'.

Imagining, but not supposing, is something one can try to do and either succeed or fail in doing. This is why, though one can ask someone either to imagine or suppose, for example, that he has been marooned on a desert island, one cannot try to suppose, as one can try to imagine, this, nor complain or confess that one cannot suppose it, as one can complain or confess that one cannot imagine it. To imagine that p, but not to suppose that p, requires the exercise of a power, which some people may possess in greater degree than others. One can be good or bad at imagining, but not at supposing.

Imagining that p can be an activity in which one can spend a few minutes; but though one may for those minutes have also been supposing that p, this is not an activity in which one was then engaged. One can exercise or use one's imagination, but not one's supposition, about exile on a desert island. One can set one's imagination, but not one's supposition, to work.

[...]

The real difference is that to say 'Suppose that p' invites or introduces a statement of the consequences or implications of p, whereas to say 'Imagine that p' sets the stage for various kinds of embroidery. Thus, on the one hand, we commonly say 'Suppose (supposing) that p, what then?' but not 'Imagine (much less 'imagining') that p, what then?'. On the other hand, we commonly say 'I want you all to sit back and imagine for the next few minutes that you are marooned on a desert island', but not, 'I want you all to sit back and suppose ...'. We are inviting our audience to give free rein to their imagination but not to their supposition.

What is creativity?

Margaret A. Boden

Source: Boden, M.A. (ed.) (1994) *Dimensions of Creativity*, ch.4, Cambridge, Mass., MIT Press, pp.75–86.

The definition of creativity

Creativity is a puzzle, a paradox, some say a mystery. Inventors, scientists, and artists rarely know how their original ideas arise. They mention intuition, but cannot say how it works. Most psychologists cannot tell us much about it, either. What's more, many people assume that there will never be a scientific theory of creativity – for how could science possibly explain fundamental novelties? As if all this were not daunting enough, the apparent unpredictability of creativity seems to outlaw any systematic explanation, whether scientific or historical.

Why does creativity seem so mysterious? To be sure, artists and scientists typically have their creative ideas unexpectedly, with little if any conscious awareness of how they arose. But the same applies to much of our vision, language, and commonsense reasoning. Psychology includes many theories about unconscious processes. Creativity is mysterious for another reason: the very concept is seemingly paradoxical.

If we take seriously the dictionary definition of creation, 'to bring into being or form out of nothing,' creativity seems to be not only beyond any scientific understanding, but even impossible. It is hardly surprising, then, that some people have 'explained' it in terms of divine inspiration, and many others in terms of some romantic intuition, or insight. From the psychologist's point of view, however, 'intuition' is the name not of an answer, but of a question. How does intuition work?

People of a scientific cast of mind, anxious to avoid romanticism and obscurantism, generally define creativity in terms of 'novel combinations of old ideas.' Accordingly, the surprise caused by a 'creative' idea is said to be due to the improbability of the combination. Many psychometric tests designed to measure creativity work on this principle.

5 The novel combinations must be valuable in some way, because to call an idea creative is to say that it is not only new, but interesting. (What is 'interesting' in a given domain is studied, for instance, by literary critics, historians of art and technology, and philosophers of science.) However, combination theorists typically omit value from their definition of creativity. Perhaps they (mistakenly) take it for granted that unusual combinations are always interesting; and perhaps psychometricians make implicit value judgments when scoring the novel combinations produced by their experimental subjects. But since positive evaluation is part of the meaning of 'creative,' it should be mentioned explicitly.

6 Also, combination theorists typically fail to explain how it was possible for the novel combination to come about. They take it for granted, for instance, that we can associate similar ideas and recognize more distant analogies, without asking just how such feats are possible. But in many of the cases that are acclaimed in the history books, it is the recognition of the novel analogy that is so surprising. A psychological theory of creativity needs to explain how analogical thinking works.

7 These two cavils aside, what is wrong with the combination theory? Many ideas – concepts, theories, instruments, paintings, poems, music – that we regard as creative are indeed based on unusual combinations. For instance, part of the appeal of the Lennon–McCartney arrangement of *Yesterday* was their use of a cello, something normally associated with music of a very different kind; this combination had never happened before. Similarly, the appeal of Heath-Robinson machines lies in the unexpected uses of everyday objects. Again, poets often delight us by juxtaposing seemingly unrelated concepts. For creative ideas such as these, a combination theory (supplemented by a psychological explanation of analogy) would go a long way, and might even suffice.

8 Many creative ideas, however, are surprising in a deeper way. They concern novel ideas that not only *did not* happen before, but that – in a sense to be clarified below – *could not* have happened before.

9 Before considering just what this 'could not' means, we must distinguish two senses of *creativity*. One is psychological (let us call it P-creativity), the other

historical (H-creativity). A valuable idea is P-creative if the person in whose mind it arises could not have had it before; it does not matter how many times other people have already had the same idea. By contrast, a valuable idea is H-creative if it is P-creative *and* no one else, in all human history, has ever had it before.

H-creativity is something about which we are often mistaken. Historians of science and art are constantly discovering cases in which other people, even in other periods, have had an idea popularly attributed to some national or international hero. Even assuming that the idea was valued at the time by the individual concerned, and by some relevant social group, our knowledge of it is largely accidental. Whether an idea survives, whether it is lost for a while and resurfaces later, and whether historians at a given point in time happen to have evidence of it, depend on a wide variety of unrelated factors. These include fashion, rivalries, illness, trade patterns, economics, war, flood, and fire.

It follows that there can be no systematic explanation of H-creativity, no theory that explains *all and only* H-creative ideas. Certainly, there can be no *psychological* explanation of this historical category. But all H-creative ideas, by definition, are P-creative too. So a psychological explanation of P-creativity would include H-creative ideas as well.

Even a psychological explanation of creativity is hostage to the essential element of value. Even a cliché (which may be P-novel to a particular person) can be valued, if it expresses some useful truth; but not all P-novel ideas will be regarded by us (or by the person originating them) as worth having. So a psychologist might sometimes say, "Certainly, little Ms. Jane Gray could not have had that particular idea before – but it's not worth having, anyway. You can't call it *creative*!" (Likewise, a historian might say, "Yes, Lady Jane Gray did have that idea before anyone else did – but so what? It's worthless, so you can't call her *creative*!".) Such value judgments are to some extent culture-relative, since what is valued by one person or social group may or may not be valued – praised, preserved, promoted – by another (Brannigan 1981).

However, our concern is with the origin of creative ideas, not their valuation (the context of discovery, not of justification). Admittedly, criteria of valuation sometimes enter into the originating process itself, so the distinction is more analytical than psychological. But our prime focus is on how creative ideas can arise in people's minds.

What does it mean to say that an idea 'could not' have arisen before? Unless we know that, we cannot make sense of P-creativity (or H-creativity either), for we cannot distinguish radical novelties from mere 'first-time' newness.

An example of a novelty that clearly *could* have happened before is a newly generated sentence, such as 'The pineapples are in the bathroom cabinet, next to the oil paints that belonged to Machiavelli.' I have never thought of that sentence before, and almost certainly no one else has either.

The linguist Noam Chomsky remarked on this capacity of language speakers to generate first-time novelties endlessly, and he called language 'creative' accordingly. His stress on the infinite fecundity of language was correct, and highly relevant to our topic. But the word 'creative' was ill-chosen. Novel though the sentence about Machiavelli's oil paints is, there is a clear sense in which it *could* have occurred before. For it can be generated by the same rules that can generate other English sentences. Any competent speaker of English could have produced that sentence long ago – and so could a computer, provided with English vocabulary and grammatical rules. To come up with a new sentence, in general, is not to do something P-creative.

The 'coulds' in the previous paragraph are computational 'coulds.' In other words, they concern the set of structures (in this case, English sentences) described and/or produced by one and the same set of generative rules (in this case, English grammar).

There are many sorts of generative system: English grammar is like a mathematical equation, a rhyming schema for sonnets, the rules of chess or tonal harmony, or a computer program. Each of these can (timelessly) describe a certain set of possible structures. And each might be used, at one time or another, in actually producing those structures.

Sometimes we want to know whether a particular structure could, in principle, be described by a specific schema, or set of abstract rules. Is '49' a square number? Is 3,591,471 a prime? Is this a sonnet, and is that a sonata? Is that painting in the Impressionist style? Is that building in the 'prairie house' style? Could that geometrical theorem be proved by Euclid's methods? Is that word string a sentence? Is a benzene ring a molecular structure that is describable by early nineteenth-century chemistry (before Friedrich von Kekulé's famous fireside daydream of 1865)? To ask *whether an idea is creative or not* (as opposed to how it came about) is to ask this sort of question.

But whenever a particular structure is produced in practice, we can also ask what generative processes actually went on in its production. Did a particular geometer prove a particular theorem in this way, or in that? Was the sonata composed by following a textbook on sonata form? Did the architect, consciously or unconsciously, design the house by bearing certain formal principles in mind? Did Kekulé rely on the then-familiar principles of chemistry to generate his seminal idea of the benzene ring, and if not how did he come up with it? To ask how an idea (creative or otherwise) *actually arose* is to ask this type of question.

We can now distinguish first-time novelty from radical originality. A merely novel idea is one that can be described and/or produced by the same set of generative rules as are other, familiar, ideas. A genuinely original or radically creative idea is one that cannot. It follows that the ascription of creativity always involves tacit or explicit reference to some specific generative system.

It follows, too, that constraints – far from being opposed to creativity – make creativity possible. To throw away all constraints would be to destroy the capacity for creative thinking. Random processes alone, if they happen to produce anything interesting at all, can result only in first-time curiosities, not radical surprises. (This is not to deny that, in the context of background constraints, randomness can sometimes contribute to creativity [Boden 1990, ch.9].)

Exploring and transforming conceptual spaces

The definition of creativity given above implies that, with respect to the usual mental processing in the relevant domain (chemistry, poetry, music, etc.), a creative idea is not just improbable, but *impossible*. How could it arise, then, if not by magic? And how can one impossible idea be more surprising, more creative, than another? If the act of creation is not mere combination, or what Arthur Koestler (1964) called 'the bisociation of unrelated matrices,' what is it? How can creativity possibly happen?

To understand this, we need the notion of a conceptual space. (This idea is used metaphorically here; later, we shall see how conceptual spaces can be described in specific, rigorous, and explicit terms.) The dimensions of a conceptual space are the organizing principles that unify and give structure to a given domain of thinking. In other words, it is the generative system that underlies that domain and defines a certain range of possibilities: chess moves, or molecular structures, or jazz melodies.

The limits, contours, pathways, and structure of a conceptual space can be mapped by mental representations of it. Such mental maps can be used (not necessarily consciously) to explore – and to change – the spaces concerned.

Conceptual spaces can be explored in various ways. Some exploration merely shows us something about the nature of the relevant conceptual space that we had not explicitly noticed before. When Dickens described Scrooge as 'a squeezing, wrenching, grasping, scraping, clutching, covetous old sinner,' he was exploring the space of English grammar. He was reminding the reader (and himself) that the rules of grammar allow us to use any number of adjectives before a noun. Usually, we use only two or three; but we may, if we wish, use seven (or more). That possibility already existed, although its existence may not have been realized by the reader.

Some exploration, by contrast, shows us the limits of the space, and perhaps identifies points at which changes could be made in one dimension or another. One modest example occurred at the Mad Tea-Party:

> 'It's always six o'clock now,' the Hatter said mournfully.
>
> A bright idea came into Alice's head. 'Is that the reason so many tea-things are put out here?' she asked.
>
> 'Yes, that's it,' said the Hatter with a sigh: 'it's always tea-time, and we've no time to wash the things between whiles.'
>
> 'Then you keep moving round, I suppose?' said Alice.
>
> 'Exactly so,' said the Hatter: 'as the things get used up.'
>
> 'But what happens when you come to the beginning again?' Alice ventured to ask.

As usual in Wonderland, Alice got no sensible reply (the March Hare interrupted, saying, 'Suppose we change the subject'). But her question was a good one. She had noticed that the conceptual space of the Mad Tea-Party involved a repetitive procedure (moving from one place setting to the next), which eventually would reach a point where something new would have to happen. That 'something' could be many different things. When there were no clean things left on the tea table, the moving round might stop permanently, and the creatures would go hungry; or it might stop temporarily, while the clock was ignored and the washing up was done; or the creatures might drop their previous qualms about hygiene, and go on using the unwashed plates, which would get dirtier with every cycle; or they might bend down to pick some grass and quickly wipe the dishes with it ... The March Hare's interruption prevented Alice from finding out which (if any) of these were chosen. The point, however, is that she had identified a specific limitation of this space, and had asked what could be done to overcome it.

To overcome a limitation in a conceptual space, one must change it in some way. One may also change it, of course, without yet having come up against its limits. A small change (a 'tweak') in a relatively superficial dimension of a conceptual space is like opening a door to an unvisited room in an existing house. A large change (a 'transformation'), especially in a relatively fundamental dimension, is more like the instantaneous construction of a new house, of a kind fundamentally different from (albeit related to) the first. Most of the changes to tea-party behavior suggested above would be small, allowing the tea party to continue but in a slightly modified form. The first, however, might destroy the space, if the participants starved to death.

A complex example of structural exploration and change can be found in the development of post-Renaissance Western music. This music is based on the generative system known as tonal harmony. From its origins to the end of the nineteenth century, the harmonic dimensions of this space were continually tweaked to open up the possibilities (the rooms) implicit in it from the start. Finally, a major transformation generated the deeply unfamiliar (yet closely related) space of atonality.

Each piece of tonal music has a 'home key,' from which it starts, from which (at first) it did not stray, and in which it must finish. Reminders and reinforcements of the home key were provided, for instance, by fragments of scales decorating the melody, or by chords and arpeggios within the accompaniment. As time passed, the range of possible home keys became increasingly well defined. Johann Sebastian Bach's 'Forty-Eight,' for example, was a set of preludes and fugues specifically designed to explore – and clarify – the tonal range of the well-tempered keys.

But traveling along the path of the home key alone became insufficiently challenging. Modulations between keys were then allowed, within the body of the composition. At first, only a small number of modulations (perhaps only one, followed by its 'cancellation') were tolerated, between strictly limited pairs of harmonically related keys. Over the years, however, the modulations became increasingly daring, and increasingly frequent – until in the late nineteenth century there might be many modulations within a single bar, not one of which would have appeared in early tonal music. The range of harmonic relations implicit in the system of tonality gradually became apparent. Harmonies that would have been unacceptable to the early musicians, who focused on the most central or obvious dimensions of the conceptual space, became commonplace.

Moreover, the notion of the home key was undermined. With so many, and so daring, modulations within the piece, a 'home key' could be identified not from the body of the piece, but only from its beginning and end. Inevitably, someone (it happened to be Arnold Schoenberg) eventually suggested that the convention of the home key be dropped altogether, because it no longer made sense in terms of constraining the composition as a whole. (Significantly, Schoenberg suggested various new constraints to structure his music making: using every note in the chromatic scale, for instance.)

Another example of extended exploration, this time with an explicit map to guide it, was the scientific activity spawned by Mendeleyev's periodic table. This table, produced in the 1860s for an introductory chemistry textbook, arranged the elements in rows and columns according to their observable properties and behavior. All the elements within a given column were in this sense 'similar.' But Mendeleyev left gaps in the table, predicting that unknown elements would eventually be found with the properties appropriate to these gaps (no known element being appropriate).

Sure enough, in 1879 a new element (scandium) was discovered whose properties were what Mendeleyev had predicted. Later, more elements were discovered to fill the other gaps in the table. And later still, the table (based on observable properties) was found to map onto a classification in terms of atomic number. This classification explained why the elements behaved in the systematic ways noted by Mendeleyev.

These examples show that exploration often leads to novel ideas. Indeed, it often leads to ideas, such as new forms of harmonic modulation, that are normally called creative. In that sense, then, conceptual exploration is a form of creativity. However, exploring a conceptual space is one thing: transforming it is another. What is it to transform such a space?

One example has been mentioned already: Schoenberg's dropping the home-key constraint to create the space of atonal music. Dropping a constraint is a general heuristic, or method, for transforming conceptual spaces. The deeper the generative role of the constraint in the system concerned, the greater the transformation of the space.

Non-Euclidean geometry, for instance, resulted from dropping Euclid's fifth axiom, about parallel lines meeting at infinity. (One of the mathematicians responsible was Lobachevsky, immortalized not only in encyclopedias of mathematics but also in the songs of Tom Lehrer.) This transformation was made 'playfully,' as a prelude to exploring a geometrical space somewhat different from Euclid's. Only much later did it turn out to be useful in physics.

Another very general way of transforming conceptual spaces is to 'consider the negative': that is, to negate a constraint. (Negating a constraint is not the same as dropping it. Suppose someone gets bored with eating only red sweets: to choose *any nonred sweet* is different from choosing *any sweet, whatever its color*.)

One well-known instance of constraint negation concerns Kekulé's discovery of the benzene ring. He described it like this:

> I turned my chair to the fire and dozed. Again the atoms were gambolling before my eyes ... [My mental eye] could distinguish larger structures, of manifold conformation; long rows, sometimes more closely fitted together; all twining and twisting in snakelike motion. But look! What was that? One of the snakes had seized hold of its own tail, and the form whirled mockingly before my eyes. As if by a flash of lightning I awoke.

This vision was the origin of his hunch that the benzene molecule might be a ring, a hunch that turned out to be correct.

Prior to this experience, Kekulé had assumed that all organic molecules are based on strings of carbon atoms (he had produced the string theory some years earlier). But for benzene, the valences of the constituent atoms did not fit.

We can understand how it was possible for him to pass from strings to rings, as plausible chemical structures, if we assume three things (for each of which there is independent psychological evidence). First, that snakes and molecules were already associated in his thinking. Second, that the topological distinction between open and closed curves was present in his mind. And third, that the 'consider the negative' heuristic was present also. Taken together, these three factors could transform 'string' into 'ring.'

A string molecule is what topologists call an open curve. Topology is a form of geometry that studies not size or shape, but neighbor relations. An open curve has at least one end point (with a neighbor on only one side), whereas a closed curve does not. An ant crawling along an open curve can never visit the same point twice, but on a closed curve it will eventually return to its starting point. These curves need not be curvy in shape. A circle, a triangle, and a hexagon are all closed curves; a straight line, an arc, and a sine wave are all open curves.

If one considers the negative of an open curve, one gets a closed curve. Moreover, a snake biting its tail is *a closed curve that one had expected to be open*. For that reason, it is surprising, even arresting ('But look! What was that?'). Kekulé might have had a similar reaction if he had been out on a country walk and happened to see a snake with its tail in its mouth. But there is no reason to think that he would have been stopped in his tracks by seeing a Victorian child's hoop. A hoop is a hoop, is a hoop: no topological surprises there. (No topological surprises in a snaky sine wave, either: so two intertwined snakes would not have interested Kekulé, though they might have stopped Francis Crick dead in his tracks, a century later.)

Finally, the change from open curves to closed ones is a topological change, which by definition will alter neighbor relations. And Kekulé was an expert chemist, who knew very well that the behavior of a molecule depends not only on what the constituent atoms are, but also on how they are juxtaposed. A change in atomic neighbor relations is very likely to have some chemical significance. So it is understandable that he had a hunch that this tail-biting snake molecule might contain the answer to his problem.

Plausible though this talk of conceptual spaces may be, it is – thus far – largely metaphorical. I have claimed that in calling an idea creative one should specify the particular set of generative principles with respect to which it is impossible. But I have not said how the (largely tacit) knowledge of literary critics, musicologists, and historians of art and science might be explicitly expressed within a psychological theory of creativity. How can this be done? And, the putative structures having been made explicit, how can we be sure that the mental processes specified by the psychologist really are powerful enough to generate such-and-such ideas from such-and-such structures? This is where computational psychology can help us.

The relevance of computational psychology

Computational psychology draws many of its theoretical concepts from artificial intelligence, or AI. Artificial intelligence studies the nature of intelligence in general, and its method is to try to enable computers to do the sorts of things that minds can do: seeing, speaking, storytelling, and logical or analogical thinking.

But how can computers have anything to do with creativity? The very idea, it may seem, is absurd. The first person to denounce this apparent absurdity was Ada, Lady Lovelace, the friend and collaborator of Charles Babbage. She realized that Babbage's 'Analytical Engine' – in essence, a design for a digital computer – could in principle 'compose elaborate and scientific pieces of music of any degree of complexity or extent.' But she insisted that the creativity involved in any elaborate pieces of music emanating from the Analytical Engine would have to be credited not to the engine, but to the engineer. As she put it, 'The Analytical Engine has no pretensions whatever to *originate* anything. It can do [only] *whatever we know how to order it* to perform.'

If Lady Lovelace's remark means merely that *a computer can do only what its program enables it to do*, it is correct – and, from the point of view of theoretical psychology, helpful and important. It means, for instance, that if a program manages to play a Chopin waltz expressively, or to improvise modern jazz, then the musical structures and procedures (the generative structures) in that program *must* be capable of producing those examples of musical expression or improvisation. (It does not follow that human musicians do it in the same way: perhaps there is reason to suspect that they do not. But the program specifies, in detail, *one* way in which such things can be done. Alternative theories, involving different musical structures or psychological processes, should ideally be expressed at a comparable level of detail.)

But if Lady Lovelace's remark is intended as an argument denying any interesting link between computers and creativity, it is too quick and too simple. We must distinguish four different questions, which are often confused with each other. I call them Lovelace questions, because many people would respond to them (with a dismissive 'No!') by using the argument cited above.

The first Lovelace question is whether computational concepts can help us understand how *human* creativity is possible. The second is whether computers (now or in the future) could ever do things that at least *appear to be* creative. The third is whether a computer could ever *appear to recognize* creativity – in poems written by human poets, for instance, or in its own novel ideas about science or mathematics. And the fourth is whether computers themselves could ever *really* be creative (as opposed to merely producing apparently creative performance, whose originality is wholly due to the human programmer).

Our prime interest is in the first Lovelace question, which focuses on the creativity of human beings. The next two Lovelace questions are psychologically interesting insofar as they throw light on the first. For our purposes, the fourth Lovelace question can be ignored. It is not a scientific question, as the others are, but in part a philosophical worry about 'meaning' and in part a disguised request for a moral-political decision (Boden 1990, ch. 11).

The answers I shall propose to the first three questions are, respectively: *Yes, definitely*; *Yes, up to a point*; and *Yes, necessarily (for any program that appears to be creative)*. In short, computational ideas can help us to understand how human creativity is possible. This does not mean that creativity is predictable, nor even that an original idea can be explained in every detail after it has appeared. But we can draw on computational ideas in understanding in scientific terms how 'intuition' works.

The psychology of creativity can benefit from AI and computer science *precisely because* – as Lady Lovelace pointed out – a computer can do only what its program enables it to do. On the one hand, computational concepts, and their disciplined expression in programming terms, help us to specify generative principles clearly. On the other hand, computer modeling helps us to see, in practice, what a particular generative system *can* and *cannot* do.

The results may be surprising, for the generative potential of a program is not always obvious: the computer may do things we did not know we had 'ordered it' to perform. And, all too often, it may fail to do things that we fondly believed we had allowed for in our instructions. So expressing a psychological theory as a program to be run on a computer is an excellent way of testing its clarity, its coherence, and its generative potential.

References

Boden, M.A. 1990. *The Creative Mind: Myths and Mechanisms*. London: Weidenfeld and Nicolson.

Brannigan, A. 1981. *The Social Basis of Scientific Discoveries*. Cambridge: Cambridge University Press.

Koestler, A. 1964. *The Act of Creation*. London: Hutchinson.

Creativity and constraint

David Novitz

Source: Novitz, D. (1999) 'Creativity and constraint', *Australasian Journal of Philosophy*, 77, 1, pp.71–8.

IV. Computers and human beings

Appropriately programmed computers are well-placed to explore conceptual spaces, to discover their limitations relative to certain goals and tasks, and to transform the prevailing generative principles in ways that will allow them to achieve specific goals and perform the requisite tasks. For this reason, Boden's account of human P-creativity applies quite well to some computer programmes. What is not nearly so clear is that her explanation applies as neatly to human beings. People are less able than computers to abide by Boden's constraint, not least because of the difficulty they experience in absorbing and integrating endless flows of information, but also because the flair and the genius that we associate with human creativity seems to be voided by Boden's requirement that humans need to be acquainted with all the possibilities and limitations of the domain of thought relative to which they are creative. This would make of human creativity the plodding, laboured and monumentally dull affair that it plainly is not.

The fact, too, that humans are social animals and that close familiarity with a complex conceptual space sometimes involves considerable investment in an associated social space, results in a range of rather special constraints on human creativity; constraints to which computational programmes are not subject. As social animals, human beings depend on others for their well-being and have a strong interest in maintaining their networks of support. In effect, this furnishes a major disincentive to human creativity that can be overcome only if humans contrive to distance themselves from some of the social consequences of their creative endeavours. Boden's account, we know, requires that P-creative thinkers should have explored, and should be maximally acquainted with, the conceptual spaces that they transform, but this ignores the fact that people are reluctant to concede that the body of knowledge that they have acquired often with difficulty, and that now affords them status in a community, could be importantly deficient. Still more, they are often sentimentally attached to their teachers and collaborators to whom they have a range of obligations that arise out of past assistance. Close acquaintance with a complex conceptual space thus carries with it very definite social expectations, some of which demand one's intellectual allegiance and one's loyalty. This, according to Jonathan Schooler and Joseph Melcher, is why humans are often P-creative precisely when they have *not* fully explored, and are not steeped in, a particular conceptual space.[1]

Contrary to what Boden says, it just is not true that radically creative human beings must always have explored and will always be familiar with the conceptual spaces that their ideas transform. Sometimes a chance remark, an image, a shape, a dream, encourage people to entertain new possibilities that cut across domains of knowledge and expertise that they have not fully explored; sometimes, too, the weight of those domains, the pressure of orthodoxy, prevent them from noticing new possibilities, new ways of doing and conceiving. Close acquaintance with conceptual spaces may actually inhibit P-creativity.

Much worse for Boden's theory, not all radically creative acts involve deliberate attempts to transform conceptual spaces. Think here of Henri Matisse, who, it is well known, developed a radically new approach to the use of colour in painting. His *Woman with the Hat* contained bold areas of flat, pure colour that outraged French critics when it was exhibited at the 1905 Salon d'Automne. In his essay, 'Notes of a Painter', he explains the way in which he paints not as an attempt to transform some prevailing style, some unified conceptual space with which he is intimately acquainted, but to achieve effects that he finds satisfying. He asks us to suppose that he has

> to paint an interior, ... and I put down a red which satisfies me. ... Let me put a green near the red and make the floor yellow; and again there will be relationships between the green or the yellow and the white of the canvas which will satisfy me. But these different tones mutually weaken one another. It is necessary that the various marks I use be balanced so that they do not destroy each other. To do this I ...[2]

It would seem from what he says here and elsewhere that Matisse's aim in what is widely regarded as extremely surprising and highly creative work, was not to transform a pre-existing conceptual space with which he was closely acquainted, still less to solve problems that could not be solved within it. His aim, rather, was to relay colour to the canvas in ways that, given his present inclinations and moods, he found satisfying. Although widely considered to be profoundly creative, Matisse's creativity, in this case, is manifested in something akin to play, and not, as some have argued, in problem-solving.[3] Even if, in so doing, he effectively transformed a given conceptual space, there is no a priori reason to suppose that he must first have explored this conceptual space, still less that it was his aim to transform it.

In just the same way, there can be no doubt that Pablo Picasso did not deliberately set out to transform a well-explored set of painterly conventions with his groundbreaking *Les Demoiselles d'Avignon* (1907) even though there undoubtedly was a tradition – a conceptual space – that he did transform. It was his fascination with tribal carvings, especially those of African origin, that led to this painting, and so to the introduction of forms that so impressed Georges Braque and signalled the advent of Cubism. If this is right, and there is no reason to doubt it, at least one paradigm example of P-creativity did not involve any attempt to transform an existing conceptual space or to solve problems posed by it; nor did it require the prior exploration of such spaces.

More damaging yet, some cases of what we would normally regard as radical creativity do not even require the existence, let alone the exploration and transformation, of a conceptual space. Think here of Edward Jenner. Prior to his development of the smallpox vaccine, there was no well-structured and unified body of knowledge or belief, no conceptual space, that dealt specifically with vaccinations and immunity. Certainly doctors wanted a cure for smallpox, and they undoubtedly dreamed of preventing the disease. It was known that one could get smallpox only once, and as a result some people had tried, with a notable lack of success, to induce mild forms of the disease through deliberate infection. But there was no well-organised body of theory or unified set of ideas according to which it was possible to induce the body to protect itself against a disease.[4] Rather, the story goes, Jenner overheard a young farm girl telling someone that she could not contract smallpox because she had once had cowpox, and it was this that set Jenner thinking and experimenting. The resultant ideas and medical procedures were startlingly new, highly suggestive, and plainly encouraged others to explore the mechanisms of infection and immunity. Indirectly it brought Robert Koch to the view that disease was caused by microbes, and it would eventually enable

Louis Pasteur to develop different and highly effective vaccines for other diseases. What we have, it seems to me, is an example of a development that most people would regard as radically, hence in Boden's terms psychologically, creative, but one which was starkly innovative rather than transformative or revolutionary; one that succeeded in developing a conceptual space *ab initio* rather than transforming an existing conceptual space.

It is open to Boden to defend her theory by pointing out that since Jenner knew of the medical impossibility of contracting smallpox twice, since he knew that people were trying unsuccessfully to protect themselves from the ravages of the disease by inducing mild forms of it in themselves, there *was* a conceptual space well-known to him, which he subsequently transformed. But this defence does not work. There is no suggestion in my argument that Jenner's discovery did not rely on earlier ideas; only that these ideas did not constitute what Boden regards as a conceptual space. For on her view, as we have seen, a conceptual space requires 'organizing principles that unify and give structure to a given domain of thinking' and so 'define a certain range of possibilities' ('WIC', p. 79).[5] She does not tell us how unified such principles and ideas must be in order to constitute a conceptual space, but even so it is clear that if she allows very loosely related, disorganised clusters of ideas to count as conceptual spaces, she will find that such spaces cannot be systemically transformed in a way that will allow computational ideas to shed light on human P-creativity. If, on the other hand, conceptual spaces are always structured sets of ideas that arise out of and depend on certain basic principles or general rules – like perspectival projection, or Mendeleyev's periodic table, or Newtonian mechanics – then Jenner was not operating within, and did not transform, a conceptual space, even though his discovery was radically creative.

Boden could, I suppose, respond by maintaining that Jenner's development of a vaccine for smallpox, since it was brought about without exploring and transforming a conceptual space, simply was not psychologically, and, in her sense, radically creative. But any such suggestion would have the wholly untoward effect of making her account of radical or P-creativity too exclusive. Jenner, after all, was responsible for developing a conceptual space pertinent to immune systems, where none had previously existed – and it seems arbitrary and deeply counter-intuitive to suggest that this was not a central instance of radically creative thinking.

The same considerations apply to Thomas Edison's invention of the phonograph in 1876. Although Edison's one thousand and ninety-three patented inventions were, for the most part, transformations of existing techniques, artefacts, and conceptual spaces, his invention of the phonograph does not seem to have involved such a transformation. The idea of developing some way of recording and reproducing the human voice was most probably occasioned by the fact that while people were able mechanically to record visual experiences with the help of the camera, there was no similar way of recording our experience of sound. But the principles and conventions of photography cannot be plausibly be regarded as the conceptual space transformed by Edison's invention, and while he certainly applied some of the laws of movement and acoustics in order to invent the phonograph, it can hardly be said that he transformed these. He would almost certainly have known that the human voice had been transmitted along an electric wire just the previous year by Alexander Graham Bell, but the phonograph did not employ, let alone transform, the electro-magnetic laws that Bell had exploited. So far as I can see, there were no existing conceptual spaces pertinent to the phonograph that he could transform; his invention, if the pun can be excused, was an invention from scratch.[6]

It is interesting to contrast Jenner's and Edison's inventions with Charles Goodyear's attempts to find a way of making rubber durable by preventing it from becoming brittle with cold or viscous with heat. Perhaps because he was in prison for debt at the time, Goodyear's research was surprisingly unsophisticated, involving only the successive combination of raw rubber with a vast array of randomly chosen additives – from witch hazel and cream cheese to black ink. It was only when he eventually stumbled on a heat-sulphur treatment for rubber (by accidentally dropping rubber mixed with sulphur on to a hot surface) that the process of vulcanization was discovered in 1839.[7]

Here, I think, we would normally resist describing Goodyear's development of the idea of vulcanization, or his subsequent discovery of vulcanization, as radically creative. For at that time, almost anyone would have known that one could alter the physical properties of a substance by combining it with other substances. Then, too, provided that there are no life-extinguishing explosions along the way, anyone is bound to come across some new and useful results by randomly combining enough different substances with rubber.

Even so, the idea and the subsequent discovery was deeply transformative of what Boden would have to treat as an existing conceptual space. Up until then, there were certain basic, law-like ideas that governed thinking about rubber, namely that rubber becomes viscous with heat and brittle with cold. And this, in its turn, affected almost everyone's ideas about what could be done with rubber. Here we have a conceptual space, where ideas about what can be done with rubber are not just interrelated, but are subtended, organised, and unified by some fundamental principles. And it is plain that Goodyear transformed that space, since he developed the idea that rubber could take a different form, need not become sticky or brittle with heat or cold, and this, in its turn, radically changed the ideas that people had about rubber and the uses to which it might be put.

Given her theory, Boden would have to regard the idea and discovery of vulcanization as radically creative. On her view, as we will see later, the relative 'depth' of transformation of a conceptual space, gives her a rough measure of degrees of P-creativity ('WIC', p.113). Since the prevailing beliefs about rubber before 1838 constituted a conceptual space, and since the idea of vulcanization could not have been thought in terms of it, Goodyear's idea and subsequent discovery would, by her own lights, have 'transformed' the fundamental organizing principles of that space. On Boden's view, therefore, Goodyear's discovery was highly creative.[8]

But this is odd. Goodyear's invention, if invention it was, was pretty lacklustre, and required very little in the way of imagination, intelligence, or endeavour. To describe it as highly creative in the way that Einstein's transformation of Newtonian physics was highly creative, and to suppose that it is somehow more creative than Jenner's development of the smallpox vaccine, or Matisse's painting, appears to be much too generous to Goodyear.

It is now clear, I hope, that where human creativity is concerned, Boden's theory is deficient in a number of respects. First, it underestimates the social constraints on human P-creativity, and so fails to recognize that people may be P-creative without exploring the conceptual spaces that they transform; indeed, that the close exploration of a complex conceptual space may on occasions inhibit rather than encourage human creativity, and is, in any event, at odds with the flair and spontaneity that is sometimes a feature of human creativity. Second, it is maintained, incorrectly, that all cases of radical, hence psychological creativity require a pre-existing conceptual space. But this tends to make the account too exclusive – as the Jenner and Edison examples show. Third, the theory is in some respects too inclusive, for while Goodyear's discovery (or invention) of vulcanization seems to satisfy all of Boden's conditions for radical creativity, it hardly warrants this praise when compared with the achievements of Edison, Jenner, Picasso, or Mozart.

V. The recombination theory of creativity

[...]

The theory that I favour allows that the starting point of human creativity is always an existing cluster of ideas or techniques, but insists that such clusters need not constitute or form part of conceptual spaces. Allowing that the term 'object' may include sensations and qualities as well as physical objects, my claim is that all creative acts require

(1) the intentional or chance recombination of such ideas, techniques, or objects – where this recombination is subsequently deliberately used or deployed

(2) in ways that result in something that is (or would have been) surprising to – hence, not predicted by – a given population, and

(3) in ways that are intended to be, and are potentially, of real value to some people.

These three conditions are each necessary and jointly sufficient for creativity. However, since (as we shall see) each condition may be satisfied to a greater or lesser degree, a high degree of creativity, like radical creativity, is not assured just by satisfying these three conditions.

There doubtless are specific psychological mechanisms that facilitate very valuable and surprising recombinations – hence a high degree of creativity. But the job of discovering these I leave to psychologists and cognitive scientists.[9] My aim in developing this theory is only to uncover the framework within which such an investigation must be conducted, and to rule out the idea that the transformative process described by Boden exhausts the notion of radical creativity.

As it stands, then, the recombination theory of creativity allows that there is an indefinitely large number of processes that constitute creative recombinations, only some of which transform the basic rules that define conceptual spaces. Others may involve recombining words or phrases according to existing grammatical and semantic rules, yet in ways that nevertheless turn out to be valuable and surprisingly insightful. Or composers may recombine notes and musical phrases in accordance with the prevailing rules of counterpoint and harmony, and may do so in ways that result in the brilliance of Mozart's music. In this way, the recombination theory can allow that many of Mozart's compositions were P-creative even though he only elaborated and explored but never actually transformed the conceptual spaces that he had inherited from Joseph Haydn. Then, too, there are recombinations that, far from being the result of detailed exploration or any great learning, are simply a matter of serendipity – sometimes the freak chance and happy result of simple play; sometimes, too, the result of comparatively uninformed trial and error strategies that are subsequently put to valuable and surprising use.

According to this theory, recombinations do not always involve the actual manipulation of words, phrases, lines, colours, notes, and physical objects. Sometimes they are purely ideational. Thus, for instance, aspection of the sort that allows me to see a duck-rabbit figure first as a duck, then as a rabbit, does not involve the actual recombination of any parts of this arrangement of lines. Rather, by considering aspects of the figure (or of any scene, state of affairs, or visual image) in terms of different beliefs or theories, and so with different emphases, the beak of the duck is thought of, or is seen as, a rabbit's ears and, as a result, everything else 'falls into place': the indentation at the back of the duck's head becomes the rabbit's mouth; the eye shifts its gaze; the lump at the back of the rabbit's head becomes part of the duck's chin. But the rearrangement, the recombination, does not involve the physical manipulation of any parts of the figure. Such manipulation as there is, is ideational, and involves looking differently, by considering aspects of the figure under different descriptions. To do this is to recombine these aspects with different ideas or beliefs in ways that may breed new, sometimes wonderful insights, innovative ways of seeing or thinking or understanding – in much the same way, I think, that the Copernican revolution did.

The second condition – the surprise condition – captures the intuition that creativity involves producing something novel or innovative from the point of view of a given population whose members were acquainted with some of the ideas or objects prior to their recombination. In other words, it captures the intuition that such an act and its outcomes could not easily have been predicted. Of course, accidents do happen, and it is well known that some recombinations will not live to see the light of day. On my view, such recombinations may nonetheless be properly regarded as creative if it is true that they would have been surprising (and of real value) to a population had they survived.

The third condition requires that a creative act be of real value to some people. Let us say that an act or an object is of real value if it possesses properties that are of actual or potential benefit to sentient beings: that either do or can increase enjoyment of life, enhance security, health, prosperity, and so on. It follows that a recombination that appears to be valuable, yet is later found to be thoroughly harmful and of no lasting benefit to anyone, will not be of real value and so will not be creative. This is why one can create something – mayhem or a mess, for instance – yet not be creative. The mad scientist who creates nothing but harm is ingeniously destructive but his actions are not properly described as creative.

Notes

[1] See Johnathan W. Schooler and Joseph Melcher, 'The Ineffability of Insight' in *The Creative Cognition Approach*, ed. Steven M. Smith, Thomas B. Ward, and Ronald A. Finke (Cambridge, MA: MIT Press, 1995), esp. p. 99 where the authors argue that not having excessive experience with a problem or in a field is sometimes helpful.

[2] I am indebted to Kevin Melchione for drawing my attention to this article. See Jack D. Flam, *Matisse on Art* (Oxford: Phaidon, 1978), p. 37.

[3] Cf. L. Briskman, 'Creative Product and Creative Process in Science and the Arts', *The Monist* 22 (1980), esp. p. 95, and T. Nickles, 'Can Scientific Constraints be Violated Rationally?' in *Scientific Discovery, Logic, and Rationality*, ed. T. Nickles (Dordrecht: Kluwer, 1980), p. 288, both of whom see creativity as conceptually linked to problem-solving. This claim brings D'Agostino, *Chomsky's System of Ideas*, p. 171, to the view that 'the degree of creativity manifested in a particular product is inversely proportional to the "strength" of the constraints on the problem for which that product is a solution'. Where the constraints strongly determine the solution to a problem, he argues, the solution is less creative than where the constraints allow the agent considerable latitude. While this is plausible for many cases of P-creativity, the strong connection made between creativity and problem-solving overlooks the fact that the explorative exercise in which Matisse engages when he paints is not directed at finding a solution to any particular problem – even in the very weak sense of

problem-solving that D'Agostino isolates on p. 170. It is not as if he sets out, for instance, to solve the problem of satisfying himself. Rather, his is a playful activity performed for its own sake, not for the sake of solving a problem. Even so, it may be properly be described as P-creative.

[4] Some semi-mystical ideas of inoculation had existed in ancient China and India, but either were not available to Jenner or were not seriously entertained by him. Homeopathic theory, it is worth noting, dates from the 1790s – just a little later than Jenner.

[5] ['WIC' refers to Margaret Boden, 'What is Creativity?' in *Dimensions of Creativity*, ed. Margaret Boden (Cambridge, MA: The MIT Press, 1994).]

[6] See Glyn Alkin, *Sound Recording and Reproduction* (New York: Focal Press, 1981). Edison's phonograph consisted of a revolving cylinder wrapped in tinfoil. A sharp point was pressed against the foil-wrapped cylinder. Attached to the point were a diaphragm and a large mouthpiece. The cylinder was rotated by hand. When Edison spoke into the mouthpiece, his voice made the diaphragm vibrate. This caused the sharp point to cut a trace in the tinfoil. When a needle replaced the cutting point, the talking machine reproduced Edison's original words.

[7] The discovery was not H-creative. The process of vulcanization was first discovered by American Indians. See Jack Weatherford, *Indian Givers* (New York: Fawcett Columbine, 1988), pp. 46-49.

[8] D'Agostino, *Chomsky's System of Ideas*, p. 171, is bound to agree with Boden on this point. He, too, would have to treat Goodyear's discovery as highly creative since the constraints on the problem that Goodyear wishes to solve do very little, if anything, to determine the appropriate solution to it. See note 3 above.

[9] See, for example, Ronald A. Finke, Thomas B. Ward and Steven M. Smith, *Creative Cognition: Theory Research and Applications* (Cambridge, MA: MIT Press, 1992). See as well their edited collection *The Creative Cognition Approach* (Cambridge, MA: MIT Press, 1995).

Is imagery a kind of imagination?

Gregory Currie and Ian Ravenscroft

Source: Currie, G. and Ravenscroft, I. (2002) *Recreative Minds: Imagination in Philosophy and Psychology*, ch.2, Oxford, Clarendon Press, pp.24–6.

We have said that mental imagery is a kind of recreative imagination. In this respect we agree with the tradition of Aristotle, Hume, and Kant, which placed so much emphasis on imagery. It is also traditional to think of mental images – visual ones, at least – as involving mental pictures. Largely because of the work of Wittgenstein, Ryle, and Sartre, the idea that having a mental image of a mountain is really a matter of seeing a mental picture of a mountain is now universally rejected. But attacks on the traditional view of mental imagery have gone beyond scepticism about mental pictures; some authors claim that imagery is not a kind of imagination at all.[1] We consider four arguments in favour of this conclusion, and reject them all.

The first argument is this:

> Imagery occurs in dreams, memory, expectation, wishing, illusion and hallucination: all cases where the subject has minimal or no control over the imagery. But imagination is under voluntary control. (A. White 1990: 91)

We all agree that imagery is sometimes under voluntary control. We should all agree that imagination is sometimes not under voluntary control; you can find yourself imagining things you very much don't want to imagine, and be surprised to find that you are imagining something you were previously unaware of imagining (Budd 1989, ch. 5). Perhaps the supposed difference between imagination and imagery is that all cases of imagination could have been under voluntary control, while some cases of imagery, namely the cases of it that occur in dreams, illusions, etc., could not have been under voluntary control. There is a sense in which imagery, as it occurs in dreams and illusions, is not under voluntary control. It does not follow that an image occurring in a dream or an illusion could not have occurred in some other context where it was under voluntary control. And the same can be said about imagination. It is true that there are episodes of imagining that are not under voluntary control. It does not follow that an involuntary episode of imagining could not have occurred in some other context where it would have been voluntary.

A slightly different argument is this.

> While my imagining may, on any particular occasion, be something beyond my control, imagining is always something that I do; imagining something involuntarily is not like having a pain. But having a mental image is not – at least not always – something that I do. (A. White 1990: 91)

Let us agree that imaginings are doings. As the objector notes, they are not always doings that one is able to control, as when one cannot help imagining something unpleasant. We see no reason to think that it is different with imagery. There is a sense in which imagery 'can come and go independently of one' (A. White 1990: 91),[2] but this is just the sense in which unwelcome imaginings can come and go independently of one. The contrast between imagining something and having a pain seems also to hold between having an image and having a pain. We have been given no reason for thinking that imagery is not imagining.[3]

It may be replied that images have features which indicate that their coming and going is less dependent on the self than is the coming and going of imaginings. For example,

> imagery has an objectivity and independence; we can scrutinize our images, which often have unexpected features. But 'One can't be surprised by the features of what one imagines, since one put them there' (A. White 1990: 91).[4]

We can be surprised by features of what we imagine. I can imagine a scheme for murdering someone and then be surprised to discover a flaw in it, and a playwright can be surprised by the richness of her own imaginative construction. I can be surprised when it is pointed out that I was imagining Sherlock Holmes to have a full set of teeth, when I was not conscious of doing so and certainly was not forming an image of them. There may well be potentially surprising features of images that are not potentially surprising features of belief- or desire-like imaginings. That is to be expected on the assumption that these are imaginings of different kinds. Once again there is no reason here for thinking that imagery is not a kind of imagining.

Finally,

> imagery is particular and determinate, while imagining can be general and indeterminate. (A. White 1990: 92)

Images are usually indeterminate in some way, as my image of a tiger ascribes to it an indeterminate number of stripes (Lyons 1984). What of particularity versus generality? The claim that imagery is a kind of imagining is, more specifically, the claim that imagery has perception as its counterpart; it is a kind of imagining which apes certain identifying features of perceptual experience. Perceptual experience is always of the particular rather than the general. So we would expect that perceptual imagining would always be particular also. The right conclusion here seems to be that there are kinds of imaginings that are always particular, and kinds of imaginings that are not. Visualising is one of the former kinds.

Notes

[1] A. White (1990) is an energetic and economical assault on imagery as imagining as well as on the picture theory of imagery. An engaging source for the history is Warnock (1976).

[2] The argument we are considering here seems to be one that White endorses, though this is not entirely clear from his exposition.

[3] See also the beginning of Ch. 8.

[4] See also Sartre (1940: 7-8).

References

Budd, M. (1989), *Wittgenstein's Philosohy of Psychology* (London: Routledge).

Lyons, W. (1984), 'The Tiger and his Stripes', *Analysis*, 44: 93–5.

Sartre, J.-P. (1940), *The Psychology of the Imagination* (London: Routledge).

Warnock, M. (1976), *Imagination* (Berkeley: University of California Press).

White, A. (1990), *The Language of Imagination* (Oxford: Blackwell).

Creativity and imagination

Berys Gaut

Source: Gaut, B. and Livingston, P. (eds) (2003) *The Creation of Art*, ch. 6, pp.148–73.

> <u>The lunatic, the lover, and the poet,</u>
> <u>Are of imagination all compact.</u>
> One sees more devils than vast hell can hold;
> That is the madman. The lover, all as frantic,
> Sees Helen's beauty in a brow of Egypt.
> The poet's eye, in a fine frenzy rolling,
> Doth glance from heaven to earth, from earth to heaven;
> And as imagination bodies forth
> The forms of things unknown, the poet's pen
> Turns them to shapes, and gives to airy nothing
> A local habitation and a name.[1]

Shakespeare, one might suppose, knew what he was talking about. In so closely linking the poet's creative act to imagination he was giving expression to a belief long maintained in Western culture. It is a view most famously celebrated by the Romantic poets (and, as we shall see, by Kant, their rather unlikely progenitor). <u>Shelley tells us that 'Poetry, in a general sense, may be defined to be "the expression of the imagination": and poetry is connate with the origin of man', indeed 'poetry creates anew the universe'</u>.[2] And the link of creativity to imagination has a history that long predates the eighteenth century, as indeed Shakespeare's enunciation of it demonstrates. Leonardo in defending painting observed that 'it is by manual work that the hands represent what the imagination creates'.[3] The view is even embodied in our common beliefs and language: when someone is stuck for a new approach to something, we might suggest that they use their imagination; and the term 'imaginative' is a near-synonym for 'creative'. This link between creativity and imagination is perhaps the most influential of the three traditional approaches to creativity – the others being the inspiration view (that the poet is literally the mouthpiece of the gods, and so does not know what he is doing, as enunciated in Plato's *Ion*, and given a secular twist in Freud's theory of the unconscious) and the derangement view (that the poet is a madman, also suggested in the *Ion*, and a view to which Shakespeare adverts).

The traditional linking of imagination to creativity invites a number of questions, which have been surprisingly little explored within contemporary philosophical discussion. I shall concentrate on two. First, is the traditional linking of imagination to creativity correct, and if so what kind of link is it? A second question arises if the link is validated: if the creative imagination exists, can we say anything about *how* it works, perhaps revealing something about its characteristic forms or modes of operation?

1. Creativity

To answer our first question about the tenability of the link between creativity and imagination, we need to clarify the two concepts in play. Creativity might seem to be a kind or way of making something; but in fact the term has a slightly wider application, as in Joseph Schumpeter's phrase 'creative destruction'. Though the term has this wider modal sense, in which even destruction can be creative, the core sense, and the one with which we will be concerned, qualifies a particular kind of making; and creative making is what we call 'creation' in the fully fledged sense of the word. Plausibly this requires that the making be a production of things which are original, that is, saliently new.

But more seems to be required to be creative than simply salient newness; for we use 'creative' as a value-term, which refers in people to a kind of excellence or virtue, in the broad sense of 'virtue'. Creativity is the virtue exhibited most fully by genius. But is the mere possession of originality sufficient to make the original object valuable? Kant, in a related discussion about genius, holds that 'Since nonsense too can be original, the products of genius must also be models, i.e., they must be *exemplary* ...'.[4] Kant's point is that originality can be exhibited by nonsense, and by implication be worthless. Now had Kant been acquainted with modern academia, he might have been more struck by the thought that even nonsense is not often original. And I am inclined to think that originality has at least some *pro tanto* merit: that even original nonsense has some merit over received nonsense, since it evinces some intellectual stirrings in its utterer, and may even produce some intellectual movement in its hearer. Be that as it may, the cutting edge of Kant's remark remains unblunted: we think of creativity as possessing considerable merit, but even if originality as I have suggested has some *pro tanto* merit, that merit is surely not commensurate with the great value we place on creativity.

That being so, we should hold that creativity is the kind of making that produces something which is original and which has considerable value. The object has this value in part because of its originality, but mainly because of its other valuable features. So we think of Picasso and Braque as exhibiting creativity, partly because of the originality of their Cubist paintings, but mainly because that originality was exhibited in paintings which, considered apart from their originality, have considerable artistic merit. The production of artworks that have little or no artistic merit, considered apart from their originality, strikes us, in contrast, as empty and not really creative.

A third condition is required for creativity to exist; for it is possible to make something that is original and valuable, but for one's making of it not to count as creative. Suppose that you daub me all over with paint and imprison me in a dark room in which there is a primed canvas. I flail around for several hours, attempting to escape; my frantic thrashings cover the canvas in such a way that it becomes, unknown to me, a stunningly good abstract painting, significantly different in appearance from any abstract painting hitherto produced. I have inadvertently produced something valuable and original, but it would be wrong to say that I have done so creatively – I made it purely by chance.[5] Or suppose that I engage in a mechanical search procedure for some desired outcome, systematically working through all the relevant possibilities, and in the course of the search come across a result that is original and valuable. Again, the upshot of such a search procedure is not an instance of creativity, for the procedure adopted is a mechanical one.[6] So *how* the original and valuable product is made plays an essential role in determining whether the act of making it is creative. And we must, at least, rule out cases of making by chance or by mechanical procedure, if an act is to count as creative. I will say that the making must involve *flair* by the maker to rule out at least these kinds of cases.

So creativity in the narrower non-modal sense is the kind of making that involves flair in producing something which is original (saliently new) and which has considerable value. Related accounts readily suggest themselves for the adjective 'creative' when applied to acts, people, processes and artefacts. A creative act is one that is the making of a saliently new and valuable thing by flair. People are creative, roughly speaking, when they have a trait disposing them to engage in creative acts. A process is creative when it is the producing of something valuable and original by flair (or, if we allow that a creative process need not always produce a creative outcome, when it is an instance of the kind of process involving flair that usually tends to produce original and valuable things). And artefacts (in a broad sense including the performance of acts) are creative when they are original, valuable and produced by flair. Originality, value and flair are the vital ingredients in creative making.[7]

2. Imagination

The notion of imagination is more slippery to handle than that of creativity. Part of the problem is that it has a variety of uses, not always closely related to its core sense. In one such use, to say that I imagined such and such is to say that I falsely believed it, or to say that I misperceived something: for instance, to say that I imagined the coatrack to be an intruder is to say that I misperceived the coatrack as an intruder. In this use, imagination involves false (propositional or perceptual) beliefs. This usage is one that is at least partly in play in the passage from *A Midsummer Night's Dream*, for the lunatic and the lover are both in the grip of false beliefs and misperceptions. But clearly this usage is distinct from the sense in which we are asked to imagine that, say, grass is red, for we are not required to believe it to be so.

A second usage is that in which 'imagination' is used virtually as a synonym for the ability to engage in creative thought; it is the usage under which 'imaginative' is employed as a synonym for 'creative'. In this usage, there is a true but analytic and trivial connection between imagination and creativity; and this use merits a deflationary account of the connection between the two realms. If this were all that there were to the connection, we need proceed no further.

There is a third use in which 'imagination' is employed to mean the same as 'imagery'. For instance, if I cannot remember how someone looks, I might be told to try to imagine her face, that is, to try to form an image of it. Some philosophers have characterised imagination simply in this sense: Mary Warnock, for instance, claims that imagination is '*that which creates mental images*'.[8] But there is a different (fourth) use of the term 'imagination' under which one needs to distinguish between imagery and imagination. In this sense, if I have remembered someone's face, it would be misleading to say that

I had imagined her face; and also one can imagine a state of affairs without having any imagery of it. It is this usage that is the one which we will now target.

Imagery is a matter of the having of sensory presentations; but these images need not be instances of imagination. A memory image of the blue front door of my previous house involves a belief about that front door, not an imagining of it. The same is true of many dream images. Perception involves perceptual presentations of the objects perceived; and such presentations though arguably images are not imaginings of the objects perceived. So memory, dreams and perception involve imagery, but are not instances of imagination. The point, then, is that one cannot *identify* imagery with imagination (though, as we shall see, *some* images are imaginings).

Conversely, imagination need not involve imagery. If I asked you to imagine that gradually your brain cells were replaced by silicon chips, you need form no mental image of this process to comply with my request; indeed, if I asked you to imagine an infinite row of numerals, you *couldn't* form an (accurate) mental image of that row.

So imagination is conceptually distinct from imagery. What, then, is imagination? A suggestion mooted by several philosophers, and one I think is basically correct, is that imagining that such and such is the case, imagining that p, is a matter of entertaining the proposition that p. Entertaining a proposition is a matter of having it in mind, where having it in mind is a matter of thinking of it in such a way that one is not committed to the proposition's truth, or indeed to its falsity. In contrast, the propositional attitude of believing that p involves thinking of the proposition that p in such as way as to be committed to the proposition's truth.[9] One can put this point in slightly different but equivalent ways. Instead of talking of entertaining the proposition that p, one can talk of thinking of the state of affairs that p, without commitment to that state of affair's (actual) existence. Or some make the point in terms of unasserted thought: to entertain the proposition that p is to think of p, but without 'asserting' that p.[10] Since assertion is strictly speaking a speech-act, not a propositional attitude, 'assertion' here, I think, should be understood in terms of commitment to the truth or falsity of a proposition (alethic commitment) in the way just outlined. These equivalent ways of presenting the view all have an important corollary: it is possible both to believe that p and to imagine that p, since one can consistently have the two distinct propositional attitudes towards the same proposition.

Thus far we have given an account of propositional imagining – imagining that such and such is the case – for instance, that it is raining. But in addition to propositional imagining there is objectual imagining: imagining an object, such as a wet cat. The account can be extended smoothly to cover such cases: imagining some object x is a matter of entertaining the concept of x, where entertaining the concept of x is a matter of thinking of x without commitment to the existence (or non-existence) of x. Equivalently, we can talk of having an 'unasserted' thought of x, where 'unasserted' thought is construed in the way just mentioned, namely, in terms of thinking of x without commitment to the existence (or non-existence) of x.

Thirdly, consider experiential imagining – the kind of case where imagining has a distinctive experiential aspect. Such imagining covers both sensory imagining (for instance, visually imagining the wet cat) and phenomenal imagining (for instance, imagining what it is like to feel soaking wet). This kind of imagining involves imagery, though we have seen that not all imagery is a kind of imagining. So what differentiates the two kinds of imagery? One might hold that visually imagining a wet cat involves having an image of a wet cat, and then thinking of that image that it is a mere imagining. But that would be false to the phenomenology of imagining, and also redundant. An image is a type of thought, possessing the hallmark of thought, namely, intentionality: an image is an image *of* something, and that thing need not exist, that is, the thought-content has intentional inexistence. A visual image is thus a kind of thought, and what makes it distinctively visual is not its content, but its mode of presentation, for I may think of how a wet cat looks without visually imagining a wet cat. When I visually imagine how a wet cat looks, the mode of presentation of that thought is visual. So what makes imagining sensory or phenomenal is the mode of presentation of the thought. The thought of the cat can be 'asserted' or 'unasserted' in the sense indicated earlier: in the former case the image may be a memory-, dream- or perceptual-image; in the latter case, the image is a kind of imagining. Thus, experiential imagining is a matter of phenomenal or sensory modes of presentation of 'unasserted' thoughts. Often when we talk of 'imagining' it is experiential imagining that we have in mind, which is a richer kind of imagining than the often minimal imagining involved in entertaining a proposition or the concept of an object. If someone says that he can entertain some proposition, but that he cannot imagine it, this shows not that imagination is never a matter of entertaining a proposition but that, in one usage of the term, to imagine involves an experiential aspect that goes beyond the minimal entertaining of a proposition.

Finally, there is what is sometimes termed *dramatic* imagining, imagining what it is like to be some person or imagining being in a person's position. This should not be thought of as a fundamentally distinct kind of imagining, for it is a structured composite of the other sorts of imagining previously mentioned. In imagining being in another's position, I have to entertain various propositions about his situation and entertain concepts of various objects, and may engage in both phenomenal and sensory imagining of his situation. The task is often a complex one, requiring considerable skills to be carried off successfully, perhaps even the skills of a great novelist. But to say that it is complex is not to say that it is irreducibly different from these other sorts of imagining.

3. Models of creativity

Given these targeted senses of 'creativity' and 'imagination', what is the relation between creativity and imagination? To take the simplest case, is there any necessary relation between them?

Does a creative act require an imagining? Not so: Bertrand Russell reported how, when he was writing *Principia Mathematica*, he would frequently go to bed having failed despite much effort to solve a difficult problem, but then wake next morning knowing the solution. Russell went from not knowing the answer to knowing the answer, without it seems any imaginative act on his part. A more subtle instance of this involves the chemist Friedrich von Kekulé, who claimed that he discovered the ring structure of the benzene molecule by dreaming in front of his fire of snakes devouring their own tails. This example does involve imagery, but being dream-imagery, and depending on the precise details of the case, it may well not have involved imagination: Kekulé while asleep may have believed that he saw snakes devouring their tails, and when he awoke, the image suggested his discovery to him.[11]

Conversely, does every imagining involve a creative act? One might hold that all imagination is creative in the sense that it can go beyond what is given to belief and to perception.[12] When I imagine a golden mountain, I am thinking of something which goes beyond my experience and my beliefs. But even so, this is not to make me creative in the sense defined earlier; for there need be nothing saliently new and valuable about my imaginings. When I peer over a cliff's edge I may, with boring and predictable regularity, just like countless other people, imagine being hurled down to the rocks below. What I imagine (luckily) goes beyond my experience and beliefs, but it is not in any even minimal sense a creative bit of imagining. The same is true of most fantasising: I may have the same fantasies as many other people, and my fantasies may be much the same each time I have them. Fantasising is a kind of imagining, but is rarely creative. Indeed, perhaps the simplest but most telling objection to Freud's influential piece 'Creative Writers and Daydreaming' is that daydreaming, a kind of fantasy, is almost never creative, and thus is not a promising model for creative writing.[13]

There thus seem to be no necessary relations at the most general level between creativity and imagination. But perhaps by examining in more detail creative uses of imagination, we might be able to find some other, more modest connections. To do so, consider two models of how imagination might operate in relation to creativity.

3.1 The display model

The first of these models I shall call the *display* model. This holds that imagination operates as a way of displaying the results of creativity to the creative person, but that creativity itself operates through some other mental capacity, perhaps in some other mental domain, such as the unconscious. The creative subject's unconscious, for instance, generates the creative idea, and this is then displayed to the subject through her imagination. In this respect at least, the display model is the heir to the traditional inspiration account of creativity, for that account holds that the creative person does not know what he is doing, and simply receives the creative result as a revelation, something that he cannot explain (as Plato tellingly argues of Ion).

One should not hold that the role of the imagination here is a necessary one in general, since, as we have seen in the cases of Russell and Kekulé, the creative idea can be displayed simply by forming a belief, or having an image. But, still, imagination would often have a display function. And that is plausible enough as an empirical claim.

However, the modest display model of the relation of imagination to creativity cannot give the whole story; for it makes imagination strictly speaking extraneous to the creative process. That process goes on in some other mental faculty, perhaps operating deep in the subject's unconscious, and then the result is displayed to the subject's consciousness through an imaginative act. It is as if imagination is just the recorder or scribe of creative processes happening elsewhere. Yet in Theseus' speech in *A Midsummer Night's Dream* it is imagination which bodies forth the form of things unknown, and the poet's pen operates as a transcriber of these imaginative acts. But on the display model the role of the imagination to creativity is merely peripheral; so we have not found the central connection between imagination and creativity for which we have been searching.

This point can be refined by distinguishing between two kinds of creativity, or perhaps aspects of creativity. *Passive* creativity occurs when the subject is unaware of the creative process, if any, which has occurred to produce the creative outcome. The outcome simply 'pops into the head' of the subject, as we say. The cases of Russell and Kekulé are like this. On a less exalted level, this kind of thing happens frequently: a solution to a thorny problem may come to someone when they are not dwelling on the problem at all, perhaps when they are on a walk or taking a shower. The display model fits this case well, at least when the medium for displaying the outcome is imagination rather than belief.

In contrast *active* creativity occurs when the subject actively searches out various solutions, consciously trying out different approaches, and in the course of this activity comes upon a solution. The solution does not emerge unbidden and unawares 'in a flash', but rather is the outcome (albeit necessarily the unforeseen outcome) of a sometimes sustained conscious process. Active creativity seems more common and important in the arts than passive creativity: a painter may for instance suddenly 'see' how his painting will look, but much of the subsequent work will involve scrutinising the painting as it is being made, imagining how it could be improved by altering it in various ways, trying out these changes, observing the results, making more alterations, and so forth. And this process may take the painting far away from its original imagined look.

In the case of active creativity, the subject uses her imagination as part of the creative process, so that imagination is not the recorder of an already completed creative process, but rather is a core aspect of that process. The role of imagination in active creativity is the locus of much of the attraction of the view that imagination is centrally involved in creativity, yet the display model signally fails to capture this role for it.

3.2 The search model

A different model of the relation of imagination to creativity appears more promising in giving imagination a role in the creative process itself: this is what I will call the 'search model'. According to this model, when one comes up with a new idea or invents a new object, one can be thought of as having worked through various possibilities ordered in logical space. The creative person has a strong, powerful imagination, capable of imagining more widely and deeper than most; her imagination is capable of grasping a set of the relevant possibilities, and selecting from them the one most suitable to the circumstances. Thus the process of 'trying out' various approaches, which we have seen is the hallmark of active creativity, is to be understood in terms of considering or surveying the relevant portion of logical space, and the process of invention is that of choosing from one of the surveyed possibilities.

Like the display model, the search model contains an important element of truth, since it takes account of the way we actively create certain things. But it also suffers from a number of defects. Most importantly, it is misleading about a very important aspect of active creativity. Contemplating Kasparov's creativity in playing chess, it is tempting to think that it lies in his ability to survey a wider range of the possible moves ahead than can anyone else. But this would be deeply mistaken. For consider Deep Blue, the chess computer which beat Kasparov in 1997. Deep Blue really does survey vastly more possible positions than any human could, and selects from them the one most likely to win the game. Deep Blue has in this sense a powerful imagination. But the problem is that it is the epitome of an *uncreative* way to play chess: it mechanically searches through the possible positions to arrive at the best. Kasparov in contrast, plays chess creatively, but cannot do so by surveying the vast numbers of possibilities that Deep Blue does. Creativity is precisely not a matter of a powerful imagination, in the sense of an ability to search through vast numbers of possibilities.

It may be objected that Deep Blue does not have an imagination at all – to have an imagination requires having consciousness and an ability to reason, and a computer has neither of these things. This may well be true, but the form of the objection stands. For consider an idiot savant, who plays chess exactly like Deep Blue is programmed to do, surveying a similarly vast array of possibilities and settling on the best. This idiot savant – let's call him 'Shallow

Pink' – has consciousness and reason, so he can and does have an imagination, which he deploys to survey a vast array of possibilities. But Shallow Pink, like his computational brother, plays chess in an uncreative, mechanical fashion.

There is something else to be learnt from this example. Let us return to Kasparov, who does play chess creatively. He may search through comparatively few moves ahead. But the ones he does survey are those which are likely to give him a significant advantage, and to be ones that may be surprising and original. Though he uses his imagination as part of the creative process, in trying out a range of selected possibilities, much of the creativity has gone into the prior selection of this small range of possibilities, rather than consisting in an ability to survey a vast array of them. And he may also use his imagination in seeing a current position as a variation of one with which he was previously familiar. So the difference between Kasparov and Shallow Pink does not lie in the fact that one uses his imagination and the other doesn't, for both employ their imaginations; rather the difference consists in *how* they use their imaginations. Kasparov uses his imagination creatively; Shallow Pink does not.[14]

This point shows that we should distinguish between imagination as a *source* of creativity, and as a *vehicle* for creativity. In being actively creative, in trying out different approaches, Kasparov uses his imagination, imagining different moves he might make. But though his imagination is a vehicle, or medium, for his creativity, it does not follow that it is the source of that creativity – that which explains why he is creative. His creativity is displayed in how he uses his imagination, but that in turn is explained largely by factors such as his vast experience, considerable knowledge of chess history, practised technique and his sheer native talent. It is these things which allow him to use his imagination creatively.

Failure to respect the distinction between the source and the vehicle of creativity explains in part the Romantic hyperbolic inflation of the importance of imagination in the creation of art, and indeed of its significance more generally. Shelley, as we noted, held that poetry, the expression of imagination, is connate with the origin of man and creates anew the universe. He thought of imagination as the source of creativity, but what we have just noted is that the imagination can be employed in an uncreative, mechanical fashion, and so cannot in itself be the source of creativity. But Shelley did see something true and important – that imagination is involved in the creative process as, I suggest, the vehicle of active creativity.

4. Imagination as the vehicle of active creativity

In being actively creative, the chess player employs his imagination in trying out various available moves ahead. The same use of imagination occurs in trying out different solutions to intellectual problems in general, and to trying out different ways to develop a painting, sculpture, novel, and so on. The painter and the musician are likely experientially to imagine their results, while the intellectual is likely to use propositional imagining; but both employ their imaginations. Imagination in such cases is the vehicle of active creativity, being that mental capacity which is used in being actively creative. If that is so, then we have found a connection between imagination and a type of creativity. The connection for which we will argue can be formulated this way: imagination is peculiarly suited to be the vehicle of active creativity. That is, it is suited *of its nature* to serve as such a vehicle, suited because of the kind of intentional state that it is. In this it differs from other intentional states, such as beliefs and intentions, which are not suited of their natures to be such vehicles.

We noted earlier that to believe a proposition is to be committed to its truth. Belief therefore aims at the truth; moreover, this end is *intrinsic* to or *constitutive* of belief: a propositional attitude counts as belief only if it has that end. (Of course, belief may not succeed in achieving this end – there are false beliefs – but belief is what it is because it has this end). It is the fact that belief has the intrinsic end of truth that helps to explain Moore's paradox, the paradoxicality, for instance, of the assertion that 'I believe that it's raining, but it isn't raining'. To assert this is ipso facto to be shown to be irrational, since it is to assert that one is in a mental state which aims at the truth while simultaneously denying that the content of that state is true. Further, it is because belief aims at the true that it is properly responsive to evidence, that is, to reasons for holding something to be true.

Intention also involves a kind of commitment, but a commitment to action, not to truth. To intend to do something involves a commitment to doing that thing *ceteris paribus*, when one can. The intrinsic end or constitutive aim of intention is thus achievable action. And this helps to explain why it is paradoxical to assert, for instance, that 'I intend to go climbing, but I won't when I can'. Again, one stands convicted of irrationality in this instance, because one commits oneself to a certain action by saying that one intends to perform it, yet simultaneously denies that one will perform it when one can.[15]

Imagination lacks the intrinsic ends of belief and intention. To imagine something is, as we have seen, not to be committed to its truth (or falsity); thus it is not in the least paradoxical to say, 'I imagine that it's raining, but it isn't'. Nor does imagination involve a commitment to performing an achievable action: it isn't paradoxical to say, 'I imagine going climbing, though I won't go climbing when I can'. Imagination is free from commitments to what is the case and to particular actions. In fact, imagination seems to lack any intrinsic end at all – that is, any end that makes it the state that it is. Imagination thus exhibits a kind of freedom in this respect. As such, imagination is peculiarly suited – suited of its nature – to be the vehicle for active creativity, since one can try out different views and approaches by imagining them, without being committed either to the truth of the claims or to acting on one's imaginings. Imagination allows one to be playful, to play with different hypotheses, and to play with different ways of making objects.

Since imagination lacks an intrinsic end, the ends of imagination are extrinsic to it: so one can use imagination for many different purposes without being irrational. (Contrast this with, for example, belief, where one cannot rationally simply choose to believe what it suits one to believe, because belief aims at truth and is consequently answerable to it.) In fantasy, the goal of one's imaginative project is to enhance one's own enjoyment, and the aim of this project determines what counts as a successful piece of fantasising. So, if despite my efforts, I keep imagining myself being embarrassingly humiliated, the fantasy has gone wrong. Alternatively, imagination can aim at learning something: here truth governs the imaginative project, but it is an extrinsic, adopted, aim of imagining, not its intrinsic aim. I may imagine myself in someone else's position *in order to* discover what she is feeling; but I do not believe that I am in her position. I can also imagine what I believe to be true; but when I do so, the aim of truth in my imagining is extrinsic. Creative uses of imagining, in contrast, need not aim at personal pleasure or at learning something. Nor need they aim at being creative: for one can be creative even though one does not aim to be so; indeed, it is likely that consciously aiming at being creative will to an extent be self-undermining, leading to a frenetic striving after shallow effects.[16] Creative uses of imagining are thus identified, not by their aims, but by their results (they produce, or are the kinds of imagining which often produce, a creative outcome). Creative uses of imagination need have no one extrinsic aim.

The claim that imagination is suited of its nature to be the vehicle of active creativity does not require that one always and necessarily employ imagination in being actively creative. Imagination, as we saw, is peculiarly suited to be the vehicle for trying out various options, because it is devoid of commitments to their truth or to acting on them. However, suppose that, instead of believing that the next option tried will be the correct solution, the creative person believes that *it is possible* that the next option tried will be the correct solution. Here the content of her belief does not commit her to the claim that the option is correct, so that her belief could be employed in being actively creative. But note what has happened: here the content of the belief mimics the feature of imagination that is crucial to explaining imagination's role in active creativity, that it be free of commitments to what is actually the case; the belief is now about the possibility of the correctness of the option. So here the *contingent content* of one intentional state, belief, mimics the *essential mode* of another, imagination. And this supports our claim that imagination is *of its nature* suited to be the vehicle of active creativity, and that belief is not. It is the nature of imagination as an intentional state, being free of commitments to truth and action, that allows it to be the vehicle of active creativity, and this is not true of the nature of belief. Individual beliefs, if they are employed in being actively creative, do not do so by virtue of their nature as intentional states, but by virtue of the fact that they have a particular content that allows them to mimic imaginings.[17]

Thus, properly understood as a point about the nature of imagination as opposed to other intentional states, the claim that imagination is peculiarly suited to be the vehicle of active creativity is correct. It establishes a constitutive connection between imagination and creativity that is the kernel of truth in the traditional linkage of the two domains. It also has the merit of explaining the appeal of the derangement view of creativity – that the creative person is literally mad. The actively creative person imagines various propositions and objects, but it would be easy to confuse her imaginings with beliefs – we have already noted that a common use of 'imagining' is in terms of falsely believing. And, indeed, given a vivid enough imagination, it would not be hard for the creative person to pass from vividly imagining something to actually believing it. The derangement view of creativity can be thought of as the degenerate offspring of the imagination view.

5. Creativity and metaphor

In answer to the first question raised at the start of this essay, we have discovered two ways in which the traditional link of imagination to creativity can be validated. First, the creative product is often made known to its creator by its display in imagination; this is an empirical claim. Second, and more importantly, we have argued that imagination is suited of its nature to be the vehicle of active creativity; this is an a priori claim, holding that there is a constitutive connection between imagination and active creativity. We can turn now to the second question mooted at the start: can we say anything about *how* creative imagination works? Perhaps surprisingly, I think we can do so, at least in part. To approach this, let us turn briefly to Kant's account of genius, perhaps the finest extended account of creativity in the philosophical canon.

In sections 46–50 of the *Critique of Judgment*, Kant investigates the relation of art to genius, and of genius to imagination. Fine art, he says, is the art of genius, 'the foremost property of genius must be *originality*' (175), and also the products of genius must be exemplary. Characteristic of genius is spirit, 'the animating principle in the mind', which is 'nothing but the ability to exhibit *aesthetic ideas*; and by an aesthetic idea I mean a presentation of the imagination which prompts much thought, but to which no determinate thought whatsoever, i.e., no [determinate] concept, can be adequate, so that no language can express it completely and allow us to grasp it' (313–14). Imagination in general, he says, is 'a power to intuit even when the object is not present'.[18] Reproductive imagination seems to be a matter of having memory images; productive imagination, to be a matter of sensory imagination. It is productive imagination which Kant has in mind in the passage about aesthetic ideas. But not just any exercise of the productive imagination is creative; indeed, Kant notes that we use this kind of imagination 'to entertain ourselves when experience strikes us as overly routine' (314), namely, to fantasise. But when aesthetic ideas, a kind of presentation of the imagination, are involved, then creativity occurs (315).

Though much in these passages is obscure, it is clear at least that Kant links exemplary originality (creativity) to a kind of imagination, without holding that all uses even of productive imagination (experiential imagination in our terms) are creative. There are thus some striking points of agreement between Kant's account and the position developed so far. But there is also something new: Kant considers under what circumstances imagination is creative, and his answer is in terms of when it exhibits aesthetic ideas. Yet his characterisation of them is less than pellucid: whatever are these things which prompt much thought, but to which no determinate concept can be adequate?

One answer is suggested by his remark of productive imagination in general that it is 'the originator of chosen forms of possible intuitions' (240). One might think of aesthetic ideas as the production of sensory forms that we lack the ability to describe adequately in literal language: think of some of the sculptural forms of Tony Cragg or the architectural forms of Frank Gehry, for instance. These are the products of highly complex uses of spatial imagination, and they are certainly examples of the creative use of imagination.

Though an attractive interpretation, this does not seem to be what Kant has in mind in talking of aesthetic ideas. He cites as examples of aesthetic ideas a 'poet [who] ventures to give sensible expression to rational ideas of invisible beings'; Jupiter's eagle with lightning in its claws as an attribute of God; a poem in which Frederick the Great asks us to leave our lives in the same way as the sun at the end of the day 'Spreads one more soft light over the sky'; and a line from a poem that 'The sun flowed forth, as serenity flows from virtue' (314–16). All of these examples involve attributing to something that Kant thinks of as the referent of a rational idea (invisible beings, God, death, virtue) a property which it does not literally possess, but which can be fruitfully attributed to it (a particular sensible expression, an eagle with lightning in its claws, the sun setting, the sun rising). In short, these examples involve a metaphorical attribution of a property to some object which does not literally possess it. And that suggests that what Kant has in mind by aesthetic ideas are metaphors. (Successful) metaphors do prompt much thought, but what they say cannot be completely paraphrased by any determinate, literal language; they involve a use of imagination; and originality is a merit of a metaphor, as it is a virtue of genius. Moreover, Kant holds that it is in the art of poetry that the power of aesthetic ideas can manifest itself to the fullest extent (314), and of course metaphors are most explicitly present in poetry, though there are visual and other sensory metaphors too.

Kant's connection of creativity with imagination in its employment of metaphor-making is intriguing, and captures an important insight. Metaphor-making, I suggest, is a *paradigm* of creative imagination. To rescue the concept of a paradigm from its Kuhnian multiple mugging, I mean by a 'paradigm' no more (and no less) than something to which we can fruitfully appeal in order to understand the phenomenon in question, or an aspect of that phenomenon. A paradigm in this sense is a heuristic notion, its application helping us better to understand the relevant phenomenon. Metaphor-making is a paradigm of the creative use of imagination, then, since it displays how creative imagination can work especially clearly and so helps us to understand creative imagination better; metaphor-making is also an instance of creative imagination.

A metaphor is an expression of imagination, since when I say metaphorically that x is y, I invite my auditors to think of, to imagine, x as y. If I say that men are wolves, I invite my auditors to think of men as wolves; the 'thinking of' here is not a matter of believing that men are wolves, but rather of imagining men as wolves. Or to put the same point slightly differently, in employing the metaphor, I invite my auditors to take up a wolfish perspective on men, to consider men as if they were wolves.[19] Besides being an exercise of imagination, the making of a good metaphor exhibits creativity: it shows flair; and originality is a prime virtue of new metaphors, creating a striking new way of looking at or thinking about some otherwise familiar object. But metaphors can also be extravagant and unconvincing, and can misfire in various ways; a good metaphor in contrast must be apt, must seem appropriate to its object. In this respect the cognitive content of the metaphor is important: if there are properties literally possessed in common between the two items linked by metaphor, then the metaphor will prove apt. It is because men really do have some salient attributes in common with (the ordinary conception of) wolves that the wolfish metaphor is an apt one. So the making of a good metaphor exhibits creativity because it shows flair and originality, and exhibits the *value* of aptness, which in turn often rests on a cognitive insight.

So metaphors involve imagination and exhibit creativity when freshly minted. Moreover, these are not independent features of metaphors: rather, the making of the metaphor exhibits creativity *through* the use of imagination. The perspective we are invited to take up on the object is the perspective of imagination – we are to imagine men as wolves – and generation of this perspective is an instance of creativity. For in a good metaphor, concepts and domains of thought otherwise far removed from each other are brought into intimate contact, reconfiguring the familiar conceptual terrain into a place both hauntingly strange yet oddly right. Wolves and men, concepts otherwise not closely related to each other, are brought strikingly together, and we are asked to imagine men as wolves. Moreover, the making of a good metaphor is not just a piece of creativity achieved through an imaginative act; the metaphor also encourages, indeed guides, further creative acts, through its encouragement of its audience's active search for the literal features that the object and its metaphorically ascribed predicate have in common (the elucidation of the metaphor), and in its propensity to support the working up of related or cognate metaphors guided by the original one (the elaboration of the metaphor).

Metaphor-making, then, is a paradigm of creative imagination, for in good metaphors an imaginative act brings together two otherwise disparate domains, and in so doing invites us to look at some object in an original yet apt fashion. As such it displays particularly clearly a central way in which active creativity operates.

This claim may seem to fall to a fundamental objection. For it seems to require that all instances of metaphor-making employ creative imagination. But surely that cannot be so: could not there be a metaphor-generating Deep Blue or Shallow Pink, mechanically grinding out metaphors, some good, some bad, some indifferent, and none of them the products of a creative imagination? And if that is possible, then it seems that metaphor-making cannot be a paradigm of creative imagination, since it need not even be an instance of creative imagination.

However, there are strong grounds for resisting the possibility of mechanically generating metaphors. In the case of chess positions, there is a set of finite, determinate rules which, together with the current position of the pieces on the board, specifies what future positions are allowed for the pieces. It is the existence of these rules that allows for mechanically searching through all of the moves ahead. There is also a clear criterion for what counts as success – checkmating one's opponent. But in the case of metaphors, there is no evident way to list all possible metaphors, since there is no similarly specifiable set of rules for what is to count as a metaphor. There seem to be no universal syntactic or semantic markers for an utterance's being a metaphor as opposed to a literal utterance. Nor can one appeal to the evident falsity of metaphors as one's criterion, both because there are plenty of evident falsities that are not metaphors, and also because there are metaphors that are literally true (for instance, 'no man is an island'). Nor would listing every sentence in English count as a way of mechanically generating metaphors, since by performing this task, one would be listing vast numbers of sentences that were not metaphors. One might as well claim that one had found a way of mechanically generating all truths, since one could generate a list of all English sentences, many of which would be true.[20] Add in the task of finding *successful* metaphors, and the difficulties of mechanical generation grow even more insuperable – though the existence of salient resemblances is one ground of success, it is not the only one, and in any case it is doubtful that there is any way of mechanically determining what is to count as salient for these purposes.[21]

I am highly sceptical, then, of the possibility of Deep Blue or Shallow Pink launching themselves on successful metaphor-making careers. But even if this were deemed possible, the claim that metaphor-making is a paradigm of creative imagination would not be materially damaged. For recall that this proposition is advanced not as a constitutive claim, grounding a universal a priori link between metaphor-making and creative imagination. Rather, it is proposed as a heuristic claim, a claim about how creative imagination, in one of its uses, can fruitfully be understood, thus illuminating how it operates. If, as the objection holds, metaphor-making is not necessarily an exercise of creative imagination, then a simple modification would hold that those instances of metaphor-making which are exercises of creative imagination are also paradigms of it. Thus restricted, the core of the heuristic claim would be undamaged. In such cases, metaphor-making would still display the process of creative imagination especially clearly. Through an exercise of imagination involving flair, such metaphors would bring together disparate domains into original and, if they were successful, apt connections. The product here illuminates the creative process; that is the core of the heuristic claim. Contrast this with, say, scientific or mathematical theorems. These may also be the products of creative imagination; but unlike metaphors, they do not similarly illuminate through their structure the process of how creative imagination works. For they are generally deductively structured from some basic propositions. Yet what we know about the creative process of making them strongly suggests that they were not generated by deductively following such steps.[22] In such cases, unlike that of metaphors, the product does not illuminate but rather occludes the process of its creation.[23]

In addition to metaphor-making being a paradigm of active creativity, metaphors are also surprisingly common in many domains of creative thought. This is obvious in the case of literature and especially poetry. But metaphors exist in other domains of art. There are visual metaphors, or visual works that function very like metaphors: Edvard Munch's painting *The*

Scream is sometimes said to be, or to function as, a metaphor for the human condition, for instance.[24] And werewolves are an embodiment of the metaphor that men are wolves. Metaphors are not just found in artworks. It is also a significant feature of our talk *about* artworks that it employs metaphors. The language of art criticism is heavily metaphorical; indeed, even basic terms of musical appreciation, such as talk of tension and resolution, high and low notes, musical space, and so on, are metaphorical. And metaphors enter into our experience of artworks, conditioning it into a kind of imaginative experience.[25] Finally, metaphors are also of considerable, though more covert, significance in science. Many philosophical and scientific theories are literal developments out of metaphors. The human mind has been variously conceived in history as a kind of hydraulic mechanism (whence some of Descartes' and Hume's psychological theories derived), as a telephone exchange, and more recently as a computational system. Sometimes these models were taken literally, but often they were treated as metaphors which would help focus intuitions, and from which a more exact literal understanding of the phenomena could emerge. Similarly, atoms have been variously thought of as billiard balls, as little planetary systems, and as waves. Science often spins its theories from a metaphorical source.

Though I have stressed the surprising frequency of metaphors in our creative practices, let me emphasise that my principal point is that metaphor-making is a paradigm of the creative use of imagination, and that this does not rest on a claim about how pervasively metaphors are employed. Paradigms are still paradigms, even when they are very uncommon. Rather, what the pervasiveness of metaphors shows is that metaphor is very influential in our creative thought; metaphor is not just a paradigm of creative imagination, but its use is a very common feature of creative imagination. However, imagination's employment in metaphor-making is not the only kind of creative imagination. We have already noted that the works of Cragg and Gehry are the products of powerfully creative spatial imaginations, but while some of their works have metaphorical aspects (Cragg's suggestion of laboratory vessels in some of his sculptures, for instance), the creativity of their forms is not exhausted by them. The claim that I am advancing purports to be only a partial answer to the question of how creative imagination operates.

Finally, it is worth briefly returning to Kant's discussion of creativity, which, I claimed, appeals to metaphors in talking of aesthetic ideas. We can now see that Kant's account has a significant defect. An aesthetic idea is characterised as a 'presentation of the imagination which prompts much thought, but to which no determinate thought whatsoever, i.e., no [determinate] concept, can be adequate...'. Kant's causal talk of 'prompting' here is inadequate as a characterisation of a good metaphor, or indeed of a good idea in general, since even excruciatingly bad metaphors and ideas can prompt much thought – for instance, thoughts about how bad these metaphors are, about how shallow and predictable their authors are, about how this kind of thing is typical of a certain banality in our culture, and so on. The causal idea of prompting, and the quantitative test of 'much thought' are inadequate standards of success in metaphor-making and of good ideas in general. A good metaphor doesn't so much *prompt* thought, as *guide* thought, asking us to think of one object in terms of something else; and its standard of success isn't the volume of thought it causes to gush from us, but the quality of that thought. For, as we have seen, a good metaphor must be apt, and a salient way in which it is apt is in fastening onto some previously overlooked features that two objects have saliently in common.

Perhaps it was Kant's hostility to the view that art can teach us anything (as opposed merely to stimulating our cognitive powers in free play) that prevented him from seeing this crucial point. But, in any case, it shows that the values necessary for creativity are in part cognitive ones. And in that respect Aristotle gives us a much better, albeit much briefer, account of the links between creativity and metaphor than Kant provides. Aristotle remarks in the *Poetics* that for a poet in respect of his use of language 'the greatest thing by far is to be a master of metaphor. It is the one thing that cannot be learnt from others; and it is also a sign of genius, since a good metaphor implies an intuitive perception of the similarity in dissimilars' (*Poetics*, 1459a5–8).[26] The link of creative thought to metaphor, and of a good metaphor to sensitivity as to how things are, could not be put much better than that.

6. Conclusion

In investigating the question of the links, if any, between creativity and imagination we have seen that some of the supposed connections have rested either on the use of 'imaginative' as a near-synonym for 'creative', or from confusing the mere use of imagination in active creativity with the claim that the imagination is in itself the source of creativity. Nevertheless, we have also seen that there are genuine links between creativity and imagination. We have seen the plausibility of the empirical claim that imagination is an important way in which creative results are displayed to the creative person. More important, we have defended the existence of an a priori constitutive connection between imagination and creativity: imagination is suited of its nature to be the vehicle of active creativity. We then investigated the question of how the creative imagination operates, and returned a partial answer to this question. We defended the heuristic claim that a paradigm of active creativity is metaphor-making, for such activity clearly displays how one can use imagination in being creative, in bringing together previously disparate domains in a way that is valuable, particularly in inviting insights into these domains. The creative product here illuminates the creative process.

The upshot is that the traditional linking of creativity to imagination is correct. Though the relation is more complex than at first appears, there are substantive and important connections – empirical, constitutive and heuristic – between the two domains. Much remains to be learned about this topic, but I hope that I have at least shown that there is a rich and interesting set of issues to be investigated here.

Notes

Versions of this paper were read at Queen's University, Kingston, and the Universities of Aarhus, Sussex, McGill, Leeds, and Sheffield. I am grateful to the audiences on these occasions for their comments, suggestions and questions.

[1] Shakespeare, *A Midsummer Night's Dream*, 5 .1. 8-17.

[2] Percy Shelley, 'A Defense of Poetry', pp. 498-513, at pp. 499 and 512, in Hazard Adams, ed., *Critical Theory Since Plato* (San Diego: Harcourt Brace Jovanovich, 1971).

[3] Quoted in Peter Burke, *The Italian Renaissance: Culture and Society in Italy*, 2nd ed. (Princeton, N.J.: Princeton University: 1987), p. 80.

[4] Immanuel Kant, *Critique of Judgment*, trans. Werner S. Pluhar (Indianapolis: Hackett, 1987), Ak. 308 (pagination of the *Akademie* edition).

[5] The stress here is on *purely* by chance; a creative procedure can involve serendipity, but for it to be creative, one must exploit chance occurrences with flair – for instance,

one must recognise the importance of an overheard remark for the solution of a problem. If the outcome occurs purely by chance, then the process is not a creative one.

[6] A real-life instance of such a mechanical search procedure was Charles Goodyear's discovery of vulcanisation. Goodyear dropped a wide variety of substances (including cream cheese) into liquid rubber before hitting on sulphur as a vulcanising agent; see David Novitz, 'Creativity and Constraint', *Australasian Journal of Philosophy* 77 (1999): 67-82 at 75. Novitz agrees that Goodyear's achievement was not radically creative, but on grounds somewhat different from those advanced here.

[7] The above account of creativity could be further developed and refined. For instance, to allow for the possibility of independent discoveries, one could distinguish between a discovery being original as far as the discoverer knows, and its being the first time that the discovery had ever been made; doing so would yield something like Boden's distinction between P- and H-creativity. For discussion of this, see the Introduction to this volume, section 2 (b).

[8] Mary Warnock, *Imagination* (London: Faber and Faber, 1976), p. 10.

[9] For this view, or variants thereof, see Alvin Plantinga, *The Nature of Necessity* (Oxford: Oxford University Press, 1974), pp. 161-2; Alan R. White, *The Language of Imagination* (Oxford: Basil Blackwell, 1990); Sabina Lovibond, *Realism and Imagination in Ethics* (Minneapolis: University of Minnesota Press, 1983), p. 198; Roger Scruton, *Art and Imagination: A Study in the Philosophy of Mind* (London: Methuen, 1974), pp. 97-8; and Nicholas Wolterstorff, *Works and Worlds of Art* (New York: Oxford University Press, 1980), pp. 233-4.

[10] For instance, Roger Scruton, *Art and Imagination: A Study in the Philosophy of Mind* (London: Methuen, 1974), p. 97, holds that 'Imagination involves thought which is unasserted...'. Scruton thinks that further conditions need to be satisfied for a mental act to be an act of imagining, something which I do not believe.

[11] It could be objected that apparent cases of creativity without imagination are really ones in which a person is imagining unconsciously – that this, for instance, was what Russell was doing when asleep. But it would be merely dogmatic to insist that this *must* be going on in all such cases, and the mere *possibility* that these cases do not involve unconscious imagining is sufficient to undermine the claim of universal necessity – that a creative act requires an imagining.

[12] For instance, something akin to this seems to be held by Scruton in his 'Imagination', in David Cooper, ed., *A Companion to Aesthetics* (Oxford: Blackwell, 1992), pp. 212-17. Scruton here distinguishes between imagination in the sense of the

capacity to experience mental images, and creative imagination, which involves the creating of mental contents which are not otherwise given to perception or judgement (p. 214).

[13] See Sigmund Freud, 'Creative Writers and Daydreaming', in *Critical Theory Since Plato*, pp. 749-53.

[14] This reinforces the point made earlier that the fantasist uses his imagination too, but rarely creatively; it is how a person uses his imagination that makes him creative.

[15] Considerations of this kind are deployed in Peter Railton, 'On the Hypothetical and Non-Hypothetical in Reasoning about Belief and Action' in Garrett Cullity and Berys Gaut, eds., *Ethics and Practical Reason* (Oxford: Oxford University Press, 1997), pp. 53-79.

[16] Compare this with the 'paradox of hedonism' – that those who strive after only their own pleasure will likely be less successful at achieving this aim than those who do not have this as their explicit or sole aim; for the latter can access other sources of value and pleasure, such as friendship, which are closed to the motive hedonist. In similar fashion, sole concern with his own creativity is likely to blind the artist to other values, such as sound technique, insight and sensitivity; and as we noted in defining 'creativity', some other values are required if creativity is to occur.

[17] One might suppose that one could also be actively creative in trying out various options physically rather than in imagination – for instance, a painter might try out various designs on a canvas, rather than imagining them. Could this also be an instance of active creativity without imaginings? Not so. The painter's activities would have to be controlled by his intentional states if they were to count as creative; otherwise they would be analogous to the paint-daubed thrashings-around in the dark room discussed in section 1. And if the painter's activities are controlled by his intentional states, then the issues to do with the nature of these intentional states resurface.

[18] *Anthropology*, 167; quoted by Pluhar in his translation of *Critique of Judgment*, p. 91.

[19] I am indebted for this point and several others in my discussion of metaphor to Richard Moran, 'Seeing and Believing: Metaphor, Image, and Force', *Critical Inquiry* 16 (1989): 87-113.

[20] Concerning the lack of surface syntactic and semantic peculiarities of metaphors when taken literally and that they can be true, see Ted Cohen, 'Figurative Speech and Figurative Acts', *Journal of Philosophy* 72 (1975): 669-84, at 671. Cohen there, and also in 'The Inexplicable: Some Thoughts after Kant' in this volume, questions the possibility of mechanically generating metaphors. He also holds that metaphors are

good examples of what Kant may have in mind by products of genius, though he does not directly connect metaphors to aesthetic ideas.

[21] Mere resemblance will not suffice: as Goodman has taught us, any two things resemble each other, since there is always some property that they share; see Nelson Goodman, *Languages of Art: An Approach to a Theory of Symbols* (Indianapolis: Hackett, 1976), ch. 1.

[22] Henri Poincaré gives an illuminating account of how during a sleepless night he discovered a fundamental mathematical theorem, a process of discovery that he expresses in terms of ideas arising in crowds and colliding, until some interlocked. The process of discovery was evidently very different from the structure of the formal proof eventually offered. See Henri Poincaré, 'Mathematical Creation', in Brewster Ghiselin, ed., *The Creative Process: A Symposium* (New York: Mentor, 1952), pp.34–42, at p.36.

[23] Even in the case of mechanically generated metaphors (if they are possible), there is a way in which their structure would still illuminate the creative process. For, even though *ex hypothesi* they would not be generated by creative imagination nor be produced by flair, they would still guide their audience imaginatively to link together two domains, and if the metaphors were successful, to discover original and apt connections between them and perhaps to elaborate the metaphors further. They would thus guide those who understood them through a process akin to the process of creative imagination that could have, but did not, produce them.

[24] Some resist calling non-linguistic signs metaphors, for they hold that a metaphor must have a subject-term which denotes the object of the metaphor (e.g., men) and a predicate-term which attributes some property to that object (e.g., being wolves). But property-attribution can be achieved not just by linguistic means, but by other methods, such as painting a property-instance (painting a wolf, for instance). Moreover, even though the object may not be denoted in all cases (the human condition is not denoted by Munch's painting), nevertheless the object of the metaphorical attribution can be *suggested* by visual means, as is indeed true of Munch's painting. So even if one were to insist that the lack of object-denotation means that one is not, strictly speaking, here dealing with a metaphor, nevertheless one can hold that certain visual signs function in a way very like metaphors, in inviting us to imagine a property of something which does not literally possess it. And the latter claim is all we need for present purposes.

[25] For the point about music, see Roger Scruton, 'Understanding Music', in his *The Aesthetic Understanding: Essays in the Philosophy of Art and Culture* (London: Methuen, 1983). See my 'Metaphor and the Understanding of Art', *Proceedings of the*

Aristotelian Society 97 (1997): 223–41, for a discussion of the role of metaphor in the understanding and appreciation of artworks.

[26] Translation from *The Complete Works of Aristotle: The Revised Oxford Translation*, ed. Jonathan Barnes (Princeton, N.J.: Princeton University Press, 1984).

Index

abstract ideas
    Hume on 73–6, 79, 116–18
    Kant on 116–18
active creativity
    and imagination 197–8, 199–200, 276, 278, 279–81, 282, 288–9
        and metaphor-making 285–6
aesthetic appreciation, and Stevenson's conceptions of imagination 8, 9, 10
aesthetic ideas
    Kant on creativity and 206, 207, 208, 209–10, 282–3, 287–8
    see also works of art
Anselmo, Giovanni, 'Eating structure' sculpture 207
Aristotelianism, and Locke 62
Aristotle 1, 6, 10, 40, 265
    Poetics 288
art *see* works of art
artificial intelligence, and computational psychology 252
aspect perception
    and the creative imagination 203, 204–5, 212
    and creativity 188–9, 193
    imagination and 124–68
    see also seeing-as; Wittgenstein, Ludwig
association/associationism
    and creativity 171
    and Hume on imagination 70, 72–3, 74, 75, 79, 80, 81, 96
    and Kant's conception of imagination 92–3, 96, 98, 120

Babbage, Charles 252
Bach, J.S. 177, 178, 179, 248
Beattie, James, *Dissertations Moral and Critical* 6
the beautiful, and the sublime 10
believing
    belief and active creativity 279, 280, 281
    and imagining 21–2

Berkeley, George 65
    A Treatise Concerning the Principles of Human Knowledge 63
    and Hume on abstract ideas 73–4
Blackburn, Simon 4, 5
Blake, William, *Songs of Experience and Innocence* 28, 29, 206
Boden, Margaret 170, 174, 174–84, 191–2
    and conceptual spaces 177–9, 180, 182–4, 211, 246–51, 256–61
    and the connection model 203
    The Creative Mind 175, 203
    'The definition of creativity' 176, 242–6
    'Exploring and transforming conceptual spaces' 177–9, 246–51
    Novitz's critique of 181–7, 188, 255–61
    and psychological and historical creativity 175–7
    'The relevance of computational psychology' 179–80, 252–5
    'What is creativity?' 175–6
Brann, Eva, *The World of the Imagination* 25–6
Braque, Georges 157, 270
Budd, Malcolm 151

Carroll, Lewis, *Alice in Wonderland* 177, 178, 247–8
causation, Hume on the principle of 72, 73
causes, and non-rational operations of the mind 7–8
changeability, and Descartes's conception of imagination 45–6
chess-playing, creativity in 197, 202, 204, 205, 209, 277, 279, 285
Chomsky, N., and linguistic creativity 176, 245
Coleridge, Samuel Taylor 1
    'On the imagination' 24
colour problems
    Hume and the 'missing shade of blue' 54, 65–8, 69, 70–1, 77, 78, 79, 81, 133–4
    Wittgenstein and the inverted spectrum 130–1
combination theory of creativity 171–2, 175, 242–3

commitment, alethic and existential
    and imagining 14–22, 165–7, 199–200, 271–4
computational psychology, and creativity 170, 179–81
computers, and chess-playing 277–8
conception
    and imagination 40–59
        see also Descartes, René
concepts
    Kant on images and schemata 110–16, 117
    in Kant's 'Transcendental Deduction' 88–90
    and seeing-as 157, 159, 163–5
conceptual spaces, and Boden's theory of creativity 177–9, 180, 182–4, 211, 246–51, 256–61
Concise Oxford Dictionary definitions
    creativity 171
    fancy 5–6
    imagination 4, 5–6
connection model, of creativity and imagination 200–2, 203, 210, 212
contiguity, Hume on the principle of 72, 73
corporeal imagination 50, 51
creative imagination 203–12
    and aspect perception 203, 204–5, 212
    in Hume 82
    and metaphor 203, 205–12, 212, 282–8
    and recreative imagination 30
creativity
    and computational psychology 170, 179–81, 251, 252–5
    defining 170–7
        creativity as exemplary originality 172–4
        creativity as novel combination 171–2, 242–3
    and Euclidean geometry 105–6, 178, 198–9, 201, 210, 214–19, 250
    Gaut's definition of 172–4, 176, 177, 180, 187, 190, 269–71
    idea of a winged horse 171–2
    and imagination 1, 5, 7, 36, 170, 192, 192–219, 271–4
        Gaut on 14–23, 193–213, 268–93
        role of imagination in creativity 193–203
        Stevenson's conceptions of 8, 9, 10, 11
    and originality 170–92
    recombination theory of 170, 187–91, 192, 203, 204, 261–3

and seeing-as 167–8
    see also Boden, Margaret
Currie, Gregory and Ravenscroft, Ian, *Recreative Minds* 30–2, 265–7

Descartes, René 287
    Compendium musicae 54–5
    Discourse on the Method 56
    Humean impressions and Cartesian images 64–5
    on imagination 1, 10, 26, 32, 35, 36, 40–59
        and imaging 40–1, 45, 48, 49–52
        intellectual imagination 52–7, 68
        and 'objects of imagination' 43
        and schemata 113, 114
        and the wax example 44–5
        and the way of ideas 60–1, 81, 84, 87
    Meditations on First Philosophy 40, 41–52, 55, 57, 60
        First Meditation 41, 56–7
        'Objections and Replies' to 50
        Second Meditation 41–6, 46, 56, 57
        Sixth Meditation 43, 46–52, 57
    Principles of Philosophy 56
    Rules for the Direction of the Mind 52–5
descriptional conceptions of imagining 68–9, 133
display model of imagination in creativity 193, 194, 196–9, 200–1, 212, 275–6
dramatic imagining 15, 18, 274
dreams, and imagination 16, 28, 274

Edison, Thomas, invention of the phonograph 183, 184, 259, 260–1
Einstein, Albert 260
empathy, and imagination 1
empirical imagination *see* reproductive, empirical imagination
empirical investigation, and Wittgenstein's conception of imagination 127
empiricism
    and Berkeley's conception of imagination 63
    and Descartes's conception of imagination 58, 84
    and images 69
    and Kant's conception of imagination 83, 84, 85, 86, 92–3, 94, 113
        and schemata 113, 114, 115–16, 122

and rationalism 40, 60
and seeing-as 156–8, 159
see also association/associationism; Hume, David; way of ideas
Enlightenment, and Kant's philosophy 83
Euclid, *Elements* 53, 54, 105, 201, 214, 217
Euclidean geometry
    and creativity 105–6, 178, 198–9, 201, 210, 214–19, 250
    transcendental imagination in 106–7, 121
exemplary originality, and Kant's account of genius 174, 180–1, 191, 205–6, 210
existence
    and imagination 24, 27
        Gaut's analysis of 20–2, 23, 35
experiential imagining 15, 17, 18, 273
external world
    Hume on imagination and the 76–80, 87
        and Kant's conception of imagination 97–8

fancy
    Greek and Latin roots of the word 6
    and imagination 4–5
        in Hume 72, 82
fantasy
    and creativity 280
    and imagination 4, 5–6, 11, 35
fictional characters, and imagination 1, 20
figurative synthesis, and Kant's conception of imagination 100, 106
first-time novelty, and Boden's theory of creativity 176, 177–8, 179
flair
    and creativity 173–4, 176, 177, 180, 181, 185–7, 190, 191, 195, 271
        and metaphor 209, 286
Forster, E.M., *Howards End* 193
Freud, Sigmund 268–9, 275

Gassendi, Pierre 50
Gaut, Berys
    on creative acts and imagining 194–5
    'Creativity and imagination' 35, 172–4, 193–213, 268–93
    and active creativity 197–8, 199–200, 276, 278, 279–81, 288–9
    analysis of imagination in 14–23
    connection model 200–2, 203, 210, 212
    and considerations of truth and existence 20–2, 23, 35
    display and search models 193, 194, 196–9, 200–1, 212, 275–8
    and metaphor-making 205–12
    definition of creativity 172–4, 176, 177, 180, 187, 190, 191, 193, 269–71
    and Kant's conception of imagination 101
    'Models of creativity' 194–5
genius
    and aspect perception 204–5
    Kant's account of 174, 177, 269–70
        and metaphor 205–8, 209–10, 282–3
geometrical methodology, and Kant's conception of imagination 104–9, 113–14
God, Descartes on the existence of 41, 46, 50, 55, 87
Goodyear's discovery of vulcanization, and creativity 173, 184–5, 188, 190, 192, 205, 259–60, 261
grammar, and Wittgenstein's conception of imagination 128

H-creativity (historical creativity) 175–7, 243–5
hallucinations, and imagining 30
Haydn, Joseph 186–7, 203, 205
Heidegger, Martin, *Kant and the Problem of Metaphysics* 103–4
historical creativity (H-creativity) 175–7, 243–5
Hobbes, Thomas
    and Descartes's conception of imagination 50
    Leviathan 6
Hume, David 40, 63–82, 157, 265
    An Enquiry concerning Human Understanding 60, 63, 67
    on imagination 10, 24, 26, 32, 35, 36, 65, 79–80
        and abstract ideas 73–6, 79, 116–18
        and the external world 76–80, 87
        ideas and impressions 63–5, 68
        liberty of imagination 70–2
        and the 'missing shade of blue' problem 54, 65–8, 69, 70–1, 77, 78, 79, 81, 133–4

pictorial and descriptional conceptions of 68–9, 133
principles of association 72–3, 74, 75, 79, 80
and Kant's conception of imagination 84, 92, 96–8, 102–3, 113
and the mind 287
A Treatise of Human Nature 63–7, 72–80
    'Abstract' to 70, 73
    and external objects 77
    'Of abstract ideas' 73–6
    'Of scepticism with regard to the senses' 76–7
and the way of ideas 63–9, 81, 87
Husserl, Edmund 93–4

ideas 73–6, 79
    and Boden's theory of creativity 184–5
    Descartes on 51–2, 61–2, 63
    and impressions
        Hume on 63–5, 68, 81
        Kant on 87, 98
    Locke on 61–3
    see also abstract ideas; way of ideas
illusory, and imagination 4–5
imaginary
    and imaginative 4–5
    and real 4–5
imagination
    Greek and Latin roots of the word 6, 11
    meanings of 3–7
    as the 'missing mystery' of philosophy 2, 25–6
    sensory and intellectual conceptions of 26–35, 36
    Stevenson's twelve conceptions of 7–14, 35
    and supposition 32–5, 40, 68, 77, 78
    varieties of imaginative experience 2–26
    see also creativity
imaginative, and imaginary 4, 5
imaging/images
    and ideas 51–2, 63, 79
    and imagination 3, 4, 6, 11, 27, 27–32, 36
        Descartes on 40–1, 45, 48, 49–52, 60–1
        Gaut on 15–16, 271–4
        Kant on schemata and 109–21, 120–1
    picture and descriptional theories of 68–9, 133
    White on 27–32, 234–9, 266, 267

Wittgenstein on 126–34, 161–2, 167
see also mental imagery and imagination
imagining
    defining 11–14
    Gaut on creative acts and 194–5
    Gaut's analysis of 14–23
    and seeing-as 165–7
    Wittgensteinian account of 21–5, 127, 165–7
immersion, and genius 204–5
impressions
    and ideas
        Hume on 63–5, 68, 81
        Kant on 87, 98
inner picture, and seeing-as 143–9, 152
intellectual imagination
    Descartes's conception of 52–7, 68
    Hume on 78–9, 80
intellectual synthesis, and Kant's conception of imagination 100
intention, and creativity 195, 279, 280, 281
intentionality of images 134
interpretation, and Wittgenstein's discussion of seeing-as 138–9, 148, 149–51
intrinsic value, and Novitz's recombination theory 190–1
introspection, and Wittgenstein on images 127
intuitions
    and Kant's conception of imagination 84–6, 85, 89–90, 101–2
        and schemata 113–14, 120

Jenner, Edward, development of the smallpox vaccine 183, 186, 188, 192, 257–8, 260–1
Johnson, Mark, *The Body in the Mind* 25, 26
Johnson, Samuel, *Rambler* 1

Kant, Immanuel
    Critique of Judgement 174, 206, 282
    Critique of Practical Reason 174
    Critique of Pure Reason (CPR) 83, 84–5, 174, 219
        'Metaphysical Deduction' 88–9
        'On the synthesis of recognition in a concept' 94
        'On the synthesis of reproduction' 91–2
        schematism chapter 109–21
        structure of 220
        'Transcendental Aesthetic' 84, 86, 88

'Transcendental Deduction' 88–9, 90, 94, 95, 96, 99–105, 120
'Transcendental Logic' 84, 85–6, 88, 110
on genius and creativity 174, 177, 191, 197, 212, 269–70
    and computers 180–1
    and metaphor 205–8, 209–10, 282–3, 287–8
on imagination 1, 10, 24, 25, 26, 32, 36, 51, 58, 81, 83–123, 265
    and abstract ideas 116–18
    as active power 99–103
    and geometrical methodology 104–9
    and German words for imagination 90
    and Hume 84, 92, 96–8, 102–3
    images and schemata 83, 84, 109–21, 121–2
    as mediation 95
    reproductive, empirical 81, 83, 84, 98, 99, 115–16, 202
    synthesis of apprehension 90
    synthesis of recognition in a concept 94
    and the synthesis of reproduction 91–4
    transcendental 81, 83–4, 98, 115–16, 121, 122, 163, 165, 170, 202
    and the way of ideas 87–8
    transcendental and transcendent in 87–8
    and Wittgenstein's discussion of seeing-as 159–60, 163, 165, 167
Kasparov, G., and creativity in chess-playing 197, 202, 204, 205, 209, 277
Kekulé, Friedrich von, discovery of the benezene ring 178–9, 194, 196, 246, 250–1, 274, 275, 276
Koch, Robert 257–8
Koestler, Arthur 246

Leonardo da Vinci 268
linguistic creativity 176, 245
Locke, John 61–3, 65, 73, 157
    An Essay concerning Human Understanding 61–2
Lovelace questions, and computational psychology 180, 252–3

McGinn, Marie 152, 159, 160
mathematics
    Descartes on imagination in 53–4, 55

and Kant's conception of imagination 104–9
    see also geometrical methodology
Matisse, Henry 182, 256–7, 260
memory
    imagining and remembering 13–14, 16, 20, 23, 28, 35, 272
    and the way of ideas 87
Mendeleyev's periodic table 178, 249
mental imagery and imagination 7
    Currie and Ravenscroft on 30–2, 265–7
    Gaut on 15–16, 271–2
    Wittgenstein on 128–30, 265
    see also imaging/images
Mersenne, Marin 50, 55
metaphor, and the creative imagination 203, 205–12, 212, 282–8
Metzler, Nancy *see* Shepard, Roger and Metzler, Nancy
the mind
    and imagination 1
    Descartes and intellectual imagination 52–7
mind/body, and Descartes's conception of imagination 40, 41, 46, 48, 49
Mozart, Wolfgang 186–7, 192, 203, 205, 261, 262
Mulhall, Stephen 152
Munch, Edvard, *The Scream* 286–7
music
    and creativity 177, 178, 179, 205, 243
        and Boden's theory of conceptual spaces 177–8, 179, 186–7, 248–9, 250
        and computational psychology 252
        recombination theory of 262
    Descartes on imagination and 54–5

natural world, and imagination 8
novel combination, creativity as 171–2, 242–3
Novitz, David
    and aspect perception 204
    'Computers and human beings' 181–5, 255–61
    'Creativity and constraint' 181–7, 255–64
    critique of Boden 181–7, 191–2
    'Explanations of creativity' 190–1
    recombination theory of creativity 170, 187–91, 192, 203, 204, 261–3
nuclear weapons development, and creativity 189, 191

objectual imagining 15, 16–17, 19–20
obsession, and genius 204–5
ordinary experiences, and imagination 3
originality, and creativity 170–92, 195, 270–1
Oxford Dictionary of Philosophy, definition of imagination 4

P-creativity (psychological creativity) 175–7, 243–5, 255–6, 257, 258, 260
pain sensation, Wittgenstein on 131–2, 155
paradigms, and metaphor-making 283–4, 287
passive creativity 196, 198, 200, 276
Pasteur, Louis 258
PDP (Parallel Distributed Processing), and creativity 203
Pentagon attack (11 September 2001) 189, 190–1
perception
    and imagination 24, 26, 60–82, 267
        actual and non-actual perceptions 118–21
        Gaut on 16, 23, 35, 272
        see also Hume, David
    see also aspect perception; seeing-as; sense perception
phantasia, and imagination 1, 6, 49, 53
phantasm, and ideas 62, 63
phantasy, and fantasy 6
phenomenal imagining 15, 17, 273, 274
Picasso, Pablo 172, 182, 185, 257, 261, 270
pictorial conceptions of imagining 68–9, 133
Plato 6
    Ion 268, 269
poetry, Romantic 268
pre-selection, and creativity 202
pretending, and imagination 35
problem-solving, Descartes on imagination and 53–5
productive imagination, Kant's conception of 81, 83–4, 98, 115–16, 202
proportionality, Descartes on problem-solving and 54–5
propositional imagining 15, 16, 17, 18–19, 68–9, 133, 272–3
psychological creativity *see* P-creativity
puzzle-pictures, and seeing-as 144–8

radical originality, and creativity 176, 177–8, 181, 182, 185–6, 187, 188, 191, 246, 261
rationalism
    and empiricism 40, 60

    and Kant's conception of imagination 83, 84
        and schemata 113, 114, 122
    and seeing-as 156–8
Ravenscroft, Ian *see* Currie, Gregory and Ravenscroft, Ian
real
    and imaginary 4–5
    and Stevenson's conceptions of imagination 7
reason, and Hume's conception of imagination 60, 76–7, 79–80
recombination theory of creativity 170, 187–91, 192, 203, 204, 261–3
recreative imagination 30, 265
Reid, Thomas, *Essays on the Intellectual Powers of Man* 134
reproductive, empirical imagination, Kant's conception of 81, 83, 84–98, 99, 115–16, 202
resemblance, Hume on the principle of 72, 73, 74, 75, 79, 81
Rogers, Carl R. 170
Romanticism
    and creativity 197, 268
    and imagination 1, 24, 35, 163, 212
    and Kant's philosophy 83, 167
Russell, Bertrand, and creativity 178–9, 194, 196, 273, 275, 276
Ryle, G. 265

Sartre, Jean-Paul 265
schemata
    and Kant's conception of imagination 83, 84, 109–21, 121–2
        and actual and non-actual perceptions 118–21
        and concepts 110–16, 117
        empirical 113, 114, 115–16
        transcendental 114
schematic cube, and seeing-as 137–40
schematism, and Kant's conception of imagination 83
Schoenberg, Arnold 177, 178, 179, 249, 250
Schouls, Peter, *Descartes and the Possibility of Science* 52, 56, 57
Schumpeter, Joseph 269
search model of imagination in creativity 193, 194, 196–9, 200–1, 212, 277–8
seeing, and seeing-as 152–3

seeing-as 12–13, 36, 124, 125, 135–68
   and the clarification of mental concepts 163–5
   and creativity 167–8
   duck-rabbit example 137, 140–3, 148, 149–51, 152, 153–4, 155, 156
      and image-formation 162
      and imagining 166
      rationalism and empiricism 157–8
      and the recombination theory of creativity 262
   and imagination 155–6, 160–2
   and imagining 165–7
   and interpretation 138–9, 148, 149–51
   and Kant 159–60, 163, 165, 167
   organization and inner picture 143–9
   problem of 135–7
   rationalism and empiricism 156–8
   schematic cube example 137–40
   Wittgenstein's solution to the problem 151–5
sensation
   and imagination 1, 24
      in Wittgenstein 131–3, 155
sense experience/sensibility, and Kant's conception of imagination 84, 85, 86
sense perception
   and imagination 6, 272
      and external objects 76–7
      Hume and Kant on 96–8
      Stevenson's conceptions of 7, 8, 9–10, 26–7
sensibility, and Kant's conception of imagination 95, 101, 103–4, 110
sensory imagining 15, 17, 273, 274
   and corporeal imagination 49, 51, 57
   Descartes's critique of 58
   and intellectual imagination 57, 78–9
Sepper, Dennis, *Descartes's Imagination* 40–1, 52, 56, 57
Shakespeare, William 268, 269
   A Midsummer Night's Dream 271, 276
Shelley, Percy Bysshe 268, 278
Shepard, Roger and Metzler, Nancy, 'Mental rotation of three-dimensional figures' 107–9
smallpox vaccine, creativity and Jenner's development of the 183, 186, 188, 192, 257–9, 260–1
spatial-temporal order, and Kant's conception of imagination 86, 107, 110, 111
Stevenson, Leslie
   and necessary and sufficient conditions for imagining 13, 14, 35
   twelve conceptions of imagination 7–14, 22, 26, 35
      and Gaut 1, 14, 15, 19–21
      and Kant 100, 101
Strawson, Peter
   'Imagination and perception' 116, 118–20, 121
   and seeing-as 159–60, 163, 204
   and metaphor 211
Stroud, Barry 67
the sublime, and the beautiful 10
supposition
   and imagination 32–5, 40, 68
      Hume on 68, 77, 78, 79, 81
      White on 32–4, 240–1
synthesis
   and imagination 83–123
   see also Kant, Immanuel

thought
   and imagination 1, 6, 23, 24, 26
      Gaut's analysis of 18
      and seeing-as 12–13
      Stevenson's conceptions of 7–8, 11, 12, 18
   and Kant's conception of imagination 85, 86, 93
transcendental deduction, and Kant's conception of imagination 83
transcendental imagination, in Kant 81, 83–4, 98, 121, 122, 163, 165, 170
transcendental schemata, in Kant 114
truth
   and imagination 24, 27
      and creativity 199–200
      Gaut's analysis of 20–2, 23, 35

understanding
   and Kant's conception of imagination 84, 85, 86, 88, 95, 101, 103–4, 110
   and schemata 111–14

value
   and creativity 173–4, 175, 176, 177, 180, 181, 191, 195, 270–1
      and metaphor 209
      Novitz on 189, 190–1

VIVIDITY

INDEX

virtue, and creativity 269
visual impressions, inner pictures and seeing-as 143–8
visualization, and imagination 35, 267, 273
vulcanization, creativity and Goodyear's discovery of 173, 184–5, 188, 190, 192, 205, 259–60, 261

Warnock, Mary 271
way of ideas 60–9, 81
    and Descartes 60–1, 81, 84, 87
    and Hume 63–9, 81, 87
    Kant's critique of the 87–8
    and Locke 61–3
    see also association/associationism
White, Alan
    The Language of Imagination
        and imagery 27–32, 234–9, 266, 267
        and supposition 32–4, 240–1
Wittgenstein, Ludwig 36, 51, 120, 121, 122, 193
    and the creative imagination 205
    on imagination and images 126–34
        and the inverted spectrum problem 130–3
        mental images 128–30, 265
        methodological claim 126–8
        and the missing shade of blue problem 133–4
        and seeing-as 161–2
    and imagining 23–4, 26
    and Kant 159–60, 163, 165, 167
    Last Writings on the Philosophy of Psychology (LW) 135, 151
    method of philosophizing 125–6
    Philosophical Investigations (PI) 126–34, 135–7, 139, 146–7, 148–9, 152, 167
        and the duck-rabbit example 140–4, 150, 151, 204
        on mental concepts 163–5
        on seeing-as and imagination 155–6
    private language argument 129
    Remarks on the Philosophy of Psychology (RPP) 135, 137, 139, 151, 156, 163
    Tractatus Logio-Philosophicus 125, 153
    see also seeing-as
Wordsworth, William 1
    The Prelude 24
works of art
    and creativity
        Gaut's definition of 173, 270
        and metaphor 207, 282–3, 286–7
    and imagination, Stevenson's conceptions of 8
World Trade Centre attack (11 September 2001) 189, 190–1

Gaut — imagination — imagination does not have to involve imagery.
1. propositional imagination
2. objectual imagination
3. experiential (sensual/phenomenal) imagination
4. dramatic imagination

imagination <u>is not</u> committed to the truth or falsity of the proposition (alethic/existential truth)

creativity = originality + value + flair

White — imagination <u>does not</u> imply imagery.
imagery <u>does not</u> imply imagination
imagination <u>is</u> voluntary
imagery <u>is not</u> essential to imagination

Currie & Ravenscroft — mental imagery <u>is</u> a kind of recreative imagination
imagination <u>is not</u> always voluntary

White — imagination <u>is not</u> the same as supposition

Hume — <u>empiricist</u>. Imagination = perception. Images are perceived by the imagination. Implied intellectual role of imagination in supposition

Locke